KANSAS POLICY CHOICES

KANSAS POLICY CHOICES

Report of the Special Commission on a Public Agenda for Kansas

EDITED BY H. EDWARD FLENTJE

UNIVERSITY PRESS OF KANSAS

Published by the University Press of Kansas (Lawrence, Kansas 66045), which was organized by the Kansas Board of Regents and is operated and funded by Emporia State University, Fort Hays State University, Kansas State University, Pittsburg State University, the University of Kansas, and Wichita State University

ISBN 0-7006-0302-6

Printed in the United States of America

Contents

Preface

On April 24, 1985, Representative Mike Hayden, Speaker of the Kansas House of Representatives, introduced House Concurrent Resolution No. 5023, which would establish a Special Commission on a Public Agenda for Kansas. The resolution was debated and adopted by the lower house the next day. On April 26, the Kansas Senate debated and adopted HCR 5023.

Through HCR 5023, the Kansas legislature created the Special Commission on a Public Agenda for Kansas, provided for its organization and the appointment of its sixteen members, and gave the special commission its assignment. Specifically, the legislature charged the special commission with the following tasks:

1. identify public issues critical to the future of Kansas;
2. identify policy choices available to Kansas in responding to these issues;
3. draw upon leadership and expertise within Kansas to analyze these public issues and policy choices;
4. solicit views from the public at-large on these issues and policy choices; and
5. report to the Kansas legislature by July 1, 1986.

On June 27, the Legislative Coordinating Council, acting under the authority of HCR 5023, took steps to provide for the operation of the special commission. Specifically, the Legislative Coordinating Council designated Dr. H. Edward Flentje, professor of public administration at Wichita State University, as coordinator for the special commission, approved an agreement with Wichita State University to assist the special commission, and authorized $36,000 for special studies to be conducted under the auspices of the special commission.

During June and July, legislative leaders appointed the membership of the special commission as provided in HCR 5023. Representative Hayden was selected as chairman; Senator Michael L. Johnston was selected as vice-chairman.

In late July and early August, Chairman Hayden and Vice-chairman Johnston through a joint letter invited the public, leaders of 160 organizations in Kansas, and the heads of nearly sixty state agencies to respond to the assignment given the special commission. At its meeting of October 3, the commission analyzed the responses to these invitations for advice and decided to focus its attention on six issues: 1) the Kansas economy; 2) the future of rural communities; 3) state and local finance; 4) capital finance and public infrastructure; 5) educational governance and finance; and 6) preventive health care. Through October and November, the commission worked in committees to define the scope and character of these public issues more precisely and at its December meeting selected seven scholars to conduct special study of each of the issues.

Progress reports on the research were made to committees of the special commission in March and April. First drafts of the studies were presented to the full commission at its two-day meeting in late April. Final reports were reviewed and approved by the special commission in early June. At its June meeting, the commission also reaffirmed its earlier agreement that its purpose was to foster discussion on a public agenda for Kansas, not to endorse specific policy alternatives with respect to that agenda.

In total, the special commission held five meetings from August 1985 through June 1986. Seven additional meetings were also held during this period by the three committees of the commission.

In closing, I wish to thank members of the special commission for the extraordinary time given to reviewing voluminous materials in preparation for meetings, for full attention and candor in guiding the studies, and sound advice to me throughout the work of the commission. I particularly wish to thank Chairman Hayden and Vice-chairman Johnston for their leadership in assuring bipartisan cooperation throughout the commission's work. Special thanks are also due Professors Fisher, Houston, Krider, Lujan, Penner, and Redwood for their sensitivity to requirements of the special commission, their exceptional performance in addition to ongoing university obligations, and their timely completion of research and reporting on schedule.

Finally, the front office of the Hugo Wall Center for Urban Studies, specifically Barbara Telford and Jo Turner, have consistently corrected my errors and assured that production deadlines were met. Fran Majors from the Fairmount College of Liberal Arts and Sciences gave outstanding editorial guidance and markedly improved the quality of the final report. Charli Frederick and her staff of the Media Resources Center produced graphics for the final report. Jennifer Hartnett, my research assistant for this project, compiled the glossary and the index. Joe Pisciotte and Nancy McCarthy Snyder, who at different times directed the Hugo Wall Center during this year, provided the atmosphere required to carry on work for the special commission through Wichita State University.

Lastly, I want to thank Wichita State University and its academic officers for allowing me to act as coordinator of the special commission as a part of my sabbatical leave from the university.

H. Edward Flentje
Editor

Contributors

Gary R. Albrecht is a research economist at the Institute for Public Policy and Business Research at the University of Kansas. He has participated in research projects with the Institute since 1984. His areas of interest include urban and regional economics, economic forecasting, and econometric models.

Glenn W. Fisher is regents professor of urban affairs at Wichita State University and a consulting economist to the Kansas Division of the Budget. His work includes numerous publications in the field of public finance.

H. Edward Flentje is professor of public administration and associate director of the Hugo Wall Center for Urban Studies at Wichita State University. His professional experience includes legislative assistant to U.S. Senator James B. Pearson, and director of state planning and research for the State of Kansas during the administration of Governor Robert F. Bennett. His research focuses upon policy making in state and local government.

Douglas A. Houston is assistant professor of business and research associate at the Institute for Public Policy and Business Research at the University of Kansas. He is currently analyzing the impact of federal deregulation on rural communities.

Charles E. Krider is professor of business and director of business research in the Institute for Public Policy and Business Research at the University of Kansas. His research specialty is the area of labor economics and demographic trends, particularly those affecting rural communities.

Herman D. Lujan is professor of political science and vice-president of minority affairs at the University of Washington. His professional and academic experience includes director of the Institute for Social and Environmental Studies and professor of political science at the University of Kansas, as well as director of the Division of State Planning and Research for the State of Kansas. He has authored and coauthored publications in the areas of resource trends, electoral politics, and legislative and agency policies.

Maurice J. Penner is assistant professor of health care administration at Wichita State University. He has served as assistant director for policy research in the Kansas Division of State Planning and Research and as the assistant director of the Department of Aging in Sedgwick County. His publications focus on the area of preventative approaches to health.

Anthony L. Redwood is professor of business and director of the Institute for Public Policy and Business Research at the University of Kansas. He has directed numerous research projects with the State of Kansas since coming to the University of Kansas in 1972. His publications include articles examining the economics of human resources, demographic economics, labor relations, the Kansas economy, and economic development.

Introduction

"When anything is going to happen in this country, it happens first in Kansas," William Allen White editorialized in 1922.[1] White's assertion was substantiated by crusading abolitionists prior to the Civil War, constitutional prohibition in 1880, populism in the 1890s, and Bull Moose progressivism in 1912. According to White, "these things come popping out of Kansas like bats out of hell. Sooner or later other states take up these things..."[2]

Neal Peirce, *Washington Post* columnist on state and local government, and coauthor Jerry Hagstrom, writing sixty years later in their book on the fifty states, take a contrary view and term Kansas "The Eclipsed State."[3] According to these authors, Kansas "is scarcely the place where things happen 'first.' Indeed, nowhere on the American continent can the eclipse of a region or a state as a vital force—a focal point of creative change or exemplar of national life—be felt so strongly and poignantly as in Kansas."[4]

Most Kansans likely would take issue with the description by Peirce and Hagstrom, as well as with their analysis. However, the divergence between their view and White's raises questions about the direction in which Kansas is moving and about state initiative in public policy. The Special Commission on a Public Agenda for Kansas was conceived by the Kansas legislature as an experiment in public policy making, one designed to frame a public agenda for Kansas by drawing upon the advice of Kansans, the guidance of state leaders, and the research talents of state university scholars. This introduction reviews the context of state policy making in the mid-1980s and gives an overview of a public agenda for Kansas formed under the auspices of the special commission.

Transition from the Federal Era

William Allen White would hardly recognize Kansas governments of 1986 based on his knowledge of them in his era. Kansas governments, like those in most states, have been transformed during the "federal era," that period of federal dominance in the U.S. ranging roughly from 1950 to 1980. As a result of federal initiative and dollars in this period, states and many localities became occupied with national objectives outlined in the Congress and specified by program managers in the federal bureaucracy. States

1

often served as federal agents in pursuing objectives as divergent as rat control, rural fire protection, and the prevention of juvenile delinquency.

The principal means for federal initiative and, ultimately, dominance in domestic policy making were federal grant-in-aid programs. In 1950, hardly a dozen such programs were authorized; by 1980, over 500 federal grant-in-aid programs were being operated—each with its own funding requirements, application deadlines, and program managers.[5] Federal expenditures for assistance to state and local governments jumped fortyfold from $2.5 billion in 1950 to $106.0 billion in 1985, a rate of growth through the late 1970s nearly five times that of the national economy. By 1980, federal dollars comprised nearly one of every three dollars flowing into state and government treasuries.[6]

Federal aid stimulated and transformed the scope and character of state government. Authority for delivering public services expanded dramatically. The number of state functions grew, and their scope became enlarged. State government in 1986 is not only bigger and more complex than it was in White's time, but also more directly affects the lives of its citizens.

Beginning in the late 1970s, federal assistance for domestic programs began to level off, and federal initiative in domestic policy making declined. Thirty or more years of rapidly expanding federal aid had created new misgivings as to whether more federal involvement could solve domestic ills. Between 1978 and 1986, federal assistance fell dramatically from nearly one-third to one-fifth of state and local budgets.[7] Measures aimed at reducing the federal deficit suggest this decline will continue, if not accelerate. As a result of this change, state and local governments are increasingly looked to for resources and initiative in responding to domestic issues.

Postfederal Era in Kansas

As Kansas enters the postfederal era, the state's agenda differs markedly from what it has been at any other time. Most of the policy issues crowded onto this agenda were not present twenty-five years ago, and many not even ten years ago. Problems demanding the attention of policy makers include:

- competing economically with other states
- controlling and disposing of hazardous wastes
- reducing teenage pregnancy
- responding to revenue shortfalls
- preventing contamination of groundwater supplies
- repairing deteriorating infrastructure
- securing international markets for agricultural products
- controlling the costs of health care
- establishing community-based treatment for those in need
- caring for the homeless

State legislative initiative in responding to these issues may be described as bounded, bounded on the one hand by the initiative of other forces at work on public policy in Kansas and on the other hand by the constraints of legislative procedure. Leading those forces shaping public policy in Kansas is the state's chief executive. Kansas now has had over ten years' experience with executive reorganization, a strengthened governorship, and a cabinet form of departmental organization, and these reforms have equipped the governor well as an initiator of public policy. Substantial influence in state policy making also resides with state agencies, with their purposes and their expertise, which may or may not be in accord with gubernatorial direction. Local governments, including schools, cities, counties, and others, are creatures of the state, but in reality circumscribe legislative action with their demands for expanded authority or funding. Federal agencies, while declining in potency, still exert substantial influence on state policy. Finally, a variety of economic interests, professional associations, and other special groups press their demands for state action before the legislature and other points of policy leverage. The collective weight of these forces severely constrains the Kansas legislature and its own initiative in public policy. Consequently, the legislature often reacts to the initiative of others in adopting public policy.

In addition to this milieu of state policy, the legislature's own procedures further restrict legislative initiative. For example, the ninety-day session forces consideration of complex proposals in accordance with strict time deadlines that may preclude adequate study, deliberation, or consideration of alternative action. The committee structure may also force proposals that impinge on numerous subjects into a committee with a single frame of reference. Partisan organization further complicates legislative initiative by drawing attention to who receives credit for legislative accomplishment.

The Special Commission on a Public Agenda for Kansas emerged from this sea of conflicting forces, on the one hand, from the vacuum left by federal retreat from participation in state and local programs and, on the other hand, from the influences which constrain legislative initiative. The special commission constitutes an experiment in agenda setting and policy making by the Kansas legislature. In carrying out its assignment, the commission first asked for advice from Kansans as to what issues were most critical to the future of Kansas. Leaders of state groups and heads of state agencies also were asked for their suggestions on this matter. The responses to these requests were synthesized into an agenda of nearly thirty items of concern to Kansans. This long agenda was then reformulated and refined by the commission into six critical issues as follows:

1. The Kansas economy;
2. The future of rural communities;

3. State and local finance;
4. Capital finance and public infrastructure;
5. Educational governance and finance; and
6. Preventive health care.

The special commission determined early in its deliberations that in identifying policy choices available to Kansas in response to these issues, the commission would not recommend a single approach. Instead, the commission would identify alternative approaches and thereby encourage, not foreclose, discussion of these issues. Within this framework, the special commission then commissioned scholars to conduct research on the six issues, as well as on alternative approaches to each issue. These studies do not, however, exhaust the range of available policy options. An overview of the resulting public agenda and policy choices for Kansas is as follows:

The Kansas Economy

The Kansas economy has provided a good standard of living for the people of Kansas during this century. Because of its traditional structure, the state economy did not suffer the degree of volatility, resulting from national business cycles, that was experienced by the industrial states. However, significant changes have occurred in the national and international economic order that raise serious questions concerning the capacity of the Kansas economy to underpin adequately the economic welfare of Kansans in the future if present trends continue. Indeed, the Kansas economy is not well positioned to go forward strongly in the next decade, so that restructuring the economic sector for a prosperous future constitutes a profound challenge for Kansans in the years ahead.

The Kansas economy has undergone significant, long-term structural change from an agricultural economy to a mixed form somewhat like the national industrial structure. The key developments in this change may be summarized as follows:

1. Farming and oil and gas continue to be important sectors, but they are no longer predominant.
2. The state has a solid manufacturing sector, but its development has not been adequate to provide sufficient alternative employment opportunities for both natural labor-force growth and labor displaced from the farms.
3. The industrial structure that has evolved is underrepresented with industries that are expected to grow strongly in the next decade.

As a result of these structural conditions, the state economy during the recent recessions fell further, started to recover later, and has grown more slowly than the national economy. Kansas can no longer be considered recession-proof, and the 1980 and 1981-82 recessions have illustrated how vulnerable the state economy now is to the national business cycle. A number of factors have caused this relatively weak economic performance in recent years. Some have been beyond state influence, such as the strength of the dollar and supply-demand conditions for traditional Kansas products in world markets. However, the state has not fostered a new industrial mix with potential for expansion and growth, and this matter resides more within the realm of our influence.

Changes in Kansas economic structure have had critical demographic consequences. Kansas has experienced net outmigration in every decade since 1890. In 1890, Kansans comprised 2.27 percent of the nation's population. The population of Kansas, which has one of the slower growth rates in the nation, is projected to fall to 0.93 percent of the total U.S. population by the year 2000. Most of those leaving the state have been young adults and persons with higher education and skill levels. Consequently, Kansas ranks ninth among states in the proportion of population 65 and over. Within Kansas, a great many people have moved to regions of employment opportunity in the eastern part of the state.

The outlook for the state economy, on the basis of likely patterns and trends, includes continued depressed prices for farm products and for oil and gas, due to chronic oversupply in world markets, modest growth at best for the aviation industry, and a secondary impact on the service sector resulting from expected softness in the core sectors. In essence, Kansas depends on a set of industries that have served it well in the past but that cannot be counted upon to "carry" the state in the future, although they will remain very important.

At the same time, under the imperative of powerful international forces, the U.S. economy is being transformed by innovation and technological change. Kansas does not have a comparative advantage that would naturally attract this type of industry, so that growth sectors in the existing economic base are underrepresented. However, the state does have strengths upon which future economic development can be based and present trends diverted. The fundamental question for Kansas, therefore, is how to foster the type and degree of economic activity that will provide a sound economic foundation for the future.

The structural changes in the Kansas economy, the demographic consequences of these changes, and the economic outlook for Kansas raise basic questions concerning the future:

1. Will a continuation of existing trends provide an acceptable level of economic welfare for Kansans?
2. What form of economic development is realistically feasible for Kansas?
3. What basic strategy will produce optimum economic development for Kansas?

A continuation of the existing trends of below-average economic performance will result in reduced income and employment for Kansans and a lower capacity to fund important state services such as education. Growth in the traditional sectors will be modest, and Kansas cannot develop a substitute industry structure for the future. Hence, a realistic form of economic development for Kansas must incorporate the old into the new. An optimum strategy for the economic development of Kansas should emphasize a balanced approach of supporting the existing economic base as well as fostering growth through the expansion of old, and the attraction of new, industry. Such a strategy would incorporate the following thrusts:

1. *Enhance and extend the traditional sectors.* The future viability of these sectors will depend on their ability to adapt to new products and processes as well as on their competitiveness with current products. An example would be diversification into new agricultural products and greater value added in food processing.

2. *Retain, sustain, and expand existing industry.* Given that 70 to 80 percent of new job creation will occur in small businesses, the Kansas structure provides a favorable basis for vitality through expansion based on modernization and enhanced competitiveness and new business formation through entrepreneurship.

3. *Develop new industry.* Despite sound fundamentals, important strengths, and limited barriers, the state is not overly attractive to outside industry. In seeking new industry, Kansas should recognize that only certain types of industry will find Kansas attractive and that foreign investment is an important source for job creation.

An optimum strategy for Kansas could include these approaches:

1. *Foster competitiveness through innovation.* Individual firms, particularly small businesses, have insufficient resources and technical capacity to learn about new technological developments and to capitalize on new ideas. Existing Kansas industry will not survive, let alone expand, unless it innovates, and the future viability of the weakened traditional sectors depends on it.

2. *Foster appropriate linkages and interrelations.* Success in economic development will depend on committed and cooperative work by many groups and purposeful leadership at many levels. The lack of an integrated approach has handicapped the state program to date in terms of level, direction, and effectiveness.

3. *Encourage entrepreneurship.* Kansas will need imaginative, risk-taking entrepreneurs able to turn ideas for new products and processes into successful business ventures. The availability of capital is critical to new business development and expansion, and the lack of capital constitutes a primary barrier to the growth of small business in Kansas. Also, a leading cause of failure for small business is lack of management competence and know-how.

4. *Provide the optimum infrastructure and business climate.* The key objective of infrastructure development and business-climate enhancement is

to influence the competitiveness and profitability of existing and potential Kansas industry. If the business environment is rewarding to existing industry, it also will be attractive to new industry.

5. *Remove barriers to development.* Significant impediments to business development, such as tax barriers, lack of risk capital, and constitutional limitations, exist in the Kansas business environment, and these retard expansion and discourage new industry. Their removal is crucial to the release of entrepreneurship and enhancement of business confidence.

Economic Prospects for Rural Communities

Rural communities in Kansas face economic problems even more difficult than the state as a whole. These problems result primarily from the replacement of labor with capital in agricultural production. Indeed, this structural change has eroded economic functions of rural communities. The dimensions of these economic difficulties may be summarized as follows:

1. Farm employment in Kansas dropped from 160,427 in 1950, or 22.7 percent of total employment in Kansas, to 62,609 in 1980, or 5.8 percent of total state employment.
2. While private, nonfarm employment rose 3.0 percent in urban areas of Kansas from 1978 to 1983, rural areas lost 3,200 jobs, a decline of 1.1 percent.
3. Net change in business establishments, that is, the number of new businesses established minus the number of business failures, grew in rural areas of Kansas at one-half the rate of urban areas from 1978 to 1983.
4. Rural areas of Kansas lost 7,803 manufacturing jobs from 1978 to 1983, a decline of 11.1 percent. The loss of primary jobs in manufacturing was not entirely offset by the creation of secondary jobs in the service sector.
5. Rural areas had varied employment experience from 1978 to 1983. A few attracted manufacturing jobs to offset losses of agricultural employment. Others replaced manufacturing jobs with employment in the service sector. Still others have lost employment in most sectors and are in rapid economic decline.

Population tends to follow employment, and slow economic growth in rural areas has meant lagging population growth. While the population of urban areas in Kansas increased by 6.6 percent from 1970 to 1980, rural areas grew only 3.7 percent. More importantly, the population cohort aged twenty to thirty-four increased 39.5 percent in urban areas during this period, compared to 32.9 percent for rural areas. These trends suggest that Kansas rural communities will not be able to retain young people unless employment opportunities are improved.

Federal deregulation in trucking, rail, bus service, and public utilities has been presumed to compound the adverse economic trends affecting rural areas by increasing the cost of doing business in rural communities relative to urban areas. The results of deregulation, however, are mixed:

1. Rural communities have benefited from deregulation of trucking. Rural Kansas shippers perceive trucking after deregulation as prompter, more reliable, and more willing to serve out-of-the-way locations. More trucking firms have entered the market and exerted a downward pressure on prices.
2. Except for communities affected by the abandonment of branch lines, deregulation of rail has generally lowered prices for rural shippers, although this drop may be due to increased competition from trucking.
3. In contrast, the effects of bus deregulation have been unfavorable to rural communities. With few exceptions, frequency of service has decreased, and the number of routes through Kansas has declined.

In addition to adverse economic trends and the impact of deregulation, state government's strategy for economic development in the past has been unfavorable to rural communities. The state's approach to industrial recruitment focuses on the attributes of urban communities and thereby places rural communities at a disadvantage.

Policy choices available to Kansas with respect to rural communities include the following:

1. *Encourage growth of businesses already in Kansas.* This strategy would include:
   a. Encouragement to entrepreneurs to start new businesses and expand existing business in Kansas;
   b. Increased investment by the state and private business in research and development to make Kansas firms more innovative and competitive and to spin off new businesses;
   c. Increased availability of financing for new and expanding businesses, especially venture or risk capital;
   d. Establishment of an existing industry program to focus on the needs and problems of business firms in Kansas;
   e. Reorganization of the Kansas Department of Economic Development to increase emphasis on rural communities, small businesses, and international trade.
2. *Recruit industry suitable to rural communities.* Certain industries have greater potential for locating in rural communities, and these could be targeted as a part of an industrial-recruitment strategy.
3. *Promote rural economic linkage.* A structure for promoting cooperation on economic development among rural communities could be established.
4. *Deregulate intrastate controls on trucking.* In the context of federal deregulation, continued intrastate regulation of trucking may be hampering trucking with respect to rural communities and is of questionable value.

5. *Consider new approaches to deregulation of public utilities.* Other states are exploring ways to increase competition in the provision of state-regulated services such as telephone. These experiments deserve consideration in Kansas and may prove beneficial to rural communities.

State and Local Finance

Kansas state and local governments have experienced large increases in expenditures and revenues since 1962. Inflation and economic growth caused a major portion of this increase; but state and local expenditures as a percentage of the personal income grew also until the trend turned slightly downward in the mid-1970s. In the last six years, expenditures stabilized around 15.8 percent of personal income. Kansas expenditures generally stayed in line with those of surrounding states and were slightly below those of the United States as a whole.

During this period, state tax rates increased somewhat, and the severance tax was added. Significant shifts in the tax structure occurred as the income tax became more important. This change was caused partly by increases in the tax rates on higher-income individuals, but much of the shift resulted from the high elasticity of the income tax. Sales taxes, including the specific excise taxes, declined in relative importance; federal grants, local nonproperty taxes, and charges and miscellaneous revenues rose more rapidly than did total revenues. Property taxes became relatively less important, and property taxes as a percentage of the market value of property actually declined. In spite of this, property taxes continue to be an important part of the state and local tax structure.

Kansas escaped the severe fiscal crises and the "taxpayers revolts" that plagued many states in the 1970s. Program improvements came about without any large tax increases or large-scale borrowing programs, but, beginning about 1981, a significant shift took place. The Kansas revenue structure, formerly adequate to support expenditures at a constant or even slightly rising percentage of personal income, began to lag. Receipts fell below estimates, some tax rates were increased, collections of other taxes were sped up, and year-end balances declined.

This revenue shortfall cannot be attributed to any one, single cause. The elasticities of most state taxes declined substantially, partly as a result of economic changes, changes in the federal tax laws, and perhaps exemptions that have eroded state tax bases. In addition, the growth in federal grants to state and local governments ceased, and the decline in interest rates reduced miscellaneous revenue.

Projections of state and local revenues suggest that Kansas governments may have to reconsider the declining reliance on the property tax or increase rates of other taxes in order to maintain current spending patterns.

Projections of general fund taxes for Kansas state government indicate that, if the tax elasticities occurring since 1980 continue, current taxes will fall short of projected expenditures in 1995 by $260 million, even with the recent increase in the sales tax. On the other hand, if longer-term elasticities continue, the current tax structure will be sufficient to meet expenditures.

In assessing Kansas taxes against criteria for a balanced tax structure, the state ranks well on progressiveness and revenue diversification. On the other hand, Kansas scores poorly on administration of the property tax and stands in the middle range on business climate. Reappraisal of property, now underway, and a proposed constitutional amendment that will elimi-nate property taxation of business inventories will significantly improve Kansas' ranking.

These analyses raise at least three major policy issues concerning state and local finance in Kansas: First, how should Kansas respond to the recent shortfalls in tax revenue relative to growth in the state's economy? Second, what direction should Kansas take concerning future reliance on the prop-erty tax? And third, how should Kansas insure that its revenue structure promotes the economic health of the state?

1. *Establish a "rainy-day" fund.* The revenue yield and the changing elastic-ities of the Kansas tax structure bear close monitoring in the immediate future. If current taxes continue to perform poorly relative to the state's economy as they have in recent years, Kansas could again be faced with revenue shortfalls. State policy makers could consider the establishment of a rainy-day fund as partial protection against revenue shortfalls in the long term.

2. *Increase or decrease reliance on the property tax.* By nearly every meas-ure, the property tax is overused and poorly administered in Kansas. Actions by the 1985 legislature move the state toward improved admin-istration of the property tax and give Kansas voters the chance to relieve the property tax burden on business. Even with these steps, the state will still be faced with the issue of future reliance on the property tax.

   Three basic choices are available to Kansas in reducing dependence on the property tax: 1) transfer local functions and responsibilities to the state; 2) provide more state financial assistance to local governments; or 3) provide local governments with more authority to levy local taxes. Each of these choices raises different difficulties and political constraints. State policy makers will have to determine if public demands to reduce reliance on the property tax are important enough to surmount the obstacles posed by these choices.

3. *Consider other options for improving business climate through the tax structure.* A critical ingredient to encouraging economic growth in Kansas is providing a tax structure conducive to the growth of all businesses. Kansas voters will have the opportunity in August and November to improve business climate through constitutional change. Other options deserving consideration include decoupling from the federal income tax,

enacting a broad-based business activities tax in lieu of the corporate income tax, or "expensing" of business capital investment.

Capital Finance and Public Infrastructure

The framers of the Kansas constitution placed severe restrictions on debt financing of capital improvements and limited state government's role in providing public infrastructure. The severity of these limits eventually motivated state lawmakers to avoid the debt mechanics of the constitution whenever possible. They have indeed devised creative means over 125 years to escape constitutional limits and adopt alternative precepts for providing capital improvements needed to achieve state purposes. The leading precepts of capital finance that evolved in Kansas may be delineated as follows:

1. Pay as we go, in other words, finance capital improvements from current revenues.
2. Authorize debt financing of capital improvements by local governments. This precept had the effect of shifting principal responsibility for public infrastructure to local governments in Kansas.
3. Pay as we go with special-purpose capital-improvement funds. These funds have been used to meet major demands for capital improvements, such as road building and construction projects at state universities.
4. Authorize state agencies to undertake capital improvements with debt financing backed by anticipated revenues. Beginning in the 1930s, state lawmakers, with the support of a friendly judiciary, created new means around the debt limits in the state constitution and initiated debt financing of capital improvements. State credit is now being used to finance improvements for a variety of state purposes.
5. Maximize federal assistance to underwrite capital improvements for state purposes. Beginning with federal land grants at the dawn of statehood, Kansas has utilized federal funds for state improvements. This source does not, however, look promising in the future.

Given these approaches to capital finance and public infrastructure, where does Kansas stand in meeting demands for capital improvements? The following findings are relevant:

1. State expenditures on capital improvements have declined consistently and dramatically relative to construction costs, overall state expenditures, and personal income over the past twenty to twenty-five years. In addition, Kansas' effort in capital investment falls substantially below various national projections of infrastructure needs.
2. With respect to highways, preservation and modernization of existing roads require virtually all available funds. The $320 million bond program for state freeways has been exhausted. Federal assistance for highways, while stable or increasing in actual dollars for the past twenty-five years, has not kept up with the cost of construction. Highway user fees

also are declining relative to costs. Requests for $700 million in system-expansion projects presently are backlogged.

3. Federal assistance for purposes other than highways is being substantially reduced. Revenue sharing for state government has been eliminated. Funding for outdoor recreation stands at one-tenth of earlier levels. Major federal water projects are on hold. Proposals for further reductions are under consideration. Federal assistance for capital improvements directed to state purposes represents a particularly vulnerable target for actions aimed at reducing the federal deficit.

4. Capital improvement requests of other state agencies are backlogged:
   - Recreational improvements, both new parks, such as one proposed at Hillsdale Reservoir, and enhancement of existing park facilities, are being postponed. State agency officials identify improvement needs of $5 million annually.
   - Proposals for resort facilities at state parks have not developed and moved forward for some years.
   - Wildlife improvements, such as minimum streamflow and protection of wetlands and riparian areas, are being postponed. State agency officials identify improvement needs of $11 to $13 million annually.
   - Preventive maintenance at state universities, state office facilities,. and state institutions is being reduced.
   - New correctional facilities have been stalled.

Existing state policy concerning capital finance and public infrastructure and the status of capital improvement spending by state government raises at least three key policy issues in this area:

1. Are those provisions in the Kansas constitution that guide and limit capital finance adequate for the future? Even for the immediate future? Will the constitution allow state lawmakers to respond to new public demands for capital improvements in areas of state responsibility?

2. Are state government's procedures for planning and budgeting capital improvements adequate for the future? Does the state have the capacity to identify new demands for capital improvements, assess their value in achieving state purposes, and set priorities among them for funding?

3. Is the current level of funding for capital improvements adequate? Are current means of capital finance adequate for the future? Is Kansas taking advantage of the variety of financing options more recently available?

These issues pose at minimum the following policy choices for Kansas:

1. *Revise constitutional provisions concerning capital finance and public infrastructure.* Should Kansas eliminate the internal improvements prohibition and reinstitute state-debt limitations that are reasonable and responsive to economic change, yet hold state lawmakers accountable when using the state's credit?

First, the constitutional ban on internal improvements has deterred state government's response to demands for public infrastructure essential to economic growth and has skewed the burden of responsibility for public infrastructure substantially toward local government in Kansas. As a result, the development of infrastructure across Kansas has been uneven, opportunities for growth likely have been lost, and important regional projects beyond the scope of a single local jurisdiction but not of compelling statewide significance have not moved forward. With the decline of federal assistance for public infrastructure, state government's role will become even more pivotal in the future; yet, the internal improvements prohibition presents a constitutional obstacle to the fulfillment of that role.

Second, the state constitution's once-restrictive debt limits have been rendered meaningless by legislative ingenuity and judicial sanction. As a result, Kansas state government has no effective constitutional limits on the level of state debt, the level of debt service, the length of debt obligations, or the extent to which major state tax funds may be committed for the future. This situation increases the likelihood of defaults in the years ahead and of demagogic challenge if problems do arise. Kansas could take advantage of its problem-free debt status and institute reasonable but effective debt limits on state government.

2. *Revamp capital planning and budgeting.* Should Kansas revamp state processes for capital planning and budgeting, augment the expertise on capital finance available to the governor and the legislature, and assure that state lawmakers receive consistent, current information on the state's capital assets and liabilities and on capital expenditures?

The value of capital stock owned by Kansas state government likely has reached a level of several billion dollars. State government is now spending over $300 million each year on capital improvements, debt service, and other capital outlays. Debts and other long-term financial obligations of the state have surpassed $400 million. Yet, Kansas still conducts capital planning and budgeting as an appendage to the consideration of operating budget requests. Minimal investments in revamping capital planning and budgeting and in improving the expertise and information available to lawmakers could pay long-term dividends in assuring that the state's infrastructure is well tended, its capital expenditures are effectively spent, and its debts are properly managed.

3. *Expand the state's investment in public infrastructure.* Should Kansas expand the level of state resources invested in state infrastructure that aids economic growth, specifically in state highways, water-resource development, recreation and wildlife improvement, and state agency facilities?

Relative to construction costs, overall state expenditure, and personal income, Kansas state expenditures for capital improvements in 1985 fell 33 percent, or $148 million, below the average level of the last twenty-five years. Declining federal assistance, a dominant pay-as-we-go philosophy, and inadequate capital planning and budgeting, among other factors, have contributed to this funding deficit. As a result, new highway projects have reached a virtual standstill, recreation and wildlife improvements have been postponed, action on new correctional facilities has been stalled, preventive maintenance of state facilities has been reduced, and a backlog of unfunded capital improvements for state purposes has occurred. To redress this capital-investment deficit, the state could explore options for expanded funding, such as increased user fees, an expanded building fund, and dedication of a portion of the state's general funds, among other options, to capital improvements. In addition, the state should augment the capital finance capacity of those state agencies responsible for water resources, state highways, and state facilities. These agencies could be assigned responsibility to expand the level of capital investment through new and existing revenues, user fees, debt financing, federal assistance, and local and private participation.

Educational Governance and Finance

The demands being placed upon education in the next decade or two will be markedly different than those of past years. Education will be expected to serve a changing clientele and to play a more vital role in the economic, social, and cultural well-being of states and the nation. These changing demands and expectations will affect educational governance and finance.

Education in Kansas will experience demographic forces now at work in the country. These forces, while not as potent in Kansas as in other parts of the country, will require response and adaptation from the educational system. Entering the system will be:

1. More children from poverty households;
2. More children from single-parent households, often headed by teenagers;
3. More children from minority cultures;
4. More children in need of different or special educational programs; and
5. More linguistically diverse children.

This changing constituency will occupy education for at least the next twenty years. Services will have to be geared to a student cohort without traditional backgrounds or preparation.

Education also fuels the economy. Job-specific training to meet local economic demands will be needed. People with broader skills in evaluation and analysis, critical thinking, problem solving, and communications, among others, will also be required. Education's agenda must include research which aids existing industry retrofit in line with changing national and international markets.

Educational governance beyond high school constitutes a major challenge facing Kansas. Education at the level of postsecondary and higher education lacks effective coordination. No authority at the state level is articulating a strategic vision of what role these critical segments of education can and should be playing in the economy and in the state's future.

Coordination is a major problem among community colleges and schools providing technical education. Authority at the state level is divided. Services are delivered by a variety of institutions without systematic governance. This confusing situation clouds responsibility for state policy, inhibits the quality of services, and impairs responsiveness to community and statewide demands as well as community needs. Further, without an effective advocate within state government this segment of education has evolved into a stepchild dilemma. One policy choice available to Kansas is to elevate this segment of education through the creation of a state Board of Postsecondary Education with authority for coordinating community colleges, area vocational schools, vocational-technical schools, and technical institutes. The board would have responsibility for developing the "strategic vision" for this segment of education in Kansas and for carrying out coordinating functions such as master planning, program review, and budget review, among others.

With respect to higher education, several policy issues have emerged in recent years to challenge the existing governance arrangement. Central among these issues are:

1. Conflicts among institutions;
2. Lack of a master plan for higher education or delineation of institutional scope and mission;
3. Reaction to intense institutional lobbying;
4. Duplication in graduate and professional programs;
5. Perceived weakness in educational leadership.

One policy choice available to Kansas is to create a Coordinating Board for Higher Education as an alternative to existing governance. This board would be charged with coordinating functions for all of education beyond high school and with providing the governor, the legislature, and institutions with an independent, analytic, and purposeful view of these segments of education as a whole. This board would have to be assigned authority commensurate with its tasks—at minimum, responsibility for master planning, program review, budget review, and the promotion of interinstitutional cooperation.

Responding to new demands will require a sound financial base for education in Kansas. Current status of educational finance may be summarized as follows:

1. Revenues available to elementary and secondary education in Kansas were estimated at $1.54 billion for 1984, an increase of 93.5 percent over 1976.
2. State aid to elementary and secondary education in Kansas increased from $306.6 million in 1976 to $681.3 million in 1984, an increase of 122.2

percent. In the same period, local and other aid increased from $352.3 to $761.5 million, an increase of 116.2 percent. Federal assistance fell from $90.4 to $68.9 million in this period, a drop of 23.7 percent.

3. From 1976 to 1984, the state share of elementary and secondary finance grew from 40.9 to 45.1 percent; the local and other shares grew from 47.0 percent to 50.4 percent; and the federal share dropped from 12.1 percent to 4.6 percent.

4. State government's share of financing elementary and secondary education in Kansas exceeds that of all neighboring states except Oklahoma but falls slightly below the national average of 49.0 percent.

5. The local property tax provides the majority of support for community colleges in Kansas, a sum of $44.6 million in 1984, which comprised 59.4 percent of operating revenues, up from 50.1 percent in 1979. Between 1979 and 1984, the state share of community college aid fell from 38.4 to 32.5 percent; the share composed of revenues from tuition declined from 9.3 to 6.3 percent; and the federal share dropped from 2.3 to 1.8 percent.

6. Kansas places a high value on education beyond high school, using 10.7 percent of state and local tax revenues for public colleges and universities and thereby ranking sixteenth nationally in this factor.

7. Students in Kansas rank thirty-sixth nationally in dollars spent for tuition; the contribution of tuition to the revenues of public colleges and universities declined 11.2 percent in constant dollars from 1977 to 1984; and the ratio of dollars spent to personal disposable income indicates that Kansans could afford to pay more for tuition.

The solid financial base has paid off for Kansas in the form of a well-educated and highly skilled work force. For example, 80.5 percent of school-age population graduate from high school, ranking the state eighth nationally on retention. Kansas ranks fifth nationally in the proportion of high school graduates who go to public colleges and universities in the state, indicating that Kansas provides attractive and accessible opportunities beyond high school. One basic issue facing Kansas is the demand to maintain educational quality in the face of declining enrollments. The critical issue for state government is continuing a stable financial base for all levels of education while responding to new educational demands.

Policy choices for financing elementary and secondary education include the following:

1. *Continue present school finance plan at present level of state participation.* This option would generally require local school districts to absorb funding reductions, for example, from federal cutbacks.

2. *Continue present school finance plan but raise state participation to the level of 50 percent.* This option would shift more responsibility for educational finance from local schools to state government.

3. *Place a surcharge on the individual income tax to meet expanding demands for resources in elementary and secondary education.*

4. *Authorize a local-option surcharge on the individual income tax to meet expanding demands for elementary and secondary education.*

Policy choices for funding community colleges and postsecondary vocational education include the following:

1. *Continue present funding plan with no change in the level of state participation.*
2. *Shift more financial responsibility for community colleges and postsecondary vocational education to the state level.*
3. *Authorize local-revenue options other than the property tax, including possibly increased user fees, a business-activities tax, or other local sources, to meet increased demands for financing of community colleges and of postsecondary vocational education.*

Policy choices for finance of higher education include the following:

1. *Continue present funding plan.*
2. *Authorize the Board of Regents to set tuition levels up to one-third of the cost of education at state universities.*

Better Health for Kansans

Kansans spend over $3 billion annually, 9.5 percent of state personal income, for health care, almost all for "sickness care," that is, the diagnosis and treatment of disease. At least half of the treated health problems could have been prevented by better lifestyle decisions and better access to preventive health care. Poor lifestyle decisions include smoking, substance abuse, poor diet, inadequate exercise, and not wearing auto seat belts. These are high-risk behaviors for heart disease, cancer, stroke, diabetes, and auto deaths and injuries.

The young face problems that are different from those of the elderly. The health of the young often depends upon their parents' decisions, about such matters as prenatal care or preventive health examinations before school entrance. Teenage pregnancy leads to health and social problems for mother and child; experts project that 40 percent of our fourteen-year-old girls will become pregnant before they turn twenty. The elderly may need assistance to be able to live on their own, but they cannot always afford or find the help they need. This aid could postpone as many as a fourth of the admissions to nursing homes.

Several ways to attack these problems are available, could improve health, and could reduce some of the expenditures for sickness care. Approaches include added state funding, incentives for healthy behavior, and preventive health requirements for families, schools, and businesses. Policy choices outlined here are based on feasibility and likely effectiveness. These options are not meant to be exhaustive but are intended to foster discussion on the prevention of health problems and available prevention alternatives.

Prenatal Care. An infant's chance of being born healthy largely depends on adequate prenatal care. Infant mortality and the risk of low birth-weight doubles where care is lacking, which is the case for 15 percent of Kansas newborns. For every low-birth-weight infant who dies, at least one other survives with a significant handicap. The following measures could increase the number who receive adequate prenatal care:

1. *Increase state support for prenatal care to high-risk mothers.* Prenatal-care programs in local health departments have insufficient resources to meet this need and cannot serve all of the poor women who seek out their services. A few hospitals offer low-cost prenatal care. If neither are available, poor mothers who are ineligible for medicaid or without health insurance receive no professional care.
2. *Require schools to foster awareness of and access to prenatal care.* Kansas schools are not required to educate students about prenatal care. Most do not refer pregnant students to prenatal-care programs, even though lack of care increases the chance these infants will need costly special education.
3. *Use nurse practitioners and physician assistants to provide care in under-served areas.* Access to obstetrical services in rural and poverty areas has deteriorated with the soaring costs of malpractice insurance. Nurse practitioners and physician assistants can effectively provide care, can screen those needing an obstetrician, and do not face as difficult a problem with malpractice insurance.
4. *Provide reminders and incentives to improve prenatal care for medicaid clients.* Medicaid clients do not make sufficient prenatal-care visits to their doctors for a variety of reasons. Reminders, transportation, and small monetary incentives could increase visits and reduce medicaid's hospital costs for low-birth-weight infants.

Child Health. Before school age, children need to be assessed regularly for growth and development, vision, hearing, and other possible impairments to learning. Unless schools require or offer health assessments, preventive health visits do not occur for many children. Also, students need to learn more about how to keep healthy. The following measures could improve the health of Kansas children:

1. *Increase the number of young children receiving health assessments.* If school districts offer or require an assessment, more health problems would be detected and treated before they could interfere with learning.
2. *Upgrade standards for school vision and hearing tests.* Many schools do not test for vision problems at near-point, a condition which interferes with reading; hearing tests sometimes are conducted in noisy areas, which reduces the tests' accuracy. Guidelines are available to improve the quality of these tests.

3. *Require comprehensive K-12 health education in schools.* Kansas does not require health education for its students; lack of school health education has been shown to increase tobacco use and likely contributes to other high-risk behaviors.
4. *Prohibit use of tobacco in school buildings.* Some Kansas schools allow students to use tobacco. Smoke-filled teacher lounges are dangerous for smokers and nonsmokers and tell students smoking is acceptable, at least for adults.

Teenage Pregnancy. Teenage parents are often unprepared to assume parenthood, as evidenced from their rates of child abuse, lack of prenatal care, and divorce. Teenage pregnancy also costs taxpayers in the form of welfare, medicaid, food stamps, and foster care. The following measures could reduce the number of teenage pregnancies:

1. *Require grandparent support for children of minors.* Currently, the teen mother's parents and welfare provide most of the financial support for the children of teen parents. This measure would shift some of this responsibility to the teen father's parents and would give parents an incentive to monitor more closely their teenage children.
2. *Counteract media romanticization of teen sex.* Many teens do not understand the pitfalls of early parenthood and do not know where to obtain counseling and, if necessary, birth control.
3. *Require sex education in Kansas schools.* Most Kansas schools do not teach sex education and will not do so without a state requirement. Teenagers' knowledge of conception and birth control is generally inadequate.
4. *Increase awareness of family planning for teens on welfare.* Few teenagers on welfare use family-planning services that are available at no cost. Relevant state agencies could be required to counsel those teens currently on welfare. Since most teen mothers are daughters of teen mothers, a strong incentive is needed to overcome this role-modeling effect.

High-Risk Adult Behavior. Unhealthy behavior or lifestyle contributes to one-half of U.S. and Kansas deaths. Heart disease, cancer, and stroke are often preventable through diet, not using tobacco, exercise, and health screening. Since most adults work, the following measures could promote health through the work place:

1. *Encourage the use of nonsmoker discounts in health insurance.* Smokers have higher health-care costs but pay the same for their health insurance. Reducing insurance costs for nonsmokers would require smokers to pay more of the costs for this habit and encourage some to quit smoking.
2. *Provide financial assistance for health promotion at work sites.* Large employers can afford health-promotion programs, but small ones rarely can. Local health departments could offer such services as health screen-

ing, help to quit smoking, and drug and alcohol counseling, among other services.

Unnecessary Placement in Nursing Homes. As many as one-fourth of all nursing-home placements could be postponed with available and affordable home-care services such as home visits and help with personal care, housekeeping, and meals. Federal and state government now pay for one-half of those in nursing homes; therefore, reducing nursing-home stays through home care could be cost-effective as well as humane. The following measures could postpone, if not prevent, many placements in nursing homes:

1. *Require preadmission screening before placement in a nursing home.* Half of the elderly are not aware of home-care services as an option to a nursing home. Requiring preadmission screening would allow more elderly to choose a lifestyle that best meets their needs. However, this requirement should not block admission for those desiring a nursing home.
2. *Increase state financial support of home care.* Affordable home-care services have waiting lists or are limited to medicaid's stringent income guidelines. Increasing state financial support could reduce future medicaid nursing-home costs.
3. *Require Insurance Department to hold forums on long-term-care insurance.* Insurance for home care and nursing-home care could spread the risk for this care among the elderly, since only a fourth ever reside in a nursing home. Holding public forums could increase the elderly's knowledge of the availability and wisdom of long-term-care insurance.
4. *Increase the use of volunteer and low-cost caregivers.* Several approaches, such as "volunteer banks" where future volunteer hours are "earned" and stored for future use, could make home care more affordable.

This overview of a public agenda for Kansas is supported by individual studies found in the six chapters that follow. More detailed analysis of the issues and of policy choices available to Kansas are contained in these chapters. Again, these analyses and the policy choices identified are not intended to be exhaustive, but to promote discussion of public issues critical to the future of Kansas.

Two ideals have guided the work and this report of the special commission. One objective has been to make more knowledge of the problems facing Kansas widely available to Kansans. Another objective has been to enhance the capacity of Kansas policy makers in responding to these problems. Ultimately, these policy makers will have responsibility for shaping the next public agenda for Kansas.

ANTHONY L. REDWOOD
GARY R. ALBRECHT

1 _____

The Kansas Economy

The Kansas economy has provided a good standard of living for the people of the state during this century. As well, because of its traditional structure, the state economy did not suffer the degree of volatility resulting from national business cycles that were experienced by the industrialized states. However, significant changes have occurred in the national and international economic order that raise serious questions concerning the capacity of the Kansas economy to underpin adequately the welfare of Kansans in the future if present trends continue.

The purpose of this chapter is to assess the Kansas economy and identify policy choices now facing Kansas decision makers as they seek to position the state for the next century. This analysis will be based on an analysis of the evolution, current status, and outlook of the state's economic and demographic environment. The bottom line is that the Kansas economy is not well positioned to go forward strongly in the next decade, so that restructuring the economic sector for a more prosperous future constitutes a primary challenge for Kansans in the years ahead.

Long-Term Structural Changes[1]

Significant long-term changes have occurred in the state's economic structure over this century, and since World War II in particular. These changes have brought in their wake a profound, albeit gradual, transformation in the state's economic character and demographic composition. The Kansas economy has evolved from a predominantly agricultural one to a mixed form somewhat like that of the national industrial structure. The trend has been one of long transition from farming to other forms of economic activity, so that today farming produces about 9 percent of state product while manufacturing produces 20 percent (see Table 1.1). These figures would have been reversed fifty years ago. This pattern of long-term

---

The authors gratefully acknowledge the assistance of Carolyn Coleman and Rob Johnson.

21

structural change may also be illustrated through trends in income and employment since 1950, with particular emphasis on agriculture.

Personal Income

Personal income in Kansas has grown substantially in recent decades, while farm-related personal income has increased only slightly. Indeed, nonfarm income grew from $2.5 billion in 1950 to more than $30 billion in 1984; farm personal income never exceeded $2 billion in this period. The relative decline in the importance of the farm sector is confirmed by the fact that farm personal income accounted for more than 20 percent of total income in 1950 but represents only 5 percent today.

Dramatic changes have taken place in the contribution of the major economic sectors to the earnings of Kansans (see Figure 1.1). Concurrently with the decline of the farm sector, manufacturing has emerged as the largest earned income generator, though this has leveled out somewhat; the service sector has continued to increase until recently and is likely to stabilize at around the U.S. average. At the same time, mining, the other key sector in the Kansas economic base, exhibited steady decline from 1950 to 1970, a resurgence to a 1982 peak, and then another decline, all within a range of 2 to 4 percent of Kansas earnings. The pattern is clear. Agriculture and mining, two key elements of the Kansas economic base, together contribute less than 10 percent directly to earnings in Kansas, and the proportion is likely to decrease further in the years ahead.

Employment

The most important employment-related measure of structural change is the distribution of jobs among different economic sectors. The significant shifts in Kansas sectors, as well as sector comparisons with national averages, are shown in Table 1.2. Kansas farm employment has decreased from 15 percent of total Kansas employment in 1960 to 5 percent in 1984 but remained above the national average of 3 percent. On the other hand, Kansas manufacturing employment increased slowly over this period from

Table 1.1
Kansas and U.S. Gross National Product by Selected Industries (%)

	1960		1970		1980	
	U.S.	Kansas	U.S.	Kansas	U.S.	Kansas
Farming	4.0	13.1	2.6	10.0	2.9	8.6
Manufacturing	28.6	19.1	25.6	19.5	22.1	20.2
Government	9.4	13.1	11.7	14.7	11.8	11.3
Mining	2.5	NA	1.8	2.5	3.7	5.3

Source: Kansas Department of Economic Development; and U.S. Department of Commerce, *Survey of Current Business*, 1981.

Figure 1.1
**Earnings in Selected Industries as a Percentage of Total Earnings in Kansas,
1950-84**

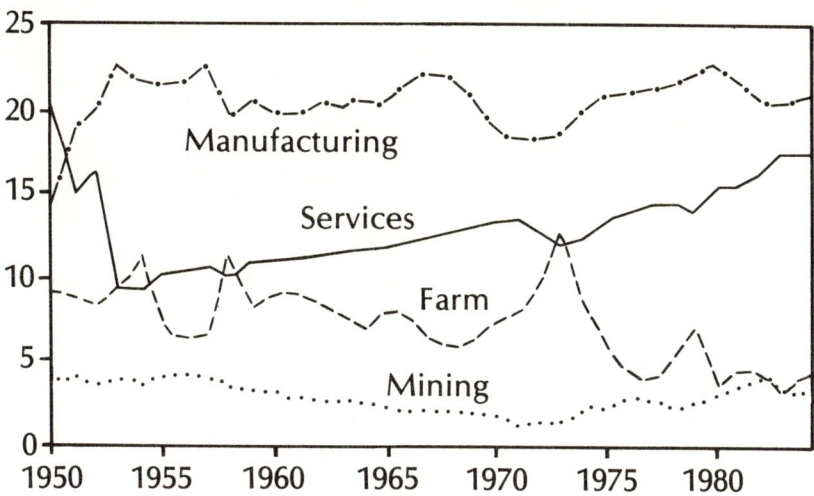

Source: Calculated from U.S. Department of Commerce, Bureau of Economic
Analysis data.

Table 1.2
Composition of Employment in Kansas and the U.S. by Industry (%)

| | 1960 | | 1970 | | 1980 | | 1984 | |
	U.S.	Kansas	U.S.	Kansas	U.S.	Kansas	U.S.	Kansas
Farm	8.3	14.8	4.4	9.4	3.4	5.7	3.2	5.2
Manufacturing	25.5	14.0	24.6	15.2	20.4	16.8	18.5	15.6
Service	11.2	8.5	14.7	11.6	19.1	14.7	19.8	16.2
Government	12.7	13.9	16.0	17.5	16.4	16.6	15.2	16.5
Trade	17.3	15.7	19.1	18.0	20.5	20.0	21.1	21.1
Construction	4.5	4.1	4.6	3.6	4.4	4.1	4.1	3.7
Mining	1.1	2.1	.8	1.2	1.0	1.4	.9	1.6
Other	19.4	27.0	15.9	23.5	15.9	20.7	17.2	20.1
Total	100.0	100.0	100.0	100.0	100.0	100.0	100.0	100.0

Source: U.S. Bureau of Labor Statistics.

14 to 16 percent of the total, while the national proportion declined from
25 to 18 percent. Employment in other Kansas sectors has increased in the
same manner as nationally, and the respective distributions tend to converge.

Two main points can be made in relation to these changes. First, in
1960, the Kansas economic bases—agriculture, mining, and manufacturing—employed 31 percent of the state's work force, compared to 35 percent

for the U.S. In 1984, these key economic sectors of Kansas employed 22.4 percent of the Kansas work force, the corresponding national figure being 22.6 percent; so the convergence is occurring. Supporting sectors in Kansas, such as service, trade and government, therefore serve an economic base today that more closely resembles the national base than ever before.

Second, the decline in agricultural employment has been steady, and employment growth in manufacturing and other expanding sectors has been chronically inadequate to offset the displacement of labor from Kansas farms. While the supporting sectors also have grown, their size is limited by growth in the primary economic base. However, as the economic bases converge, the intensity of this problem may now be lessening.

Mining employment in Kansas has been relatively insignificant, ranging around 1 or 2 percent of total employment (see Table 1.2). While still proportionately greater than the national average, Kansas mining employment has also converged with the national pattern of mining employment. In addition, employment in Kansas mining, which is predominantly oil and gas, has exhibited considerable sensitivity to price changes, which are beyond the control of Kansas producers.

Manufacturing as a percentage of total employment for the U.S. has seen a steady downward trend since 1960 (see Figure 1.2). In Kansas, manufacturing has remained a more stable proportion of employment, although it has also experienced a slight downward trend. Fluctuation in Kansas manufacturing employment has been substantial. This volatility reflects movements in the aircraft component of durable goods manufacturing, beginning in the early sixties. Coincidental with the Vietnam War, a major expansion in aircraft employment in Kansas occurred, lasting until the late sixties, and followed by a dramatic fall in the early 1970s, a further surge about 1980, and a significant decline thereafter.

The manufacture of durable goods constituted 60 to 70 percent of Kansas manufacturing, and one subsector, aircraft, has comprised over 20 percent of total manufacturing employment. The nondurable component, dominated by food and meat products, also has exhibited greater volatility than the U.S. average, but its decline being much more modest than nationally (see Figure 1.2).

The Changing Kansas Farm[2]

Because of its central significance to the evolution of the Kansas economy, changes occurring in the farm sector deserve further examination.

In a context of relatively constant total acreage in Kansas agriculture, the Kansas farm has undergone transition in terms of the number of farms and farm size (see Figure 1.3). The number of farms under 500 acres in size has been declining steadily since World War II. Only farms 500 acres and larger have increased in number over this period. By 1978, farms with

Figure 1.2
Employment in Manufacturing, Durable Goods Manufacturing, and Non-durable Goods Manufacturing as a Percentage of Total Employment, for Kansas and the U.S., 1960-84

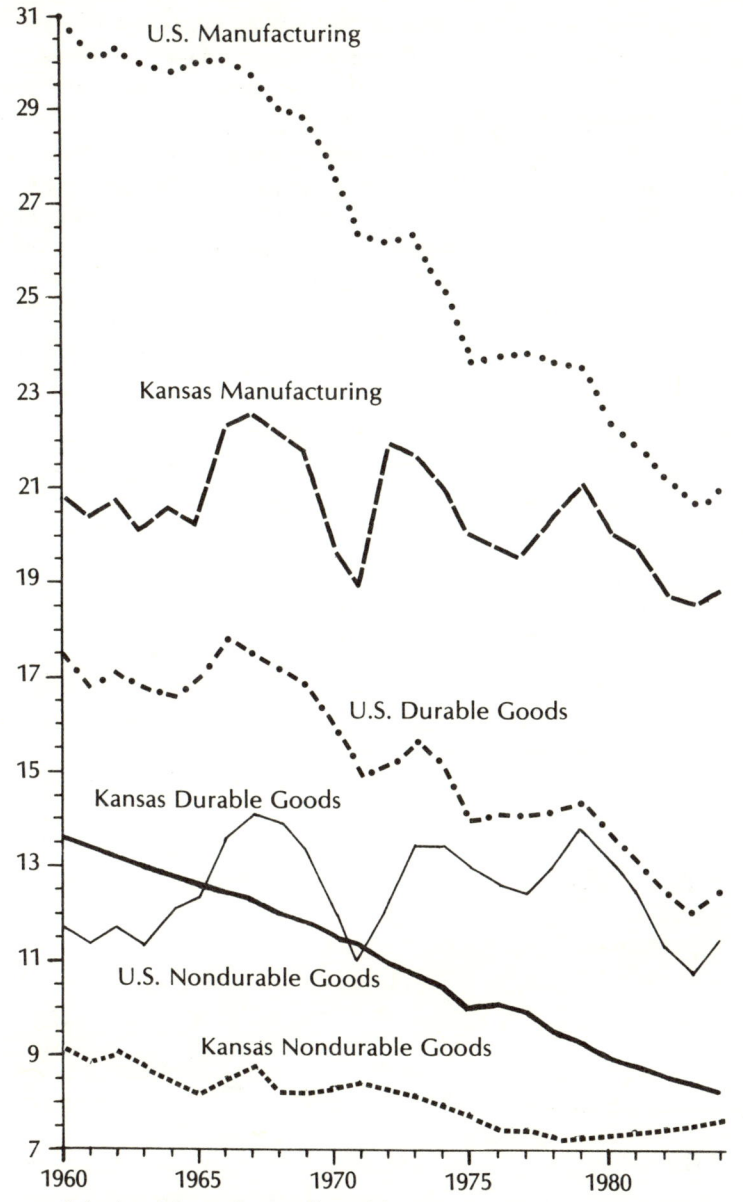

Source: Calculated from data collected by U.S. Bureau of Labor Statistics and Kansas Department of Human Resources.

$500,000 or more in agricultural sales, less than 1 percent of the total number of farms, accounted for over 45 percent of total farm production in Kansas.

In addition, the structure of production inputs in Kansas agriculture has been altered markedly over time. Farming in Kansas has undergone a transformation from self-sufficient enterprises of settlement days—which relied almost exclusively on land, family labor, and animal power as inputs—to market-oriented establishments that depend more and more heavily on outside, purchased inputs. Technological change has been the principal catalyst in this structural revolution. In part, the result has been a substantial decline in the labor requirements for agriculture and a commensurate increase in machinery use. In addition, technological breakthroughs, such as chemical fertilizers, herbicides, and pesticides, have increased production and also saved labor costs, replacing, for example, time-consuming, manual methods of cultivation.

Figure 1.3
Number of Farms in Kansas by Size of Farm, 1945-78 (in thousands)

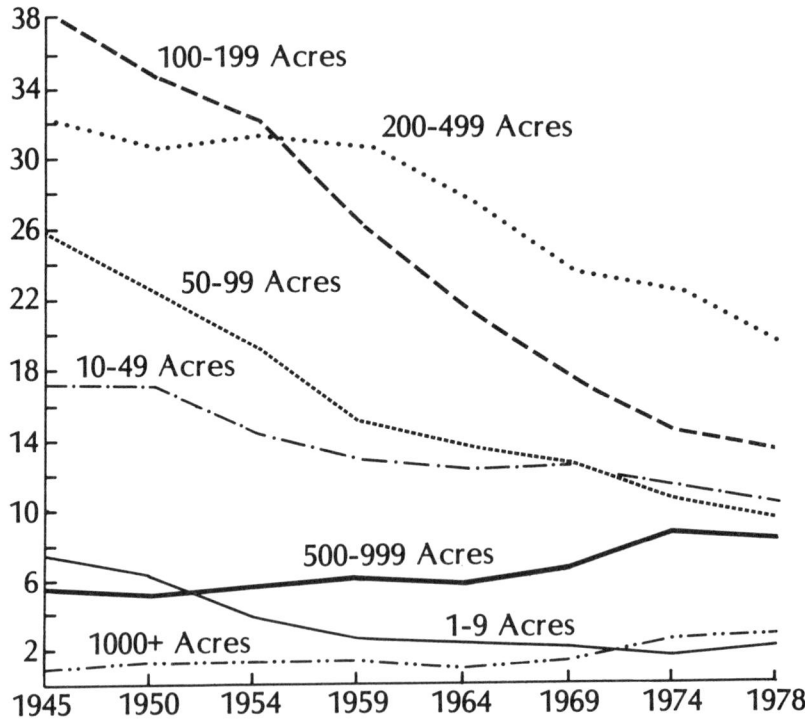

Recent developments in the revolution of the farm economy are detailed in Table 1.3, which shows changes in the use of farm inputs since 1950 for the Northern Plains region (Kansas, Nebraska, and the Dakotas). In 1950, agriculture was still heavily labor-intensive, but this requirement had declined dramatically by 1983. In contrast, chemical usage designed to enhance agricultural yields had shown a twenty-fivefold increase, and the relative importance of machinery also increased, though not as significantly.

Two major consequences follow from this restructuring of agriculture. First, the larger, capital-intensive farms are more vulnerable to the vagaries of the national business cycle, especially with respect to variation in interest rates. Second, farms dependent on machinery and chemicals employ fewer and fewer people.

Recent Economic Performance

During and following the 1980 and 1981-82 recessionary periods, the Kansas economy fell farther, started to recover later, and has grown more slowly than the national economy. This pattern contrasts with the traditional view of Kansas' enjoying a stable economy, somewhat insulated from national cyclical fluctuations. This section reviews recent performance of the Kansas economy with reference to its immunity to national recessions.

Stability in the Kansas Economy[3]

The period from the late 1950s to the early 1970s was characterized by stable growth in Kansas. Although the period 1958-72 was marked by three recessions at the national level, none was particularly severe or long-lasting. In Kansas, either farm income or wage and salary income ameliorated the effects of recessions, and the state economy grew at a relatively smooth, steady rate throughout this period. In other words, Kansas was relatively recession-proof.

Table 1.3
Indexes of Farm Inputs for Northern Plains Region, 1950-83
(1977 = 100)

Year	Labor	Machine	Chemicals
1950	240	77	4
1955	211	90	9
1960	164	85	16
1965	132	78	31
1970	117	84	65
1975	106	100	78
1980	92	99	123
1983	78	91	96

Source: U.S. Department of Agriculture.

Strength in either farm income or wage and salary income insulated the Kansas economy from flucuations in national business cycles. For example, real wage and salary income in Kansas was flat during the 1957-58 recession but took sharp dips coincident with the national recessions in 1960 and 1970. The farm sector propped up the Kansas economy in the latter two instances with growth in receipts from beef and wheat. The fluctuation of wheat and beef receipts *happened* coincidentally to offset the sharp downturns that hit the nonfarm sector during both the 1960 and 1970 recessions. Specifically, wheat earnings in 1960 reached a peak, one not approached again for thirteen years. In 1970, although wheat receipts had fallen, beef income, in the midst of a strong, long-term increase, offset the decline in the nonfarm sector, causing total Kansas income to continue its upward trend through the recession.

Examination of only the direct influence of the Kansas farm sector belies its importance, because farming, like manufacturing, is a primary industry and, as such, forms the life-blood for a number of secondary industries in Kansas. As with any other primary income source, farm income magnifies and creates multiple impact throughout the economy.

Earned personal income, propelled by rapid increases in farm income, grew at an unusually rapid rate from 1971 to 1973, but, as the severe 1973-75 recession set in, Kansas earned income turned sharply down. The downturn occurred principally because of sharp declines after 1973 in wheat and beef earnings; real wage and salary income in Kansas actually rose slightly during this recession.

The decline in Kansas earned income from 1973 to 1975, although steep, represented for the most part a return to the level income would have occupied had it not risen sharply above trend during 1971-73. Therefore, in contrast to the previous two recessions, the 1973-75 contraction was characterized in Kansas by a declining farm sector with a fairly strong nonfarm sector tending, this time, to soften the state's overall decline. In this recession, strong wage and salary income supported the Kansas economy, in contrast to the 1970 recession when wage and salary income fell while farm income supported the economy.

The fact that wage and salary income did not fall during the 1973-75 recession may be attributable to strength in aircraft employment over this time period. The aircraft industry, although based in Wichita, affects employment in all of Kansas. During the 1970 recession, aircraft employment fell dramatically, affecting total employment in Kansas and thereby adding to the decline in wage and salary income during the recession.

Following 1975, Kansas embarked on another period of growth above trend-rates, sparked by a strong surge in the nonfarm wage and salary income, and by another sharp increase in income from beef. The peak was reached in 1979 with beef, wheat, and the nonfarm sector all attaining local maximums.

Kansas' relative stability in the three most recent recessions prior to 1980 is somewhat misleading in that the state's unstable sectors tended to offset each other. For example, rising farm receipts offset the fall in aircraft production, producing an apparent stability (relative to the nation as a whole) that enhanced Kansas' recession-proof image. During 1980-82, however, when both farm income and aircraft production took a downward turn, the result was a major slump in the state's economy. As Sexton and Glass conclude, the "historical tendency for Kansas to be recession proof may, in many cases, have been the result of a fortuitous combination of events rather than the effect of an inherently stable economy."[4]

Economic Performance over Recent Recessionary Periods

The Kansas economy has not recovered as well as the national economy from the 1980 and 1981-82 recessions. Recent employment trends illustrate how Kansas has lagged behind the national economy (see Figure 1.4). The brief respite between the 1980 recession and the 1981-82 recession allowed the number of employed in Kansas to increase from 1980 to 1981. However, the effect of the 1981-82 recession was a decline in overall employment for both the U.S. and Kansas, and the decline in Kansas was much steeper than in the U.S. as a whole. Further, the steep decline in Kansas from 1981 to 1982 began at a level of employment similar to the 1979 level of employment. In the U.S., on the other hand, employment fell in 1982 to a level of employment that was still above the 1979 level. The entire year of 1983 was a recovery year, but in 1983, as in 1984, the expansion was more rapid for the U.S. than for Kansas. As a result, Kansas lost jobs between 1979 and 1984, while the U.S. made substantial gains in the number of people employed.

The declines in both the level of employment in Kansas and Kansas employment relative to the U.S. have reduced the size of the labor force. From 1979 to 1984, the U.S. labor force increased by approximately 8 percent compared to a Kansas rate of growth of about 1 percent over this time period. Kansans leaving the state for employment have probably kept the state labor force from growing apace with the nation's. The reason the unemployment rate in Kansas normally falls below the U.S. rate is that the Kansas unemployed often leave the state to find work.

As the state economy becomes more reliant upon manufacturing employment for its economic health, it becomes more like the U.S. economy and cannot withstand recessions better than the nation as a whole. Manufacturing employment decreased continuously from 1979 through 1983 in both the U.S. and Kansas before picking up in 1984, as shown in Figure 1.4. However, the final level of manufacturing employment falls well below the 1979 level for both the U.S. and Kansas. The 1984 level of manufacturing employment for Kansas was approximately 90 percent of its 1979 level.

Figure 1.4
Change in Total Employment and Manufacturing Employment in the U.S. and Kansas, 1979-84 (1979 employment = 100)

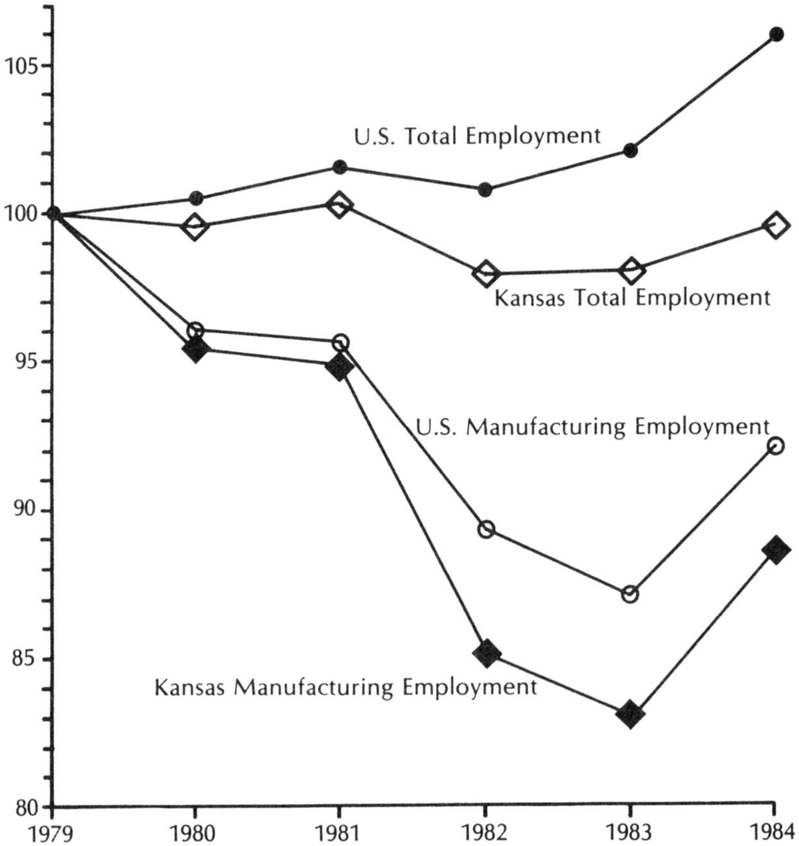

Source: Indexes calculated from data collected by the U.S. Bureau of Labor
   Statistics and the Kansas Department of Human Resources.

Manufacturing employment may be divided into nondurable manufacturing employment and durable manufacturing employment. Employment
in durable goods has been falling since 1979, both in Kansas and nationally,
but the level in Kansas fell about 10 percent more in 1981 and has never
caught up. In Kansas, aircraft and automobile manufacturing comprise a
more significant component of durable goods than in the nation as a whole.
These industries were hit particularly hard during the 1980 and 1981-82
recessions, which would account for Kansas' sharper declines in durable
goods employment. In Kansas, the level of employment in durable goods

for 1984 was around 80 percent of the 1979 level, while the corresponding figure for the U.S. was 90 percent.

Employment in nondurable manufacturing held up well in Kansas relative to the U.S. over the recessionary periods. As a result, the employment level in Kansas in 1984 was approximately 3 percent higher than the 1979 level compared with national employment in nondurable goods at about 95 percent of its 1979 level. Kansas' relatively strong showing in nondurable manufacturing employment is attributable to food products. In particular, the meat packing industry in Southwest Kansas has grown continuously between 1979 and 1984.

Mining employment in Kansas, dominated by oil and gas extraction, has significantly outperformed the U.S. The average well-head price per barrel of oil was $12.64 in 1979, rose to $31.77 in 1981, and then began to taper off to $26.17 in 1983. Mining employment in Kansas followed the price level. Employment in mining fluctuates more in Kansas than the U.S. as a whole because of the volatility of oil prices. Kansas has the largest number of stripper wells in the nation, and these wells produce an average of three barrels per day. Because of this low output, many wells are marginally profitable, and, as the price of oil declines, the number of operating wells drops rapidly. With oil at $14 per barrel, the low profit margin of Kansas wells will induce a precipitous fall in employment levels in Kansas mining.

Although mining employment did perform better than the U.S. over the 1979-84 period, this performance could not offset the poor performance of manufacturing in Kansas. These industries serve as Kansas' export base and as such determine the wealth of Kansas. With such weakness in the state's primary industries, one would not expect employment in secondary industries in Kansas to perform as well as their U.S. counterparts. Indeed, employment in construction, finance, service, trade (wholesale and retail), and transportation and utilities all lagged behind national trends. In not one of these industries did employment in Kansas perform as well as in the U.S. from 1979 to 1984.

The rate of employment growth in a state can differ from the rate of employment growth in the nation for two reasons: on the one hand, the industrial mix of the state can be different from the nation, or on the other hand, a particular industry's rate of growth may be different between the state and nation. A state may, for example, have a disproportionate share of slow-growing industries; yet these industries may be growing at the same rate as their national counterparts. On the other hand, a state's proportion of slow- and fast-growing industries may be the same as the nation's; yet the particular industries may grow at a slower rate than their national counterparts.

If employment in Kansas had grown at the same rate as U.S. employment from November 1979 to November 1984, 1,019.0 thousand people

Table 1.4
Actual and Projected Employment in Kansas, by Industry, November
1979 - November 1984

	Actual 1979	Actual 1984	Projected 1984	Difference between Actual and Projected
Manufacturing	203.2	177.6	193.8	-16.2
Stone, clay, glass	8.3	7.1	7.2	-.1
·Primary metals	4.4	3.3	3.1	.2
Fabricated metals	14.3	11.5	12.4	-.9
Machinery	37.3	27.3	36.6	-9.3
Transportation equip.	57.0	45.0	54.6	-9.6
Other durables	12.4	11.3	12.1	-.8
Food and kindred products	23.4	26.8	22.2	4.6
Apparel	3.7	3.5	3.4	.1
Printing and publications	16.6	18.0	18.2	-.2
Chemical	9.1	8.5	8.7	-.2
Petroleum and coal	4.7	3.3	4.1	-.8
Other nondurables	12.0	12.0	11.2	.8
Mining	14.2	18.0	14.6	3.4
Construction	52.1	43.8	50.5	-6.7
Transportation	65.6	64.8	66.0	-1.2
Wholesale trade	63.5	66.8	67.8	-1.0
Retail trade	165.6	179.6	180.7	-1.1
Finance	46.7	52.1	53.0	-.9
Services	167.4	186.0	203.6	-17.6
Federal government	25.9	26.4	26.0	.4
State and local government	162.5	165.8	163.3	2.5
Total	966.7	980.9	1,019.3	-38.4

Source: Calculated from data collected by the U.S. Bureau of Labor Statistics and
the Kansas Department of Human Resources.
Note: Projections of Kansas employment by industry assume that the rate of
growth from November 1979 to November 1984 was the same as the U.S.
rate of growth in the industry.

would have been employed in Kansas in November 1984. However, only
980.9 thousand people were employed in Kansas in November 1984, a
shortfall of 38,400 employed. Table 1.4 shows, further, the number of
people who would have been employed by each industry in Kansas if each
industry had grown at the same rate as its national counterpart.[5] The summation of projected employment by industry shows that particular industries
in Kansas have, in general, been growing at a slower rate than their national
counterparts and that the industrial mix in Kansas is, practically speaking,
merely neutral in terms of its effect on growth. The different industrial mix
in Kansas, therefore, is not the reason for the slower Kansas growth; the
reason is simply that the industries in Kansas grew more slowly than their
national counterparts.

In particular, manufacturing industries are not keeping up with the rates
of growth by their national counterparts. Manufacturing has, over time,

become the principal source of the state's economic health and was not strong enough either to resist or to respond vigorously to the recessions of the early 1980s. As a result, jobs lost in manufacturing initiate a significant "multiplier" effect throughout the state economy.

The pattern found in employment is also reflected in business formation. As shown in Table 1.5, the number of firms increased more rapidly in the U.S. than in Kansas from 1979 to 1983. A notable exception was in mining, in which the number of firms increased by 42.0 percent in Kansas and by 32.6 percent in the U.S. In terms of the surrounding states, Kansas is on par with Missouri and Nebraska. These three states, however, lag considerably behind Colorado and Oklahoma in terms of recent growth in the number of establishments. Colorado and Oklahoma significantly outperform the other states except for agricultural services, forest, and fisheries, an industry in which Kansas excels. Kansas performs well relative to Missouri and Nebraska in mining, transportation, and wholesale trade.

In sum, recent performance in the Kansas economy has, with few exceptions, lagged behind national economic trends. While Kansas had been insulated somewhat from the effects of national recessions in the past, recent weakness in manufacturing employment, particularly, has not been offset by comparable strength in other core industries. Indeed, the lack of vitality in Kansas' primary sectors has slowed employment growth in secondary industries as well. Kansas is no longer positioned to ride out fluctuations of the national business cycle.

Demographic Trends

While the Kansas population level has increased each decade since the first census, Kansas' share of the total U.S. population has declined from 2.27 percent in 1890 to 1.04 percent in 1980, as shown in Table 1.6. Projections indicate that Kansas will have 0.93 percent of U.S. population in 2000 and possibly as low as 0.75 in 2030 based on existing trends.

Table 1.5
Percentage Change in Number of Establishments by Industry for Selected States, 1979-83

	Agriculture	Mining	Construction	Manufacturing	Transportation	Wholesale trade	Retail trade	Finance	Services	Total
Kansas	40.3	42.0	-4.5	8.3	20.5	10.7	11.6	8.4	22.1	13.4
Colorado	37.3	64.3	4.6	21.9	28.3	20.1	21.1	21.1	33.9	26.7
Missouri	24.3	14.6	-5.1	6.2	12.1	5.7	10.7	7.0	21.3	12.1
Nebraska	33.0	15.7	-9.5	8.0	14.8	4.1	9.7	5.7	18.9	10.4
Oklahoma	34.1	68.1	7.2	17.0	13.5	18.7	15.8	18.6	28.5	23.2
U.S.	28.7	32.6	-0.1	8.9	14.8	12.9	14.5	10.5	26.3	17.0

Source: Figures are calculated from *County Business Patterns,* 1979 and 1983.

Kansas has also had one of the lowest population growth rates among the states, a situation likely to continue if present trends persist. In comparison to neighboring states, Kansas' growth rate has been well below that of Colorado and Oklahoma, and about the same as Nebraska and Missouri (see Table 1.7). This pattern is projected to continue.

Given that Kansas birth and death rates approximate those of the nation, slow population growth has been caused largely by net outmigration, which has been chronic over time, occurring each census decade since 1890. The level, nature, and location of economic activity largely determines the level and distribution of a population, so that people stay or migrate according to the availability and attractiveness of economic opportunities at home and elsewhere. During the decade 1960-70, Kansas experienced a net outmigration of 130,000 people, which was over 6 percent of the 1960 population; estimates of net outmigration between 1970 and 1980 range from 20,000 to 25,000.

Table 1.6
Kansas Population and Percentage of U.S. Population, 1890-2030

Year	Kansas population	% of U.S. population
1890	1,428,108	2.27
1900	1,470,495	1.93
1910	1,690,949	1.83
1920	1,769,257	1.66
1930	1,880,999	1.53
1940	1,801,028	1.36
1950	1,905,299	1.26
1960	2,178,611	1.21
1970	2,249,071	1.10
1980	2,363,679	1.04
1990[a]	2,463,500	0.99
2000[a]	2,494,400	0.93
2030[a]	2,668,300	0.75

Source: U.S. Bureau of the Census.
[a] Projected.

Table 1.7
Population Growth Rates in Selected States (%)

	1950-60	1960-70	1970-80	1980-90[a]	1990-2000[a]
Kansas	14.4	3.2	5.1	4.0	1.3
Colorado	32.4	25.8	30.7	29.5	24.0
Missouri	9.2	8.3	5.1	3.0	0.1
Nebraska	6.5	5.2	5.7	4.2	1.4
Oklahoma	4.3	9.9	18.2	15.5	12.6
U.S.	18.5	13.2	11.4	9.7	7.3

Source: U.S. Bureau of the Census, Series P-25, No. 937.
[a] Projected.

Net migration will ebb and flow over time according to how well the state's economy is doing relative to other states. For example, significant net outmigration occurred from 1970-75 as employment growth weakened, but from 1975 to 1980, when job creation improved, more people moved into Kansas than left the state. However, net outmigration has been modest in the 1980s, despite below-average economic growth, suggesting that the underlying cause of the past outflow, namely labor displacement from the farm sector, is no longer the dominant force it once was.

Outmigration is concentrated heavily in the 25-35-year age group and reflects the departure of out-of-state youth who come to Kansas for college. However, many of those leaving are Kansas youth, including the better educated, who have been unable to secure appropriate job opportunities in the state. Even when the state experiences net inmigration overall, as for the period 1975-80, net outmigration tends to occur for the 25-29 age group. The implication is clearly that the state must not only create an adequate number of jobs, but also jobs of high quality.

Regardless of the interstate migration situation, most counties in the state have experienced continuing net outmigration. For some, the outflow has ranged up to 25 percent of a county's population in a single decade. Over half of Kansas' counties suffered net outmigration in both decades 1960-70 and 1970-80. This substantial population loss over a wide area of Kansas raises profound policy questions over the future of rural communities, a subject addressed in Chapter 2.

Population Structure and Distribution

The population of the state has been redistributed in recent decades as agriculture has become much less labor-intensive and as other economic sectors have evolved. New economic activity has become concentrated in the area roughly bounded by Interstates 35, 135, and 70. Serious losses of population have occurred primarily from the western half of the state, although 33 percent of the state's population is still rural, compared to 26 percent for the nation as a whole.

The population of the nation and the state has also been aging. In 1970, the median age of Kansans was 28.7 years, compared with a median age of 28.0 for all U.S. residents. By 1980, Kansans' median age was 30.1, that for the nation as a whole 30.0. This narrowing is a favorable movement, though it could be explained by the relatively strong influx of college-age students to our public and private colleges from other states during the 1970s.

The age distribution of Kansans has not been uniform across the state. The median age of the Kansas population in 1980 ranged from 22.8 years in Riley County to 44.8 years in Elk County. In general, median ages were much higher in north-central and southeastern Kansas than in other regions of the state.

Statewide, the percentage of the population aged 65 and over was 13 percent in 1980 as opposed to 11 percent in the nation as a whole. Again, the age distribution of Kansans was not uniform, ranging from 5.5 percent of the Riley County population's being 65 years and over to 26 percent in Elk County. The north-central and southeastern portions of the state had the highest concentrations of older Kansans. This aging phenomenon has important social policy implications for the state.

The age structure of the Kansas population for 1980 and projections for the year 2000 by the U.S. Census Bureau are given in Table 1.8. Several aspects are worth noting: First, the 15-24 age group will decline from 19.1 percent of the Kansas population in 1980 to 14.7 percent in 2000. Second, the 25-44 age group will increase from 26.5 percent in 1980 to 31 percent in 1990 and 27.6 percent in 2000. And third, the group aged 45 and over will increase from 32.2 percent in 1980 to 35.7 percent in 2000. These developments will mirror changes in the U.S. population age structure except that, if anything, the Kansas population and work force will continue to be slightly older than that for the U.S.

One of the great challenges facing Kansas in the next 15 years will be to adjust our education and training, as well as other social and economic policy, to this changing population structure and aging work force in an era of rapid technological change.

Economic Outlook

As noted above, the wealth-creating industries in Kansas, which serve as a foundation for the Kansas economy, are currently weak. Historically, the basic industries of aviation, oil and gas, and agriculture have served Kansans well. However, recent trends and current performance of these industries raise policy issues for Kansans with respect to future economic development. This section examines these industries, their inherent strengths and weaknesses, and their outlook for the future.

Table 1.8
Kansas Population by Age Group, 1980 and Projections for 2000

Age group	1980	%	2000	%
under 5	180,877	7.7	174,200	7.0
5-14	344,378	14.5	374,100	15.0
15-19	217,721	9.2	192,900	7.7
20-24	232,788	9.9	175,100	7.0
25-34	374,618	15.9	308,500	12.4
35-44	249,600	10.6	379,800	15.2
45-59	351,300	14.9	458,900	18.4
60-69	200,241	8.4	180,100	7.2
70 and over	212,055	8.9	250,800	10.1
Total	2,363,679	100.0	2,494,400	100.0

Source: U.S. Bureau of the Census.

Traditional Industries

The traditional Kansas industries of aviation, oil and gas, and agriculture are not currently in a strong position. A key question in the economic development of Kansas is whether further decline in these industries is anticipated.

Aircraft. The aircraft industry in Kansas consists of two elements, commercial aviation and general aviation, the former being large commercial-transport aircraft, that is, large commercial jets, and the latter being smaller recreational, business, and regional-carrier aircraft.

The commercial aircraft industry delivered an estimated 275 aircraft in 1985, up sharply from the 188 units delivered in 1984. The Boeing 737 is a particularly successful model in this market. Fortunately for Kansas, a large portion of the assembly of 737s occurs at Boeing's Wichita plant. The U.S. Department of Commerce predicts that world traffic growth and the need for replacement aircraft will keep demand strong for large transport aircraft. Due to the fact that Boeing and McDonnell-Douglas are the only domestic builders of these large transports, Boeing in Wichita will be anticipated to provide growing employment opportunities.

The vigor of the commercial transport market contrasts with general aviation. Approximately 60 percent of general aviation aircraft that are produced in the United States are made in Kansas. In 1979, 17,048 general aviation aircraft were shipped; this number fell to 2,691 by 1983 and to 2,050 by 1985. The U.S. Department of Commerce estimates that 2,200 units will be produced in 1986.

The reasons for this decline are not clear. Initially, the market downturn for general aviation aircraft was believed to reflect the general downturn of the 1980 and 1981-82 recessions. Evidence now suggests that, although the recessions may have aggravated the negative trend, there are other factors involved.

Partial explanations of the reduction in general aviation aircraft shipments include the changing nature of the regional airline industry, the strong dollar favoring increased imports of foreign-produced aircraft, and declining demand being satisfied by products in service. In 1980, imports of general aviation aircraft accounted for 20 percent of the market; in 1985, imports increased to 37 percent of the market. Several foreign manufacturers are aiming at the growing market of aircraft with twenty to sixty seats.

The U.S. Department of Commerce expects more structural shifts in the general aviation industry; in particular, the department forecasts a growth in the industry of 3.6 percent for each of the next five years. In terms of units, this growth would be quite small since current production is low. Consequently, the general aviation industry is unlikely to attain in the near-term its former level of production.

The prospects for the aircraft industry in Kansas are mixed. The general aviation sector has been weak, and the first quarter of 1986 was the worst ever for the industry and for the production of general aviation aircraft. However, the recent decline in the strength of the dollar will be a source of strength for general aviation. Kansas should continue, however, to benefit from the strong market for large transports.

Oil and Gas. As noted above, the Kansas petroleum industry is extremely sensitive to variations in the price of crude oil. When oil prices fall, the number of operating wells drops rapidly. One study estimates that, when the price of crude falls to $18 a barrel, over 15 percent of Kansas wells will be abandoned; if the price falls to $15 a barrel, approximately 23 percent of the wells will be abandoned.[6] Another measure of the sensitivity of the Kansas petroleum industry to prices is the correlation between the number of active drilling rigs and the price of crude oil. In 1979, when the well-head price of oil averaged around $13 per barrel, the average rig count for Kansas was 66; in 1980, when the average price jumped to $22 per barrel, the number of rigs was 120. More recently, the number of active drilling rigs has been declining steadily from a high of 224 rigs attained in 1984. In mid-February 1986, the count of active rigs fell to between fifty to sixty as oil prices continued to fall. Collins and Eck estimate that for every dollar change in the price of well-head crude, the rig count will change by ten in the same direction.[7]

During the second half of the 'seventies, many developing countries became dependent on oil revenues. The demise of the oil cartel—with the resulting price decline—has forced these countries to attempt to maintain oil revenues by increasing output. The chronic oversupply of oil will keep downward pressure on the price of oil. This price consideration, combined with the nature of the Kansas oil industry, suggests that this important source of wealth for Kansas cannot be relied upon to generate income much greater than the present level.

Agriculture. Wheat and cattle have been the mainstays of Kansas agriculture, historically producing 70 to 75 percent of agricultural receipts. The worldwide supply of wheat has been continuously increasing. Countries such as India and China, which historically imported wheat, now export it. This increasing supply of wheat has outpaced the demand, and stockpiles have been increasing, as shown in Table 1.9. Unless there are interruptions in the worldwide supply, a continuing increase in the stock of wheat is anticipated. This growing wheat surplus will, or course, put downward pressure on price. The decline in the value of the dollar will offset partially the effect of growing wheat surpluses and increase the demand for U.S. wheat. As a result, further significant decline is unlikely, but little improvement in the current situation is foreseen.

The U.S. Department of Agriculture anticipates rising beef prices, which is certainly good news for cattle producers. This improvement will not solve the agricultural problem in Kansas; it will, however, help offset weaknesses in other economic sectors.

Table 1.9
World Supply and Demand for Wheat (metric tons)

	Production	Exports[a]	Consumption[b]	Ending stocks[c]
1979-80	422.8	86.0	443.5	80.4
1980-81	442.9	94.1	445.7	78.2
1981-82	448.4	101.3	441.4	85.1
1982-83	479.1	98.6	467.9	96.5
1983-84	491.0	102.9	486.6	100.8
1984-85[d]	513.9	107.2	500.6	114.1
1985-86[e]	505.2	90.9	494.2	125.1

Source: U.S. Department of Agriculture.
Note: Data not available for all countries.
[a] Excludes trade within European Common Market.
[b] Where stocks data are not available (excluding USSR), consumption includes stock changes.
[c] Stocks data are based on differing marketing years and do not represent levels at a given data.
[d] Estimated.
[e] Projected.

Kansas as a Place to Do Business

While Kansas faces adverse economic and demographic trends, the state has important strengths to build upon in formulating economic development policy. One of the most important strengths of Kansas, if not the most important strength, is its people. Kansans have a strong work ethic: they perform a day's work for a day's pay.

Kansas has a relatively high wage rate, but this should not impede development. Kansas and neighboring states have hourly manufacturing wage rates higher than the U.S. average, and, regionally, Kansas is second only to Iowa (see Table 1.10). However, the average hourly wage rate in Kansas is distorted by the high-paying aviation, auto, and rubber industries. The frequency distribution of hourly wage rates in Kansas is bimodal: there is a large group of Kansas workers who are highly paid and a large group with moderate wages.

For every dollar paid to a Kansas manufacturing employee, dollars are added to the value of the product. In terms of productivity, Kansas ranks higher than any of the neighboring states and fifth among all states based on the value added by manufacturing employee per dollar of payroll. These data demonstrate that Kansas workers are productive in return for being well paid (see Table 1.11).

Many manufacturing firms prefer to locate where the unemployment rate is high, thus ensuring an adequate supply of labor. While, historically, the unemployment rate in Kansas has been lower than the nation, a hidden supply of labor is available in many counties of the state. A study by Francke

Table 1.10
Average Hourly Manufacturers Wage Rates, 1983

	Hourly wage	State rank[a]
Kansas	$ 9.28	35
Colorado	8.97	28
Iowa	10.09	42
Missouri	8.89	26
Nebraska	8.75	21
Oklahoma	9.21	34
U.S.	8.71	-

Source: U.S. Department of Labor, Bureau of Labor Statistics, *Employment and Earnings*.
[a] Lowest wage ranked first.

Table 1.11
Value Added by Manufacturing Employee Per Dollar of Production Payroll, 1982

	Value added	State rank
Kansas	4.69	5
Colorado	4.27	17
Iowa	4.55	8
Missouri	4.14	21
Nebraska	4.44	13
Oklahoma	3.92	33
U.S.	4.05	-

Source: U.S. Department of Commerce, Bureau of the Census, 1982 Census of Manufacturers, *Preliminary Report Summary Series*.

indicates that for Kansas the low unemployment rate may be misleading concerning available labor supply.[8] In many counties, a large supply of "latent labor," persons who would enter the labor force under certain economic conditions, exists. Therefore, low unemployment should not be a constraint on attracting new industry to Kansas.

The high educational level of Kansans constitutes another quality of the Kansas work force. Most firms seeking a location require the availability of a technically qualified, trainable work force. Kansas ranks seventh in the U.S. in median years of schooling. A higher proportion of Kansans also pursues graduate and professional work, such as engineering and business degrees, than the U.S. population as a whole.

Concerning the weight firms attach to taxes when making location decisions, the evidence is mixed. Certainly, however, any expense of doing business affects the bottom line and will influence location decisions to some degree. Experience suggests that a state's taxes should not stand out on the negative side. In general, Kansas taxes do blend with those of neighboring states. There are exceptions, however, which form barriers to development and should be removed. For example, Kansas is one of few states in the nation that have a sales tax on machinery and equipment used in manufacturing. Another tax detrimental to business development is the property tax on inventories. Kansas is unique in the region for having this tax. Although Kansas taxes tend to be slightly high for business, removal of these anomalies, which is under consideration, will bring Kansas more into line with neighboring states.

The geographical location of Kansas is often cited as an advantage Kansas holds in attracting firms. However, exploiting geographical location requires a good transportation network. Kansas must maintain its highway network to take advantage of this inherent strength and find resources to fund major highway access to the southeast and southwest regions of the state. Further, many areas of the state lack air service.

In sum, further deterioration of the industries that have historically served Kansas well is not anticipated, but growth will be modest. These industries remain an important feature of the Kansas economy but should not be relied upon to provide sufficient employment opportunities for Kansans in the future. By building upon the strengths that Kansas has, the state can succeed in the competition to provide economic opportunities for its citizens.

Policy Choices for Economic Growth

The preceding analysis raises certain policy issues concerning the economic future of Kansans. Will a continuation of existing economic trends provide an acceptable level of social and economic welfare for Kansans? Should Kansas allow these trends to continue, or attempt to influence them for the better? What is the cost of "doing nothing"?

With few exceptions, Kansas economic performance has been below the U.S. average during the 1980s with respect to income and employment. From 1979 to 1985, personal income grew at an average annual rate of 2.57 percent in the U.S., while for Kansas it grew at 2.06 percent. If Kansas had grown at the same rate as the U.S. over this period, Kansas personal income would be larger by $4.6 billion in 1985 dollars. This level of income would have meant an additional 40,000-50,000 jobs and additional revenues of $240-250 million (1985 dollars) for state government. These rough estimates are indicative of the consequences of relatively weak economic performance. This revenue "loss," for example, seriously affects the capacity of the state to provide basic social services to those in need, to fund public schools and higher education, and to maintain roads and other physical infrastructure at a level enjoyed by other Americans.

Extrapolating into the balance of this decade, if Kansas could achieve a 0.5-percent increase in the annual growth rate of personal income for

1986-91, that is, approximate average U.S. performance, personal income five years hence would be greater by $2.7 billion (1985 dollars), 30,000-40,000 more jobs than expected would be created, and $135-140 million (1985 dollars) in state government revenues would be added, based on tax provisions prevailing prior to the 1986 changes. These ballpark estimates illustrate the serious consequences for Kansans if recent trends continue into the 1990s.

Potential Economic Structure

What form of economic development is feasible for Kansas in the future? What type of economic structure can the state realistically develop? Should an industrial structure based on our existing economy be envisioned, or is it feasible to aim for a relatively different economic composition based on new industry?

The state's economic base provides the ultimate source of jobs and income in Kansas. The economic base comprises those industries that produce goods and services that are "exported" from Kansas to other states or countries and hence bring new money to Kansas. Also included are those industries that supply other Kansas industries with goods and services, which would otherwise be imported, and economic activities, such as tourism, in which services are provided to non-Kansans.

All other industries can be characterized as the local-market economy, which involves trade within the state. They do not bring new money into the state, but simply recirculate that which is already here. The size of the local-market economy is largely determined by the size of the economic base and will contract or expand in response to changes in that base.

A state achieves economic growth, therefore, by increasing the value of output from its economic base. The increased earnings of Kansans arising from that expansion then circulate in the local-market economy, creating additional jobs and income in that sector. The primary focus of a successful economic development strategy, therefore, must obviously be on the expansion of the state's economic base.

The Kansas economic base consists of agriculture, mostly wheat and beef; mining, primarily oil and gas; manufacturing, particularly aviation and food processing; and exported services, such as engineering, software development, and tourism. Kansas has clusters of producers, suppliers, skills, knowledge, infrastructure, and institutions that are geared to these industries. The attributes of our state have provided a competitive advantage in the past to the production of these particular goods and services within Kansas compared with other localities.

The outlook for this Kansas economic base suggests, at best, relatively weak growth in the future. This base has not been able to generate adequate income and employment in the recent past; nor will it provide a sole foundation for the future. In essence, the vision of a future Kansas economy with the same structure as today does not represent a viable alternative in itself. The traditional sectors can no longer carry the state as they did in the past.

Should Kansas countenance an approach of allowing our current base to fade away and be replaced by a completely new structure? This situation could occur only if the substitute industries were also based on comparative advantage. If a substitute economic structure were based on artificial comparative advantage, such as developing a wine industry in competition with California, it would be expensive and vulnerable. Abandoning our traditional sectors is simply not a viable option for Kansas.

Kansas cannot rely on its traditional base; nor can the state depend on the development of a radically different industrial mix. A realistic form of economic development for Kansas must incorporate the old into the new. If the current economic base of Kansas is conceived as a "stool" having three legs, namely, agriculture, oil and gas, and manufacturing (particularly aviation and food processing), the future stool must have a foundation of four legs, the present sectors plus a fourth sector comprising some share of the new evolving industries in this era of technological development and application. Kansas has important traditional industries; yet these industries need to be enhanced with new basic industries.

A Kansas Economic Development Strategy

What strategy will produce an expanding economic base for the future comprising a mix of traditional industry and new development? How can Kansas retain, nourish, and strengthen traditional sectors and concurrently attract and nurture new industry?

The traditional sectors will survive and remain as the primary components of the economic core only if they become the gateways or conduits through which new products or processes emerge. This course necessarily involves the application of science and technology to the core industries so that resources are utilized to compete in world markets in the most competitive and innovative manner.

Fostering timely adaptation to change therefore beomes a leading objective of an economic strategy for Kansas. The harsh reality of the world economic order is that those industries which develop and apply new and existing knowledge rapidly and efficiently will be the ones with a competitive edge. For Kansas, providing an environment and support for innovation in, and the application of science and technology to, the existing economic base will be required to develop new industry.

Where will the impetus come from? What is the role of the state, the private sector, other key institutions, and groups in Kansas? First, the role of the state is limited, but it is vital. State government does not have the capacity or power to conduct a comprehensive industrial policy that makes broad, strategic allocation decisions affecting all aspects of economic development. Nor does the state have control over commodity markets, tariffs, capital markets, or the money supply. Moreover, the prevailing philosophy of free enterprise and the traditional perception of the function of state government limits the scope of state government in being an active partner in the development of business enterprises. The state can, however, play a vital role by creating the preconditions for economic development to flourish, which are

1. establishing an optimum foundation for development, such as tax structure and physical infrastructure;
2. fostering productive linkages, for example, private sector-state government cooperation and university-business research;
3. cultivating a favorable business climate; and
4. removing barriers to entrepreneurship and innovation.

While state government can and must establish the preconditions for economic growth, the state cannot be the main party to development. The private sector and other groups must respond to the opportunity that the state will open for profitable venture.

Consequently, an optimum strategy for the economic development of Kansas should emphasize a balanced approach of supporting the existing economic base as well as fostering growth through the expansion of old, and the attraction of new, industry. Such an approach could incorporate the following thrusts:

1. *Enhance and extend the traditional sectors*, for example, through diversification into new agricultural products and greater value added in processing. The future viability of these sectors will depend on their ability to adapt to new products and processes, as well as on their competitiveness with current products.
2. *Retain, sustain, and expand existing industry.* Businesses of small-to-medium scale seem to be highly compatible with the Kansas environment. Given that 70 to 80 percent of new job creation occurs in small businesses, Kansas provides a favorable basis for vitality through expansion based on modernization and enhanced competitiveness and new business formation through entrepreneurship.
3. *Develop new industry.* Despite sound fundamentals, important strengths, and limited barriers, the state is not overly attractive to outside industry. Some improvement in attractiveness will occur with any enhancement of the fundamentals and strengths, or removal of barriers. In seeking new industry, the state should recognize that only certain types of industry will find Kansas attractive and that foreign investment represents an important source for job creation, one being actively pursued by other states.

Given this focus on development from within, complemented by the attraction of new industry to the state, the key elements of an optimum strategy for Kansas would seem to be as follows:

1. *Foster competitiveness through innovation.* Individual firms, particularly small business, often have insufficient resources and technical capacity to learn about new technological developments and capitalize on new ideas. New technology will not be a separate industry but will rather be at the heart of every industrial sector. Existing Kansas industry will not survive, let alone expand, unless it innovates, and the future viability of the weakened traditional sector depends on it.

   Economic development initiatives to foster competitiveness and create a culture of innovation would include: increasing the pool of innovation, through university research, both basic and applied, and joint university-business research; improving access to innovation, through mechanisms for technology transfer and industry liaison; and creating incentives to innovate, such as tax credits for research and development and tax exemptions for research and development facilities.

2. *Foster appropriate linkages and interrelations.* Success will depend on committed and cooperative work by many groups and purposeful leadership at many levels. The lack of an integrated approach has handicapped the state program to date in terms of level, direction, and effectiveness. Linkages and organization can be improved significantly by more directed policy formation, through legislative committees and the establishment of a blue-ribbon policy-advising group; by broader input to policy formulation, through private sector and other key group participation; and by greater operational effectiveness, through better organization of the state effort, and closer involvement of and with the local communities.

3. *Encourage entrepreneurship.* Kansas will need imaginative, risk-taking entrepreneurs who are able to turn ideas for new products and processes into successful business ventures. Entrepreneurs exist in all communities, but the vigor with which they emerge depends on the entrepreneurial environment—the availability of the role models, access to financial institutions, rewards for risk-taking, and above all the absence of barriers. The availability of capital is critical to new business development and expansion, and the lack of capital constitutes a primary barrier to the growth of small business in Kansas. A primary cause of failure is lack of managerial competence and knowhow. Initiatives to cultivate homespun entrepreneurship include encouraging university connections and settings, for example, research parks and research incubators; developing risk- and venture-capital pools; and providing technical assistance and support for managerial development.

4. *Provide the optimum infrastructure and business climate.* A key objective of infrastructure development and business climate enhancement is to improve the competitiveness and profitability of existing and potential Kansas industry. The task is to cultivate both the notion and reality that

Kansas is a good place to locate economic activity. If the business environment is rewarding to existing industry, it will also be attractive to new industry. Kansas will lose attractiveness relative to other states if its tax structure and levels contain significant anomalies or fail to send the right "signals" about business climate. In particular, the state must avoid having a tax that generally is not found in competing states and negatively affects business in a significant way. Initiatives of the following kind can improve the business environment:

a. making physical infrastructure development compatible with state economic goals, by supporting infrastructure development related directly to business activity, loan pools for transportation, and industrial park development and by establishing priorities for road and other physical investment based on economic purpose;

b. moving the state tax structure into line with regional patterns, for example, through sales tax exemption for purchase of capital equipment and removal of the property tax on inventories;

c. providing special assistance for individual firms and small businesses, for example, information and technical services and marketing support;

d. creating relevant and effective incentives to encourage business location in Kansas, for example, an option for property tax abatement to local government, venture capital, and tax credits for research and development;

e. retaining commitment and support for public schools and higher education, to maintain one of the state's greatest assets;

f. ensuring that work-skill development meets industry needs; and

g. enhancing the quality of life.

5. *Remove barriers to development.* Significant impediments to business development, which retard expansion and discourage new industry, can be found in the Kansas business environment. Examples include tax measures impacting Kansas business unduly, for example, the sales tax on plant and equipment and the property tax on inventories; lack of nontraditional capital; lack of technical assistance and support for small business management; and constitutional limitations on the involvement of state government in economic development. Removal of such barriers is crucial to the release of entrepreneurship and enhancement of business confidence.

Economic development initiatives should be evaluated in terms of their contribution to these basic elements of strategy.

Conclusion

To achieve long-term improvement in the economic base, the state will need to make a large and sustained funding investment over the next decade to support a well-designed package of economic development initiatives. Even so, there is no absolute guarantee of success from a large-scale effort. Patience will be necessary because the specific payoffs will be long-term and uncertain.

In addition, transition through structural change can be uneven and painful. While the strategy outlined above provides the opportunity for development anywhere in the state, success is more likely in certain parts than in others. Appropriate social policies may therefore be necessary to ensure that all Kansans share the fruits of economic development, with a particular focus on displaced persons and distressed areas.

While the challenge facing Kansas is not an insurmountable one, it will be difficult. The path to progress will require substantial investment, patience, leadership, and commitment. It can be done.

CHARLES E. KRIDER
DOUGLAS A. HOUSTON

2

Economic Prospects for Rural Communities

Kansas rural economies are growing at a slower rate than Kansas as a whole or United States averages and in many cases are experiencing actual declines in employment and population. A major underlying source of weakness in rural communities is ongoing structural changes in agriculture. During this period of change in agriculture, numerous federal deregulatory initiatives have begun, for example, in transportation, and these have been alleged to exacerbate an already difficult problem.

Replacing labor with capital in agricultural production has been a long-term trend in the United States. The proportion of Kansans employed in agriculture has declined steadily throughout the century, from 54 percent in 1900 to approximately 5 percent at the present time. The system for providing farms with supplies and in distributing farm products has changed as well. The result is that many small communities that provided services to the agricultural sector of the economy and homes for farm workers have lost an important segment of their economic function. Additionally, federal farm policies are undergoing changes that, coupled with the growing importance of export markets, likely will make farm-based communities more susceptible to open-market influences. The current problems of agriculture have resulted in substantial declines in the value of farmland and in the serious deterioration of banks that have relied upon agricultural loans.

Federal deregulation policies have the potential to compound problems in the agricultural economy by increasing the cost of doing business in rural communities relative to urban areas. If a rural area has been receiving services under regulation at prices less than the incremental cost of providing them, then moves to open the entire market will push rural prices upward and, perhaps, reduce frequency and quality of services. The loss of these "cross subsidies" in transport, telephone service, and other sectors can raise the cost of living and of doing business in rural areas relative to

49

urban areas. Further, a declining willingness of the federal government to subsidize directly or indirectly organizations such as the rural electric co-operatives will raise costs to rural communities. On the other hand, dere-gulated markets and competition often lead to increased innovation in service provision and downward pressure on prices because of more alert management, increased efficiency, and the removal of numerous direct and indirect regulatory costs. Deregulation effects typically are a "mixed bag" and must be examined carefully in the context of the changes in rural communities.

This chapter will examine the economic situation of rural communities in Kansas and prospects for the future. The focus is upon current economic and demographic trends and what these imply for the ability of rural com-munities to adapt to changing conditions. Certain essential services pro-vided to rural Kansas, for example, transportation and public utilities, are then analyzed. Finally, the policy choices posed by these analyses are presented with emphasis on stimulating economic development in rural communities. The choices for Kansas are clearly tied to an overall agenda for economic development in the state and include the less visible but critical framework for sustained long-term prosperity.

Rural Economic Growth

The essential economic problem for rural communities in Kansas is that the continuing decline in agricultural employment has not been offset by growth in other industries. Since declining agricultural employment is a long-term structural change that will not be reversed, rural communities will either continue to decline or will have to develop alternative, nonagri-cultural employment opportunities. Agriculture's diminishing importance as a source of employment is being compounded by the sharp drop in oil prices in 1985-86 that will make an impact on oil and gas drilling and production in Kansas, most of which has been concentrated in rural areas. The economic problems of rural communities thus are multidimensional.

Employment. Rural areas of Kansas have not had any growth in em-ployment in recent years. The data in Table 2.1 show employment changes in the state's urban and rural areas[1] from 1978 to 1983 for the private-sector, nonagricultural labor force. Over this six-year period, employment in urban areas rose by 12,003 (3.0 percent) but fell in rural areas by 3,200 (-1.1 percent).

Thus, all of the state's employment growth has occurred in urban areas, particularly in the Kansas City area. Clearly, a substantial imbalance exists in the state's economy that has negative implications for Kansas rural com-munities.

The loss of employment in the private, nonfarm sector of the rural Kansas economy is occurring in the context of declining agricultural em-

Table 2.1
Private Nonfarm Employment for Urban and Rural Areas in Kansas, 1978-83

	Employment 1983	Change in employment, 1978-83	
		Total	%
Urban areas (by SMSA)[a]			
Kansas City	164,988	12,788	8.4
Wichita	171,844	-1,299	-0.8
Topeka	58,842	-591	-1.0
Lawrence	16,762	1,105	7.1
Total	412,436	12,003	3.0
Rural areas	301,495	-3,200	-1.1
Kansas	713,931	+8,803	1.2
United States	72,971,318	+2,618,875	+3.7

Source: U.S. Department of Commerce, *County Business Patterns.*
[a]SMSA is standard metropolitan statistical area.

Table 2.2
Farm Employment in Kansas, 1950-80

	Total	As a percentage of total employment
1950	160,427	22.7
1960	101,462	12.9
1970	68,251	8.0
1980	62,609	5.8

Source: U.S. Bureau of the Census, *Characteristics of Population.*
Note: Farm employment includes farmers, farm managers, laborers, and foremen.

ployment, which has not been offset by increased nonfarm employment. Table 2.2 shows that farm employment has declined from 160,427 in 1950 to 62,609 in 1980. This rapid decline from 22.7 percent of total employment in Kansas to 5.8 percent in a thirty-year period has had a major impact on rural economies and particularly on population growth. Farm employment has been declining in rural communities while nonfarm employment has been expanding primarily in urban areas.

Business Establishments. An additional measure of economic growth is net change in business establishments, which roughly shows the number of new businesses established minus the number of business failures. Data on net changes in business establishments for rural and urban areas of Kansas, presented in Table 2.3, show that the rate of new business formation is lower in rural communities than in urban areas of Kansas. Establishments in rural areas increased by 3,228, or 10.5 percent, a smaller increase than for any of the state's urban areas. The increase in establishments during a period when employment fell indicates that the average business in rural areas was smaller in 1983 than in 1978. Indeed, virtually all of the increase in rural establishments occurred in small firms with one to nineteen employees. The number of establishments with 100 or more employees actually fell in rural areas.

Industry Patterns. While rural areas in Kansas have experienced a decline in employment for 1978-83, a look at employment trends by industry identifies those sectors that are expanding and contracting. For economic development to occur, rural communities will need to generate employment in primary industries that export goods or services beyond the local community, bring new wealth to a community, and form the basis for local growth in such areas as retail trade and services. In Kansas rural communities, the export industries have been primarily in agriculture and oil and gas. With the decline of these industries, manufacturing will be an increasingly important source of primary jobs. Rural economies cannot grow by relying on service and retail jobs that simply recycle dollars within a community.

Table 2.4 shows employment changes in rural areas by major industry group from 1978 to 1983. Significant declines in manufacturing and construction took place, but major increases were recorded in mining (mainly oil and gas) and services. Manufacturing lost 7,803 jobs, a decline of 11.1 percent over this six-year period, but this loss was offset by an increase of 5,510 jobs, or 9.0 percent, in services. However, the loss of primary jobs in manufacturing is not entirely offset by the creation of secondary jobs in the service sector. The substantial increase in mining employment through 1983 has not been sustained with the reduction in oil prices in 1985 and 1986.

These data suggest a serious erosion for Kansas rural communities: industries most likely to contain primary jobs are declining, while some sectors with secondary jobs are expanding.

Growing and Declining Industries. The relative decline of primary employment and growth of secondary, service employment in rural areas is

Table 2.3
Net Change in Establishments in Urban and Rural Areas of Kansas, by Size of Establishment, 1978-83

| | Size of establishment | | | | Net change |
	1 to 19	20 to 99	100 and up	Total	(%)
Urban areas (by SMSA)					
Kansas City	2,443	203	30	2,676	29.5
Wichita	1,634	49	1	1,684	17.8
Topeka	619	-3	1	617	15.6
Lawrence	250	16	1	267	22.2
Total	4,946	265	33	5,244	21.5
Rural areas	3,138	119	-29	3,228	10.5
Kansas	8,084	384	4	8,472	15.6

Source: *County Business Patterns.*

Table 2.4
Employment in Rural Areas of Kansas, by Industry, 1978 and 1983

	1978	1983	Total change	% change
Agricultural services	1,145	1,429	284	24.8
Mining	8,929	12,602	3,673	41.1
Construction	17,963	13,736	-4,227	-23.5
Manufacturing	70,141	62,338	-7,803	-11.1
Transportation	19,115	20,176	1,061	5.5
Wholesale trade	24,640	24,341	-299	-1.2
Retail trade	73,040	71,373	-1,667	-2.3
Finance	16,825	18,089	1,264	7.5
Service	61,039	66,549	5,510	9.0
Not classified	1,301	1,353	52	4.0
Total	295,818	292,285	-3,533	-1.2

Note: Column totals are statewide totals for rural areas. The summation of individual industry figures does not equal the column totals, because in smaller counties data from certain firms are excluded to avoid disclosing confidential data on those firms.

also shown by examining these data in terms of standard industrial classification. Table 2.5 shows growth industries, while declining industries are in Table 2.6. Only three manufacturing industries showed growth in the period, and only printing and publishing had substantial growth. In mining, oil and gas extraction increased by 2,711; whether that growth has been maintained is doubtful. Most growth in rural communities has occurred in retail trade and services. Employment rose in food stores and in eating and drinking places. Banking has increased employment of 1,076. In services, health services were up by 5,333, and business services by 2,194.

Several manufacturing industries experienced major employment declines, including food and kindred products, machinery (except electrical), and transportation equipment. Certain retail and service industries also fell, particularly general merchandise stores, automotive dealers and service stations, furniture and home furnishing stores, real estate, and social services.

The overall pattern of employment gains and losses suggest that rural communities have not succeeded in developing employment in primary sectors to offset the decline in agricultural employment. With few exceptions, employment gains have been concentrated in retail and service, while significant manufacturing industries, including food and kindred products, have had employment losses.

Regional Differences. Not all rural communities have experienced the same economic problems in recent years. Southeast Kansas has consistently had the most serious employment problems, while many counties in the southwest have had substantial employment growth. Table 2.7 shows employment changes for six regions of Kansas. The greatest growth was in the

Table 2.5
Industries with Employment Growth in Rural Areas of Kansas, 1978-83

Industry	Employment increase	% increase
Mining		
Oil and gas extraction	2711	59
Nonmetalic minerals, except fuels	21	17
Manufacturing		
Printing and publishing	1320	51
Chemical and allied products	47	9
Rubber and miscellaneous plastic	72	11
Transportation and utilities		
Local and interurban passenger transit	35	13
Transportation services	33	70
Electrical, gas, and sanitary services	226	17
Retail trade		
Food stores	958	9
Apparel and accessory stores	462	13
Eating and drinking places	880	4
Finance and insurance		
Banking	1076	15
Credit agencies	87	6
Security, commodity brokers and services	27	33
Insurance agents	279	22
Services		
Business services	2194	95
Auto repair, services, and garages	128	8
Miscellaneous repair services	75	10
Amusement and recreation services	147	10
Health services	5333	21
Legal services	355	29
Educational services	566	34
Miscellaneous services	271	14

northeast, which had an employment gain of 14,174. The southeast and south-central regions had employment losses of 5,516 and 4,341, respectively. The rural areas of Southwest and Northwest Kansas both had employment gains, particularly the southwest region, with a 3,175 gain.

The basic pattern for all regions except the southwest was to lose manufacturing employment and gain service and finance and insurance jobs. Only the northeast was able to increase employment in retail and wholesale trade. Perhaps the most interesting finding is that Southwest Kansas was able to increase manufacturing employment and consequently had a substantial increase in overall employment, all of this manufacturing gain in food processing (beef) in Finney County. The importance of such jobs is that they bring new dollars into a rural community and provide the basis for employment in the retail and service sectors.

Further detail for six specific rural counties is shown in Table 2.8. Clearly, Finney County's substantial gain of 35.1 percent in employment is

Table 2.6
Industries with Employment Losses in Rural Areas of Kansas, 1978-83

Industry	Employment decrease	% decrease
Construction		
General building contractors	2113	37
Heavy construction contractors	432	23
Special trade contractors	1062	14
Manufacturing		
Food and kindred products	1884	33
Apparel and other textile products	765	75
Lumber and wood products	283	28
Furniture and fixtures	449	80
Stone, clay, and glass products	325	40
Fabricated metal products	780	19
Machinery except electrical	1389	15
Transportation equipment	1591	87
Transportation and utilities		
Trucking and warehousing	108	2
Communication	255	10
Wholesale trade		
Durable goods	71	1
Nondurable goods	140	1
Retail trade		
Building material and garden supply	597	17
General merchandise stores	1372	20
Automotive dealers and service stations	2295	18
Furniture and home furnishing	867	38
Miscellaneous retail	257	3
Finance and insurance		
Insurance carriers	134	19
Real estate	903	42
Combined real estate and insurance	65	24
Holding and other investment	75	65
Services		
Hotels	52	2
Personal services	76	2
Motion pictures	23	79
Social services	865	23
Membership organizations	772	11

attributable to the gain of 2,069 manufacturing jobs and the 597-job increase in services. The employment increase in Pottawatomie County is mainly due to the gain in transportation and utilities (Jeffery Energy Center), which offset the decline in manufacturing. Thomas County, in contrast, has had an increase in employment only because of services, mainly health services.

The other three counties in Table 2.8 all had employment declines. Cheyenne County is almost entirely agricultural, and new jobs are not being created there to replace those lost in agriculture. Cheyenne had no employment gains in primary sectors of the economy that would bring dollars into

Table 2.7
Employment Change in Kansas, by Region, 1978-83

	North East	South East	North Central	South Central	North West	South West	Total
Agricultural services	245	13	144	83	0	-15	657
Mining	389	667	898	2,272	171	172	6,134
Construction	-4,012	-870	-807	-4,069	-211	-372	-10,485
Manufacturing	-8,490	-4,632	-687	-11,242	42	2,278	-22,693
Transportation	3,113	-499	-680	1,210	-5	-282	3,550
Wholesale trade	2,662	174	-432	560	-44	23	2,534
Retail trade	2,566	-2,323	-292	-145	-114	-19	-367
Finance	3,057	247	423	1,497	111	193	5,561
Service	13,454	1,239	1,577	5,433	310	1,036	23,083
Not classified	187	110	108	71	27	116	829
Total	14,174	-5,516	-361	-4,341	277	3,175	8,803

Source: Institute for Public Policy and Business Research, University of Kansas.
Note: Column totals are statewide totals for rural areas. The summation of individual industry figures does not equal the column totals, because in smaller counties data from certain firms are excluded to avoid disclosing confidential data on those firms.

Table 2.8
Employment Change in Selected Kansas Counties, 1978-83

Industry	Finney	Thomas	Pottawatomie	Cheyenne	Allen	Smith
Agricultural services	-21	0	3	0	0	-3
Mining	-27	0	0	0	70	0
Construction	-45	-19	-28	-6	-63	-31
Manufacturing	2,069	-40	-106	0	-149	-29
Transportation	42	-62	298	-36	38	9
Wholesale trade	-94	-16	10	-5	-199	-14
Retail trade	-44	-25	-42	31	-741	-61
Finance	6	37	-27	4	23	26
Service	597	169	47	6	31	-48
Not classified	19	11	1	0	0	0
Total	2,502	82	156	-17	-977	-166
Percentage change in employment, 1978-1983	35.1	4.0	6.9	-2.8	-21.0	-15.0

Note: Employment is private-sector, nonagricultural employment. Also, the summation of individual industry figures does not equal the column totals, because in smaller counties data from certain firms are excluded to avoid disclosing confidential data on those firms.

the county, its employment gains being all concentrated in retail trade and services. Allen and Smith Counties both had losses in manufacturing and wholesale and retail trade. Allen had small gains in service and finance but still had a 21-percent decrease in employment. In Smith County, services declined; and with finance the only industry to show an employment gain, total employment fell by 15 percent.

This review of selected individual counties suggests rural counties have had varied employment experience from 1978 to 1983. Some, such as

Thomas, have been able to stress growth in services to offset losses in manufactures, but others have not been able to pursue that strategy successfully. Other counties, such as Allen, are in rapid economic decline. On the positive side, Finney County has attracted new manufacturing jobs related to the agricultural economy of Western Kansas and is growing.

Implications of Slow Rural Economic Growth

Although slow economic growth has numerous implications for rural communities, one major concern is population change. Population tends to follow employment. If employment is declining in rural communities, and it is in most, population growth will lag.

Rural counties in Kansas have generally experienced slow population growth and in some cases have experienced actual declines. As shown in Table 2.9, U.S. population increased by 11.4 percent from 1970 to 1980 in contrast to 5.1 percent in Kansas. Within Kansas, rural counties grew slower than the state average. Population in rural counties increased by 43,269, or 3.7 percent, while urban counties increased by 71,339, or 6.6 percent.

While population growth was relatively low in rural Kansas counties from 1970 to 1980, counties varied considerably, some rural counties showing rapid growth and others actual declines. Evidence that population change follows employment change may be found in those rural counties examined earlier (see Table 2.8). In Pottawatomie County, for example, population increased by 25.7 percent, in Finney County by 25.2 percent. On the other hand, population fell by 13.4 percent in Cheyenne County and by 12.0 percent in Smith County. Thomas County grew 12.6 percent, and Allen County shrunk 4.1 percent.

The age composition of the Kansas population is changing more dramatically in Kansas than the population as a whole, as shown in Table 2.10. As with total population, rural communities are showing slow population growth for persons aged twenty to thirty-four, the most mobile segment of the population. From 1970 to 1980, rural counties in Kansas saw an increase of 71,434 (32.9 percent) in this age group in contrast to an increase

Table 2.9
Population in Rural and Urban Counties of Kansas, 1970-80

| | | | Change | |
	1970	1980	Total	%
Kansas				
Rural counties	1,166,953	1,210,222	43,269	3.7
Urban counties	1,082,118	1,153,457	71,339	6.6
Total	2,249,071	2,363,679	114,608	5.1
U.S.	203,302,031	226,545,805	23,545,805	11.4

Source: U.S. Bureau of the Census, *Census of Population Characteristics.*

of 90,284 (39.5 percent) for urban areas. These population trends closely follow the ability of urban and rural areas to create employment opportunities. The policy implications are clear: Kansas rural communities will not be able to retain young people unless employment opportunities are improved.

Impact of Deregulation

Actions over the past ten years to deregulate formerly regulated services have sparked controversy as to whether such actions simply compound the adverse economic and demographic trends affecting rural communities. Critics of deregulation argue that governmental regulation assures that consumers in smaller, rural communities will receive high-quality service at reasonable rates. Proponents of deregulation argue that free competition will provide better service at lower rates. This section assesses the impact on Kansas of deregulation in a number of formerly regulated industries, such as trucking, rail, bus, and telephone services, and one regulated industry that soon may be substantially deregulated — electric power.

The ability of the small business in a rural community to survive and grow depends critically upon high-quality transportation services. Our far-flung communities cannot "connect" into the national and international economy unless the flow of materials is relatively low cost and adaptable to changing circumstances. For example, the development of a Kansas manufacturing base, such as a baked-products industry, closer in the chain of distribution to the final consumer will be dependent upon fast, flexible transport, especially rail and trucking.

Trucking. The trucking industry has been regulated heavily by the Interstate Commerce Commission (ICC) since the Motor Carrier Act of 1935. That legislation was intended primarily as a response to the railroads' justifiable fear that trucking represented a major competitive threat. Thus, the intent of the regulation was to "rationalize" the industry by balancing the interests of railroads and truckers. Additionally, some shippers believed that

Table 2.10
Population 20-34 Years of Age in Rural and Urban Areas of Kansas, 1970-80

	1970	1980	Change Total	%
Kansas				
Rural counties	217,207	288,641	71,434	32.9
Urban counties	228,481	318,765	90,284	39.5
Total	445,688	607,406	101,718	36.3
U. S.	41,278,450	58,400,543	17,122,093	41.5

Source: U.S. Bureau of the Census, *Census of Population Characteristics.*

rate regulation would stabilize the "cut-throat" competitive practices of certain truckers during the depression. Interestingly, the only group to oppose regulation was farmers, who found trucking an excellent remedy to the substantial market power of the railroads.[2]

The trucking industry underwent deregulation with passage of the Motor Carrier Act of 1980, legislation intended to correct numerous defects in the ongoing rate and route regulation of the ICC. These problems included rates far above cost, misallocation of transport resources due to distortion of transport mode selection by shippers, and concentration of economic power in those truckers able to control operating rights to various routes. The law has, in brief, directed the ICC to liberalize the granting of operating permits; eliminated obstacles to free entry into markets, such as entry tests that forced the entrant to explain why current service is inadequate; relaxed numerous route and commodity restrictions; and provided the carriers with flexibility in establishing rates.

The results, six years later, have been gratifying to most shippers nationwide. Thomas Moore, in a survey of shippers across the United States, found they mainly agreed that service quality had improved and that prices had declined.[3] In a random-sample survey conducted in November 1985, small shippers in rural Kansas were asked whether transportation services had improved, remained the same, or become worse as a result of deregulation. Sixty-two percent responded that overall service had improved; only 5 percent found it worse (see Table 2.11). The perceptions of those using deregulated trucking services is resoundingly positive. Deregulation has made trucking in Kansas prompter, more reliable, and more willing to serve out-of-the-way locations. Although the survey did not specifically ask about prices, those who commented strongly believed that prices were lower than before deregulation.

Few respondents were located on heavily traveled routes on which the truckers' costs obviously would be lower. Indeed, further analysis of shippers located outside urban areas (i.e., outside SMSAs) and off of interstates found that 67 percent thought overall service had improved, while only 10 percent felt it had declined.

One reason for this perceived increase in trucking value for the dollar has been the rapid creation of small trucking firms since deregulation. Table 2.12 shows the growth in the number of trucking firms in Kansas. In particular, the 60-percent growth in the smallest firms from 1979 to 1983 demonstrates the tendency of smaller trucking firms to enter the market. Other data indicate this industry trend is continuing. For example, 1,027 intrastate common carriers were registered with the KCC as of June 30, 1980; 1,395 were registered as of February 26, 1986.[4] Many of these smaller carriers do not last long, often departing quickly due to a lack of working capital and knowledge of the marketplace. Nevertheless, many have stayed and con-

Table 2.11
Survey of Small Shippers in Rural Kansas Concerning Quality of Truck and Rail Service after Deregulation

	Truck			Rail		
	Improved	Unchanged (% response)	Worse	Improved	Unchanged (% response)	Worse
Quality of vehicles	62	38	0	26	60	14
Promptness of service	60	31	9	14	43	43
Availability of service	62	31	7	14	52	34
Reliability	45	51	4	18	48	33
Adjustment of claims	24	66	10	6	69	25
Willingness to serve off-line points	42	39	19	N.A.	N.A.	N.A.
Overall service	62	33	5	18	47	35

Note: A random sample was drawn from small shippers (i.e., those employing less than 250) operating in rural areas and in towns of less than 20,000 population. Sample size varies from 33 to 35 for rail and from 50 to 55 for truck.

Table 2.12
Number of Trucking Firms in Kansas, 1979 and 1983

Size of firm[a]	1979	1983	% change
1 to 4	990	1,581	60
5 to 9	464	385	-17
10 to 19	138	146	6
20 to 49	111	80	-28
50 to 99	14	26	86
100 to 249	9	8	-11
250 to 499	6	3	-50
500 to 999	3	1	-67
1,000 or more	1	1	0
Total	1,736	2,231	29%

Source: U.S. Bureau of the Census. *Census of Manufacturers.*
[a] Based on number of employees.

tinue to put downward pressure on prices throughout the state. Among the big winners of truck deregulation have been small towns in Kansas.

Rail Service. Railroads have been subject to inter- and intrastate regulation since the latter part of the nineteenth century. Regardless of the intent of those who have supported economic regulation of rail, the essential economic rationale has been based on "natural monopoly." Although the service of only one railroad in a region may be less costly than competitive duplication of rail service, a single supplier has great economic power over customers. While this argument might have been a reasonable justification for regulation in the past, the emergence of trucking as a good substitute mode of transport has weakened that argument. Deregulation of trucking has allowed motor carriers to price aggressively against the railroads and forced the rails to respond in kind. Thus, although the railroads in Kansas seldom experience direct competition by other railroads, they exercise considerable restraint because of the existence of a vigorous, competitive trucking industry.

The economic well-being of railroads would have been impaired dangerously had they not been allowed to respond competitively to the newly deregulated truckers. Two key federal acts brought rail service into a more open marketplace: the Railroad Revitalization and Regulation Act of 1976 (the 4R Act) and the Staggers Rail Act of 1980. The 4R Act permitted the railroads greater rate flexibility, and the Staggers Act reinforced the principle. Significantly, the latter act allows railroads to enter into long-term contracts with freight shippers and also permits the abandonment of uneconomical rail routes more easily. Whereas in the past the ICC would not allow abandonment without protracted hearings, the procedure for dropping service may now take only a few months.

The general trend of rail investment in Kansas has been long-term decline in rail mileage. As Figure 2.1 shows, the mileage has fallen steadily since 1930, suggesting low returns on these railroad assets. Since passage of the Staggers Act, abandonment has proceeded at an accelerated clip. For the fifty-year period of 1930-80, the net loss in track in Kansas was thirty-nine miles per year. In the five years after Staggers, the railroads have dropped an average of eighty-two miles per year.[5] The vast majority of rail abandonments in Kansas have occurred in the eastern part of the state.

How have rural shippers fared under partial rail deregulation? The picture is less clear-cut than for trucking. In the survey of small, rural Kansas shippers, rail service under deregulation was also assessed. As Table 2.11 shows, only 18 percent of these rail customers felt that service was improved. On the other hand, only 35 percent felt that service had worsened. Many who were dissatisfied with rail service mentioned that they were using trucking far more than in the past, a finding confirmed by the tonnage shifting toward trucking—especially agricultural products moving to centralized rail depots. An unintended consequence of this move toward trucking may be more rapid deterioration of rural Kansas highways and bridges, in part caused by overloaded trucks. That condition, in turn, may require a closer examination of Kansas highway funding (the subject of Chapter 4), load limits on trucks, and traffic enforcement.

Of particular concern to rural Kansas is the impact of rail deregulation on agriculture. The state's distance from major grain markets and limited access to waterways make us much more dependent upon rail than is the rest of the nation. About 80 percent of total Kansas wheat shipments travel by rail, and nearly all the major western railroads serve the state. A recent study from the U.S. Department of Agriculture indicates that several major changes have occurred in the transport of Kansas wheat:[6]

Figure 2.1
Railroad Mileage in Kansas, 1930-85

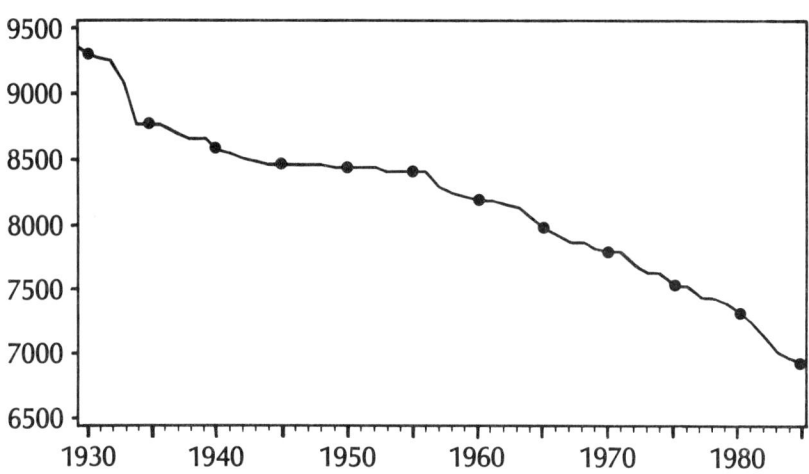

Source: Kansas Corporation Commission.

1. Railroad rate changes used to be virtually simultaneous across firms; now one line's changes are usually followed by others', suggesting more competitive behavior.
2. Closely correlated with the new pricing procedures is a significant drop in published rates for shipping Kansas wheat. For example, the authors calculated a 34-percent decline for shipping to Gulf of Mexico ports from 1981 to 1984. This figure compares with a 64-percent increase in the four years before the Staggers Act.
3. More contracting is evident since deregulation. Generally, these contracts carry volume commitments that work to the advantage of large contract shippers, and many Kansas contract shippers are large. Contract rates to the Gulf of Mexico were 17-percent lower than published rates.
4. With the lower rail rates, middlemen have offered a higher price for grain than they would have otherwise. In other words, a substantial portion of the rate savings has been passed back to the farmers.
5. The impact on smaller shippers is, at best, mixed. For those who cannot obtain contracts, rates are higher, and they consequently lose business.

Forces other than deregulation have affected the transportation of wheat in Kansas, and, thus, precision about deregulation's impact is not possible. The evidence suggests, however, that greater competitiveness generally has lowered prices and has made the railroads far more sensitive to market forces than in the past.

Bus Transport. Bus service was deregulated at the federal level through the Bus Regulatory Reform Act of 1982. Briefly, the law allows any "fit and able" bus operator to enter and to withdraw from routes in most circumstances, although the interests of small communities without alternative transport are to be considered before a service is discontinued. Rates are essentially allowed to be set competitively.

In Kansas, many small communities have no low-cost alternative mode of passenger transport, and the results of bus deregulation have been largely unfavorable. The greatest loss in bus service to rural portions of Kansas was the reduction of routes by Continental Trailways (specifically, Wichita to Kansas City, Wichita to Manhattan, Kansas City to Tulsa, Wichita to Liberal, Liberal to Dodge City, Salina to Lincoln, Salina to Hutchinson, Hutchinson to Stockton, and Hutchinson to Dodge City) and the discontinuance of Trans State Bus (previously operating routes throughout central Kansas).

Table 2.13 indicates changes in daily frequency of bus service through eight rural Kansas communities over the past three-and-a-half years. In all but one case, frequency has decreased, with an overall decline of 35.3 percent. The number of routes by all companies with service into Wichita also dropped from 35 to 24 in the same period, a 31.4-percent decline, which also suggests a loss in service throughout the state.

Further declines in bus service may occur in the state as private carriers adjust routes according to the dictates of profitability. This "shakeout" allowed by eased regulatory restrictions resembles the railroad abandonments after the Staggers Act. But, unlike rail service discontinuation, bus service abandonment can be accomplished more quickly because altering bus routes does not involve disposition of large capital investments. Thus, greater variability in bus operations should be expected in the future.

Because entry into service is relatively easy, significant increases in bus transport likely will occur where markets are anticipated to become profitable, a small example of which is the Hutchinson Shuttle Service that

Table 2.13
Daily Frequency of Bus Service to Selected Communities in Kansas, June 1982 and December 1935

Community	Number of buses	
	June 1982	December 1985
Dodge City	13	7
Garden City	10	4
Goodland	6	7
Great Bend	6	3
Hays	10	8
Manhattan	18	12
Newton	14	8
Pittsburg	8	6
Total	85	55

Source: *The Official Bus Guide* (Cedar Rapids, IA. Russell's Guides).

recently began operation, primarily between Hutchinson and Wichita. This firm is working on routes previously discontinued by larger operators. Another recent outgrowth of deregulation, totally unregulated charter service, may also be picking up some service discontinued by the major carriers. Unfortunately, little information on these operations is available at this time.

Telephone and Electrical Service. As the telephone business has become increasingly complex technologically, the regulation of this industry has become an intricate maze. Briefly, the divestiture of the various Bell operating companies from AT&T in 1982 left long-distance communications that are moving toward unregulated price competition and regional operating companies that are still closely regulated on rates and services by the state utility commissions. Many consider that these telephone operations embody the characteristics of "natural monopoly," wherein one provider is better than two or more. By contrast, the demise of the AT&T long-distance monopoly has resulted, in part, from the unconvincing nature of the natural monopoly argument given the new technologies in communications.

One of the anticipated effects of the AT&T breakup was that the charges for local service would rise, because prices would be determined by cost. Whereas previously the local rates were supposedly cross-subsidized by long-distance revenues, now the local rates, at "full cost pricing," would be forced upward significantly.

How have prices for local service in smaller Kansas communities been affected? According to the Kansas Corporation Commission, residential rates in selected Kansas cities[7] increased from January 1984 to June 1985 by 15.1 percent for one-party lines, 22.9 percent for two-party lines, 18.2 percent for rural, four-party lines, and 9.8 percent for the flat trunk rate. Increases for the same period in business rates ranged from 6.1 percent to 15.3 percent depending on the class of service. Business increases have been moderate and generally less than for residential customers.

Concerning electrical service, Kansas appears to be in line with neighboring states, as shown in Table 2.14. Our statewide average electricity rates, both residential and industrial, are lower than the U.S. average but higher than surrounding states except for Iowa. Some towns, such as Garden City, have high rates due to local utility developments. Rates in towns serviced by KG&E now run substantially higher than the average since the Wolf Creek nuclear generating plant is included into that utility's rate base.

Policy Choices Concerning Rural Communities

Before policy choices for addressing the economic problems of rural communities are considered, the limitations of current state policy should be understood. For at least the past twenty years, state economic development policy has been based on a strategy of industrial recruitment of firms from outside the state to locate in Kansas. The Kansas Department of Eco-

Table 2.14
Average Typical Electrical Bills for Residences in Selected States,
January 1, 1985

	250 kWh	500 kWh	1,000 kWh
Kansas	$21.19	$37.76	$68.83
Colorado	18.98	34.44	65.28
Iowa	22.36	40.69	71.00
Missouri	18.78	33.30	57.94
Nebraska	19.49	32.94	55.35
Oklahoma	19.69	34.28	58.49
U. S. average	22.61	41.86	76.37

Source: Energy Information Administration, U.S. Department of Energy.

nomic Development (KDED) has implemented this strategy by working with companies that have expressed an interest in locating a facility and "selling" them on the advantages of coming to Kansas. By this conception of economic development, Kansas rural communities suffer severe disadvantages relative to urban areas and, in fact, have not enjoyed many benefits from this strategy. An industrial-recruiting strategy may work for urban areas, but different approaches are needed for rural communities.

This conclusion is based upon several considerations. First, Kansas' location limits the viability of industrial recruitment for the state in general. Even though the state is in the center of the country geographically, it is not near the major population centers. A crucial factor in plant location is low-cost access to major consumer markets. Plants located in such states as Kentucky or Tennessee may have substantial cost advantages given their quicker, lower-cost access to heavily populated areas of the county.

Second, rural communities, in many cases, hold less attraction for firms considering locating in Kansas than do the state's urban areas, whose major advantage is that they are all located on interstate highways an hour-and-a-half's driving time from a major airport with regularly scheduled air service. Further, the cultural, educational, and entertainment opportunities available in urban areas of Kansas offer an added attraction to many firms. Considerations such as these often lead firms to specify that they will consider locating only in a community (1) near an urban area, (2) near an interstate highway, or (3) with access to a major airport.

Given these constraints, KDED has responded to requests about possible locations in Kansas by providing information on such communities as Olathe, Lawrence, Wichita, and Topeka. KDED is much less likely to recommend rural communities, because they usually fail to meet one of the criteria set by firms considering a Kansas site. KDED must be responsive to a firm's selection criteria in order for a Kansas site to be selected rather than one in Missouri, Oklahoma, or another state.

These comments do not, of course, apply to all firms seeking to locate a plant or other facility in Kansas. Firms related to agriculture may view rural communities differently. The analysis is, however, accurate in most cases and strongly suggests that Kansas' rural communities suffer disadvantages in comparison to urban areas particularly when the state's economic development program is defined as recruiting firms from out of state to locate in Kansas. The alternative is to redefine economic development to include state policies to promote internal economic development within the state.

Policy Choices for Economic Growth

The crucial question concerning the economic prospects of rural communities is what role, if any, state government should have in prompting economic development. Historically, the state has not played a substantial role in assisting development within rural counties, and this policy could be continued. The implications of such a policy, however, are fairly clear: current trends will continue—low or no employment growth and slow population growth. Overall, the rural population would be expected to age as young persons migrate to areas of greater economic opportunity. Further, the tax base in rural areas would show relative deterioration, making it difficult to finance public services in rural communities and further shifting the state tax burden to growing urban areas.

Alternatively, the state could decide that an economic development strategy is not a good policy in rural areas. If a state investment has a greater return in growing urban areas of the state, then one option would be to target those areas as key to the state's strategy. Such a "go with the winner" strategy would maximize the state's economic growth if policies promoting rural communities could not lead to growth levels comparable to growth levels in urban areas. In essence, such a policy would recognize that the transfer of capital and population from slow-growing rural communities to faster-growing urban areas would improve economic efficiency and overall personal income in the state. The state as a whole would gain, even if rural communities did not.

A third policy option is for the state to begin an active role in the economic development of rural communities. Previous state actions—such as decisions on building roads—have had an impact on rural economic development, but the state has not created a deliberate and sustained policy designed to promote rural economic development. Several considerations might justify such a policy change. First, Kansas is primarily a rural state, with only four major urban areas covering 8 of 105 counties. To accept the continued economic decline of a vast portion of the state implies a negative outlook for Kansas as a whole. Second, all Kansans would benefit by greater economic activity in rural areas, because the basic infrastructure in rural communities—highways, public schools, hospitals, and water systems—would need to be maintained. If the tax base in rural areas were inadequate to generate sufficient local revenues, then increased state assistance would be required. In essence, the expanding tax base in urban areas would be used in part to support public services in rural areas. Similarly, urban areas would incur an increasing proportion of state expenses for general state purposes, such as state universities. Finally, rural communities might offer good opportunities for growth in particular areas, and not all growth necessarily would occur in urban areas. Opportunities exist for current firms in rural areas to expand and for new firms to establish themselves, especially those relating to the state's agricultural and natural-resource bases. We conclude that it would be a mistake for the state to place primary emphasis only on economic growth in urban areas, where most recent growth has occurred. Several state strategies are possible for rural communities.

Subsidize Industries. The crucial question is what type of strategy the state could adopt to assist economic development in rural communities. A policy choice based on resisting the significant structural changes now occurring in rural Kansas, for example, changes in agriculture, oil and gas, and deregulation in transportation, is not advisable. Policies could be designed to subsidize rural firms, declining industries, or entire rural communities. Such policies would relieve some economic difficulties in rural areas but would not have long-term beneficial impacts. A policy based on resisting adverse economic trends would likely fail in the long run and delay the type of economic adjustments that must occur if rural communities are to compete in the emerging economic order.

New York State perhaps has the most ambitious proposed legislation for rural development in the United States, with four bills before the state legislature in 1986. These represent elaborate attempts to channel and stimulate investment into rural New York State for a variety of purposes. Proposals that head the list would create two new executive-branch organizations to spearhead the various programs: an office of rural affairs and a rural development authority.[8]

The New York approach contains significant drawbacks. First, new agencies will create new bureaucracy that must be integrated with existing political administrations, all vying for scarce government dollars. Second, once created, regardless of the wisdom of their original creation, the new structures take on a life of their own, defended by the employees who staff the agencies and the interest groups who gain from the programs. And third, the rigid specification of "rural" programs creates barriers to growth. The subsidization of rural areas necessarily must take tax dollars from those in other areas whose use of the funds is now foregone. Strict rural criteria for receiving subsidies freeze resources in particular locations, the selection of which is based on political definitions. This reduced mobility will impede market efficiency and growth in general.

If explicit subsidies for rural communities are rejected, one implication is that some smaller communities likely will cease to exist. Those small rural communities that were established to serve an agricultural economy may have no economic future as changes in agriculture undermine the reasons for their continuation. Although larger communities—Hays, Garden City, Great Bend, and Pittsburg, among others—have the means to diversify their economies, the very small communities do not. We see no reason for the state to resist this consolidation in rural areas by providing explicit subsidies to the smaller communities whose economic reason for existence is diminishing. Such a policy, if tried, would eventually fail.

Recruit New Industry. While recruitment of industrial firms from outside of Kansas to locate in the state historically has favored urban areas, this result is not inevitable. Part of the state's industrial recruitment could be devoted specifically to communities in rural areas, which would require targeted marketing to identify firms suitable for rural areas and attract them to Kansas. The Midwest Research Institute (MRI) has begun this effort as a part of the economic development study commissioned by the 1985 legislature. In that study, MRI identified several growth industries that have the greatest potential for locating in rural areas. This work should not only be continued, but KDED should further be encouraged to develop a long-run strategy for attracting firms to rural communities when appropriate. Such targeted marketing could be tried first on an experimental basis to determine its cost effectiveness.

Encourage Internal Economic Development. The most important policy initiative for rural economic development would be to emphasize internal growth for all of Kansas. Included would be policies encouraging entrepreneurs to establish new businesses and encouraging existing businesses to expand within the state. If economic development is defined in this way, then rural communities have a better chance to participate in state programs than if economic development means only recruiting from without. Rural communities do have existing businesses that could expand and entrepreneurs who could start new businesses. An appropriate role for the state is to stimulate such activity while maintaining minimal state involvement.

Such a policy of internal growth was adopted by the legislature and governor in 1986. The key elements are

1. Increased investment by the state and private business in research and development to make Kansas firms more innovative and competitive and to spin-off new businesses;
2. Increased availability of financing for new and expanding businesses, especially venture or risk capital;
3. Establishment of an existing industry program to focus on the needs and problems of business firms in Kansas;

4. Reorganization of the Kansas Department of Economic Development to increase emphasis on rural communities, small businesses, and international trade.

These initiatives could be beneficial for rural communities as well as urban areas.

The 1986 legislative initiatives recognize that state government should have a more active role in stimulating economic development in Kansas. In effect, a new partnership will be created involving the state, private business, and educational institutions to resolve economic problems affecting all parts of the state, rural and urban. The strongest argument in support of the initiatives is that the alternative is continued economic stagnation and decline in rural communities.

Promote Rural Economic Linkage. An unresolved issue is how rural communities should organize for economic development. Small towns in particular do not have sufficient resources to hire staff to coordinate economic development. Yet, rural communities must have staff devoted to economic development (1) to insure that they participate in state initiatives already passed by the legislature, (2) to actively recruit new firms in their area, and (3) to develop local strategies for development. To be successful, rural communities must make bold efforts to adjust to economic changes, which suggests that a regional strategy covering a number of counties may be most efficient.

Several regional institutions already exist that could play an important role in rural economies. The Certified Development Corporations, Inc. (CDCs) are organized in most parts of the state to assist small businesses with financing. They have also, in some cases, assumed additional responsibilities for economic development, such as recruiting firms to their area. Regional planning commissions also perform some functions relating to economic development. In addition, some larger cities and counties in rural areas have hired economic development coordinators. Obviously, overlapping responsibilities and rural communities' working against each other and depleting scarce resources are potential problems. Although state government should probably not impose a structure for cooperation among rural counties, incentives could be offered to multicounty areas throughout the state in order to coordinate strategies and programs for economic development.

Policy Choices Concerning Deregulation

Deregulation has been initiated over the past decade largely through federal action. Although deregulation has critics, the movement to deregulate formerly regulated industries has momentum and does not appear at all transitory. The issue of deregulation as well as its impact in Kansas raises a number of questions concerning state action. For example, although transport has *not* been deregulated at the state level in Kansas, federal deregulation has removed the statutory basis for state control by the Kansas Corporation Commission (KCC) and reduced significantly the effectiveness of most state regulatory programs that do continue. Thus, trying to regulate rates and service intrastate, while interstate transport is largely open to market forces, is difficult at best and counterproductive at worst. This section examines policy choices facing Kansas as a result of deregulation, particularly with reference to rural communities.

Intrastate Regulation of Transport. The future of trucking deregulation will offer more of the same at the federal level. Indeed, the Reagan administration budget for fiscal year 1987 calls for "sunsetting" the ICC, a fate that befell the CAB at the end of 1985. With the death of the ICC, most remaining economic regulation of surface transport in the United States would cease.[9] Thus, a major policy issue will be the state's stance toward trucking given interstate competitiveness.

The trend toward more competition in trucking is one that should perhaps be duplicated elsewhere in the rural Kansas economy. Small businesses in rural areas and agriculture have benefited. Rural economies depend far more on transport than do metropolitan communities, and quality transport becomes a critical factor for rural economic success as conditions become more competitive. Thus, rural Kansans appear to owe a large debt to the deregulation of motor carriers.

A recent study of the effects of intrastate deregulation of motor carriers in Florida suggests the gains Kansas might anticipate from deregulating intrastate trucking.[10] Intrastate carriers in Florida were deregulated in 1980, when a sunset review led to the termination of the Florida Public Service Commission's authority in this area. The study estimates that the removal of economic regulation on intrastate freight reduced prices by approximately 14 percent and that price discrimination among markets diminished because of deregulation.

A major policy choice is whether Kansas should take actions to deregulate trucking further. Currently the state, through the Transportation Division of KCC, spends over $1 million controlling transport. A large part of this regulation involves intrastate licensing, handling rate filings, and issuing citations to those motor carriers not following the commission's regulations. This intrastate regulation appears to serve no useful public purpose and may instead hamper flexibility and adaptiveness of the Kansas trucking industry, particularly with respect to rural communities. With the ICC withering away, a continuation of state transport regulation has questionable value.

Within Kansas, public policy toward the railroads is severely constrained, because virtually all railroads engage in interstate commerce and therefore are regulated at the federal level by the ICC. The KCC does act as an intervenor in ICC hearings on rail-line abandonments, but in general has had little success in preventing such line terminations. Although the loss of trackage is troublesome to smaller communities and their shippers, the railroads have argued that the forced continuance of such service has weakened them greatly, leading to bankruptcy in certain cases. Since the Staggers Act and more rapid abandonment, no further bankruptcies have occurred.

The concern for rural communities and small shippers has led Congress to consider more regulation in the form of the Railroad Antimonopoly Act of 1986. This bill would allow shippers to attempt, under some conditions, to redress in the courts their grievances about high rates. Remedy could be to force a railroad to pay damages or to allow another railroad to serve the shipper over the guilty party's lines.

Although this type of legislation is, on the surface, an attractive way to constrain costs, significant pitfalls exist. Restriction of rail rate-setting flexibility would jeopardize the benefits under deregulation discussed above. This rate freedom seems to have worked to the advantage of rural Kansans, and farmers in particular. Further, the low contract rates now negotiated by large shippers in Kansas act as a competitive restraint on other railroads' pricing. Additionally, the lower rates of railroads constrain trucking prices, much as competitive trucking prices act on railroad prices.

Given Kansas' limited authority in rail regulation, the state could take a more active role in rehabilitating those rail lines considered essential to the economies of rural communities and in the economic interest of the state as a whole. Under the 4R Act, the state has planned for rail rehabilitation and acted as a conduit for federal assistance to specific projects, but no state financing has been made available. Also, the state legislature has conditionally guaranteed a federal loan for major rail rehabilitation in North Central Kansas. These options and others deserve exploration as rail abandonments eliminate service to rural communities.

In terms of regulation, state-level public policy toward private bus service is similarly quite limited. It is unreasonable to expect that closer regulation of private bus firms will improve service intrastate. Certainly, Kansas cannot affect the decisions of the major crosscountry providers, such as Greyhound or Trailways. Thus, if feeder service to and from small communities is considered desirable, policy makers should clearly understand that this will require either subsidization or direct service provision by government.

Encouragement to bus operators willing to serve areas currently suffering from loss of service could be considered. A simple, direct approach might be most useful. For example, drawing upon the program of risk capital enacted by the 1986 Kansas legislature could serve this purpose by expanding available capital for such businesses.

Regulation of Telephone and Electrical Service. State government has clearer authority and more available policy choices in regulating telephone services and electric power, and each area presents unique issues.

In the field of telecommunications, technology is challenging traditional approaches to state regulation. For example, whether Southwestern Bell will be able to retain its monopoly status over local-exchange service in the future is uncertain. The rapidly evolving technology of telecommunications and the concurrent flux in demands for new services leaves the static concept of local natural monopoly far behind. If the Bell companies cannot provide the best service quickly, commercial users look elsewhere. New technology gives large telecommunications users the capability to "bypass" the local exchanges of Southwestern Bell and form minitelecommunications networks outside the jurisdiction of the phone company. Increasing tariffs give them the incentive to do so. This behavior is understandable and perhaps desirable, for it suggests that new technology is reaching into the industry quickly, stimulating growth and employment. On the other hand, this "bypass" puts the remaining regulated customers, possibly smaller rural users, in the unfortunate position of having to cover the telephone company's operating costs plus a return on investment. Prices to these consumers will rise in this situation.

A direct solution to this problem would be to force businesses to stop circumventing the phone company. Yet, that might damage severely the growth and prosperity that a dynamic, open economy could provide. Another response would be for state regulators to allow phone companies to price "flexibly" among their customers. Nebraska, for example, has a new law giving local telephone exchanges authority to raise basic rates by up to 10 percent without state approval. Possibly, a gradual shifting away from public utility regulation of telephone companies might ease the pain of movement into a more competitive environment. Before deregulation occurs, however, more study of the impact of deregulation on low-volumn users is needed. Predictions in this area are difficult, but the Federal Communications Commission has called on states to consider allowing expanded competition in intrastate telecommunications, and a Kansas study of the potential gains and risks of opening the intrastate telephone markets to competition would be valuable.

Although to date no states have completely deregulated electric power, many are experimenting with more market-oriented approaches. The Federal Energy Regulatory Administration (FERC), which has authority over interstate sales of electricity, has expressed interest in pursuing more competitive approaches. For example, an experiment sponsored by FERC in the southwestern states has allowed investor-owned utilities there to sell and buy electricity among themselves free from regulatory constraints. Intrastate, a number of state public utility commissions have examined means to put market forces to work. For example, California has begun to consider pricing new power on the basis of average rates in a region rather than the traditional regulatory approach of covering all costs plus an allowable return on investment. With a number of other states considering such significant reforms, competitive pricing schemes seem to be a developing national trend. Such state-level policy initiatives are forced in part by changing economic conditions.

Future competitive pressures are likely to build as major industrial customers seek lower-cost electricity either by cogenerating or purchasing outside the serving utility's territory. Forcing these firms to conform to rigid state utility regulation might lead to higher production costs, lower growth within the state, and ultimately lower employment opportunities for both metropolitan and rural citizens alike. According to Phillip O'Connor, recently resigned chairman of the Illinois Commerce Commission, "A greater reliance on market forces could correct one of the most critical deficiencies of traditional regulation—its inherent inability to match [customer] prices with the economic costs of production."[11] One of the anomalies of this failure is the spectre of one utility's customers paying rates far higher than neighbors who are fortunate to have service from a "low-cost" producer. Competitive pressure could act to remove such pricing variances.

Kansas could consider the proactive, competitive options being debated or introduced in other states. These include (1) placing new plant and equipment outside the KCC regulatory domain, thus allowing competitive-pricing flexibility, (2) encouraging the exchange of electricity, based on low-cost availability, among utilities and other producers, and (3) placing, for a fee, the electricity-transmission lines of each utility at the service of outside users so they may "wheel" electricity from distant generating plants to any industrial customers or local utility districts. None of these options is without problems. However, all have been or are being examined elsewhere, and some have been implemented. At the least, Kansas should begin a discussion on the desirability of policy designed to increase competition in the state. If other states greatly change their regulatory stance and we remain mired in the traditional approach, our attractiveness as a location for new business will decline.

Although the electricity issue may seem only peripherally related to small Kansas communities, it is not. Indeed, small, municipal utility districts and towns in Kansas face the greatest risk of rate increases from continued utility regulation. When competitive alternatives are offered to the small users, they may receive electricity from distant sources at the best price available. In both California and Texas, such innovations are becoming realities.

In summary, this study has provided a view of the changing economic structure of rural Kansas and its demographic impact, the effects of federal deregulation, and policy choices for the future. Two assumptions have been made throughout: first, that policy choices of the State of Kansas with respect to rural conditions should be *directed at long-term economic growth*; and second, that subsidization of rural communities will not be an effective means of achieving the above goal unless these incentives are transitional in nature, leading to a termination of subsidy by enhancing the capability of the rural economy to become self-supporting. Our emphasis has been upon economic efficiency and growth. Implementing these twin virtues can provide the basis for prosperity, a high quality of life, and rewarding employment prospects for future generations. No master plan for the separate economic development of rural Kansas communities has been presented. Rural "separatism" would be inadvisable. Instead, the policy choices presented here are consistent with coherent economic development for both rural and urban Kansas.

3 _____ GLENN W. FISHER
State and Local Finance

Tax and expenditure questions are seldom absent from the public policy agenda. State and local governments finance many services important to the residents of the state. Without services such as police and fire protection, education, highways, and public health services, few persons would care to live in Kansas. Lack of government services would make it impossible to carry on the business and agricultural activities of the state. On the other hand, the levy and collection of taxes deprive individuals of income which could otherwise be utilized to purchase and consume goods and services. Taxes on businesses deprive firms of funds which might otherwise be invested in expansion and the creation of jobs and sometimes influence the decision of a firm to move or expand operations.

The difficulty of balancing these considerations is compounded as economic growth slows and industry becomes more mobile. States and localities are more conscious of the effect of expenditure and revenue programs upon economic growth, and both business firms and individuals are becoming more skillful in taking advantage of concern about economic growth to secure the "best deal."

Analyses of the revenue structure of a state and its localities often begin with a list of criteria of "a good revenue system." Such a list might include the following characteristics:

1. Revenue productivity;
2. Economic neutrality;
3. Equity;
4. Amount of tax exported to other states or localities;
5. Effect on investment and economic growth;
6. Administrative feasibility; and
7. Taxpayer compliance costs.

Some of these qualities of a revenue source can be measured with a certain precision—others cannot. An attempt to evaluate accurately every

This chapter was prepared with the skillful assistance of Becky Allen and Susan Penner, research assistants in the Hugo Wall Center for Urban Studies, Wichita State University.

revenue source might find that sources ranking high on one criterion do not rank high on others. The above list focuses mainly on economic factors. How the public perceives a revenue source and its long-run effect on the structure of governments are other, elusive variables.

The time and resources available for this study do not permit a detailed criterion-by-criterion examination of the Kansas revenue structure. Instead, this chapter focuses upon two questions: "Is the Kansas state and local revenue structure adequate?" and "Is the Kansas state and local revenue structure well balanced?" Obviously, the meaning of these questions requires further definition. But before turning to those questions, a brief look at Kansas revenue policy in a historical and regional perspective is appropriate..

Kansas Finance in Its Historical and Regional Setting

Government expenditure, measured in dollar terms, has grown tremendously in the last two or three decades, but much of the apparent growth merely reflects changes in the economy. As population grows, government expenditure must grow to provide the same level of services. Inflation has reduced the value of the dollar, and expenditure had to expand to maintain services. In addition, the postwar years have been years of unprecedented real economic growth. The fact that a large part of the economic resources of our society has been devoted to governmental purposes is therefore not surprising.

Academic and popular writers have sought the reasons for the more rapid growth of the governmental sector. The following explanations, among others, have been advanced:

The growing interdependence in our society. The great depression, with unemployment levels reaching as high as 25 percent, made it clear to most people that every individual is dependent upon others for economic well-being and security. The degree of interdependence continues to grow. The importance of the world market to Kansas farmers and oil producers and the potential harm that can be inflicted by nuclear power or hazardous substances demonstrate the circumstances that lead to demands for government intervention.

Preferences for governmental goods and services. Governments produce goods and services different from those of the private sector. As a nation grows wealthy, the demand for the consumption of governmentally provided goods and services grows rapidly. Public preference for education, public parks, health services, and assistance to the disadvantaged may grow more rapidly than the demand for the consumption of privately produced goods and services.

Differential rates of inflation. The price of goods and services purchased by governments has risen more rapidly than the price of all goods and services. Public services are more labor-intensive and concentrated in areas such as construction in which costs have risen the fastest. To maintain the same relative level of services, governmental revenues must increase faster than private-sector expenditures.

Bureaucratic and political factors. Governmental expenditures established through the political process are not subject to the test of the market as are expenditures for items produced in the private sector. Governmental agencies rarely discontinue programs. Agency heads and representatives of special-interest groups often form alliances with sympathetic members of legislative bodies to protect and expand agency budgets, even when general interest in a program is small.[1]

Expenditure and Revenue Trends

According to U.S. Bureau of the Census figures, the general expenditure of Kansas state and local governments increased by 601.3 percent between fiscal years 1962 and 1984 (see Figure 3.1).[2] Although the yearly increases have varied a good deal, the period falls roughly into three phases. The four-year period 1963-66 showed an average annual growth rate of 6.2 percent. In the next fifteen years, 1967-81, the annual average growth rate was 10.1 percent. In the last three years for which data are available, 1982-84, the rate of growth has slowed to an average of 6.5 percent. Figure 3.1 also shows total taxes for the same period. Taxes have grown less rapidly than expenditures, a fact made possible because federal intergovernmental revenue and charges and miscellaneous revenue have grown more rapidly than taxes. Also, Kansas local governments have increasingly used debt financing.

The rapid growth in state and local government expenditures in the 1962-84 period is due in part to a dramatic rise in prices during this period. When adjusted for price inflation, the growth in governmental expenditures is more modest (see Figure 3.1). Kansas state and local government expenditure, adjusted for price change using the Consumer Price Index (CPI), increased by 107.3 percent between 1962 and 1984. If the government purchases deflator is used to adjust expenditures, the increase is only 73 percent.[3] These data show that prices have increased significantly in the period under consideration and also emphasize that cost increases encountered by governments are significantly greater than those encountered by the average consumer.

Kansas has experienced not only substantial inflation during the last twenty-five years but also real economic growth, which is best indicated by personal income. Other good measures of growth in government are expenditures and taxes as percentages of personal income, as shown in Figure 3.2. These measures automatically take account of population change, economic growth, and general price change, but unfortunately

Figure 3.1
State and Local General Expenditures and Taxes,
Actual and Deflated Dollars, 1962-84 (in billions)

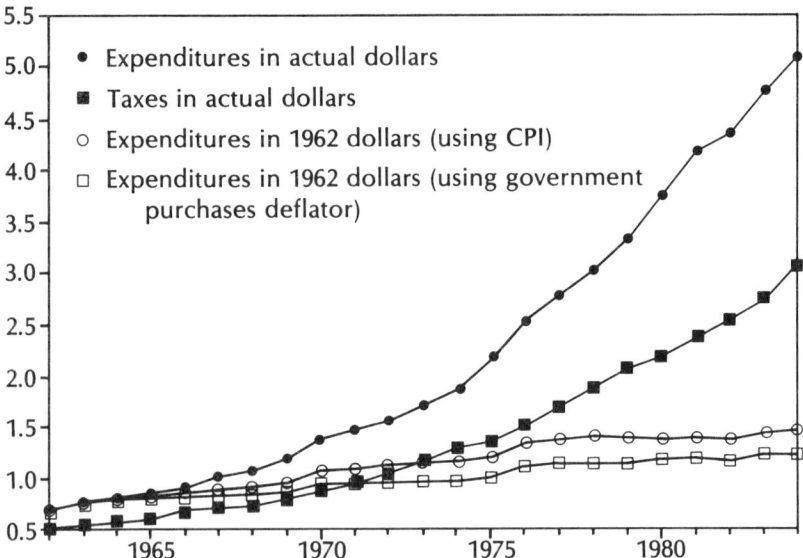

Source: U.S. Bureau of the Census [Census of Governments], *Government Finance.*
Note: General expenditure does not include insurance trust or utility expenditure.

make no allowance for the more rapid price inflation of government purchases.

Figure 3.2 shows that Kansas state and local government expenditures have risen from 13.8 percent of personal income in 1962 to 15.7 percent in 1984. This rise is not insignificant but may surprise those who have not looked carefully at the numbers behind the headlines about increasing governmental expenditure. Relative to economic growth, total expenditures have increased modestly in the period but appear to level off in the last six years. Surprisingly, taxes as a percentage of personal income have actually declined. Celebration should be postponed until the reason for the increasing gap between taxes and expenditures has been examined. To the extent that the explanation lies in greater dependence on federal funds, this gap may have been good news to Kansas taxpayers. However, recent reductions in federal assistance may bring gloomy prospects. To the extent that the differential represents greater revenue from fees and charges or from proceeds of borrowing, it merely means that different individuals within the state are paying, or will pay, for state and local expenditures.

Figure 3.2
State and Local Expenditures and Taxes in Kansas
as Percentage of Personal Income, 1962-84

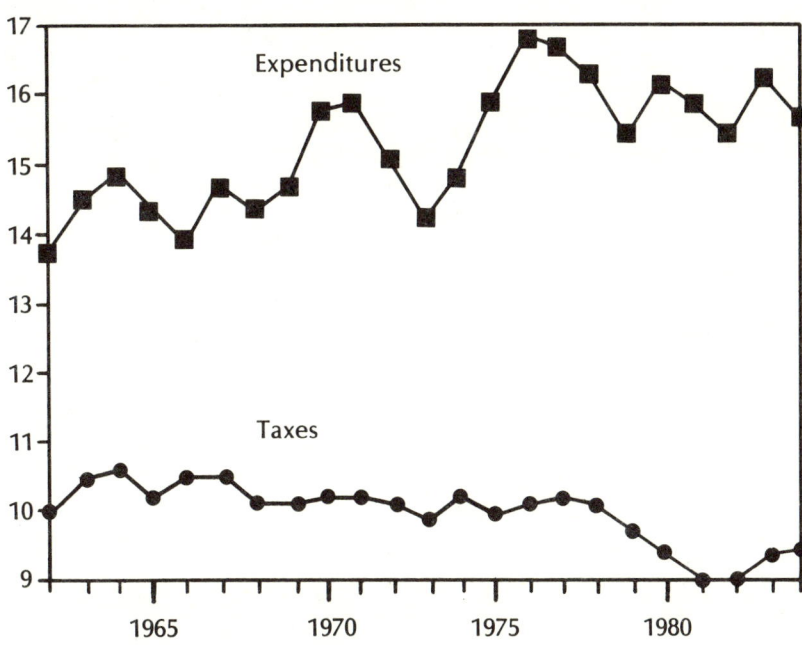

Source: Computed from data in Figures 1 and 4.

The data presented above appropriately analyze the total level of taxation and expenditure in the state but do not reveal the increasing centralization of state and local finance. Data presented in Figure 3.3 measure centralization of state and local finance by showing state expenditures as a percentage of state and local expenditures; and state taxes as a percentage of state and local taxes. The top line of Figure 3.3 shows a substantial rise in the percentage of state and local taxes levied at the state level. In 1962, state revenue sources generated only about 40 percent of state and local revenue, but this percentage rose to about 58 percent in 1984.

The percentage of direct expenditure occurring at the state level always has amounted to substantially less than the percentage of taxes. These figures demonstrate that the state returns substantial amounts of its collected revenue to local government for expenditure. Although the percentage of state government's expenditure has risen over the period, it has grown irregularly. The jump that occurred in 1972-73 reflected changes in school finance and the administration and finance of welfare, but the centralization of expenditure has declined in the last few years.

Figure 3.3
State Expenditures and Taxes as a Percentage of State and Local
Expenditures and Taxes, Respectively, 1962-84

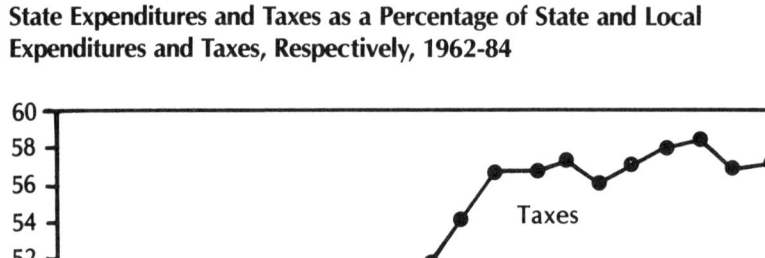

Source: U.S. Census of Governments, Governmental Finances in (various years).

Changes in Expenditure by Function. From 1962 to 1984, expenditures of Kansas state and local governments increased for every function, but not uniformly. Table 3.1 shows the expenditures for major functions in 1962 and 1984. Interest on general debt shows the largest increase and is almost entirely local expenditure, since the state constitution restricts state government from borrowing. Governmental administration expenditure also has increased greatly, perhaps partly because of changes in data classification and reporting. Expenditures for higher education, public welfare, and police have increased more rapidly than has total general expenditure. Expenditures for elementary and secondary education, local fire protection, and sewerage and sanitation have increased less than has the total, but by far the smallest increase is in expenditures for highways. Expenditure for highway purposes has increased by only 262 percent, less than one-half the 601-percent increase in all direct general expenditure.

Changes in Revenue Structure. Although some changes have occurred in the relative importance of the various purposes for which Kansas state and local governments spend, even greater changes have taken place in the sources of revenues, as shown in Table 3.2.

Table 3.1
Kansas State and Local Direct General Expenditure by Function,
1962 and 1984 (dollar amounts in millions)

Function	1962	1984	Increase (%)
Education	$292.9	$1,986.3	578
Higher	70.9	664.3	837
Elementary and secondary	217.7	1,302.6	498
Other	4.3	19.4	351
Public welfare	57.7	471.9	718
Highways	158.8	575.1	262
Health and hospitals	49.9	419.5	741
Police protection	16.5	149.9	808
Local fire protection	9.2	59.4	546
Sewerage and other sanitation	20.2	133.8	562
Financial administration	12.6	110.9	780
Other governmental administration	14.6	174.5	1,096
Interest on general debt	21.7	374.2	1,624
Miscellaneous	68.8	614.3	793
Total	$722.9	$5,069.9	601

Source: U.S. Bureau of the Census, [Census of Governments] *Governmental Finance in [1962 and 1984].*
Note: Functions shown are those for which definitions seem to be consistent for both years. "Miscellaneous" includes the census category "Other and Unallocable" and others items not consistently defined.

Table 3.2
Kansas State and Local Revenue by Major Source,
1962 and 1984 (dollar amounts in millions)

Revenue source	1962	1984	Increase (%)
From federal government	$ 93.6	$ 802.9	755
Property taxes	290.8	1,140.8	292
State sales and gross receipts[a]	145.1	662.3	357
Income taxes	36.1	704.2	1,853
Other state taxes	37.9	399.1	954
Local nonproperty taxes	8.8	165.6	1,780
Charges and miscellaneous	110.5	1,461.3	1,223
Total	$722.7	$5,336.2	638

Source: U.S. Bureau of the Census, [Census of Governments] *Governmental Finance in [1962 and 1984].*
[a]State sales and gross receipts includes selective sales taxes such as those on alcohol, cigarettes, and gasoline, as well as the general sales tax.

Revenue from income taxation grew the fastest, increasing by 1,853 percent in the period. Revenue from local nonproperty taxes increased by 1,780 percent, largely because of the widespread adoption of local sales taxes. Charges and miscellaneous revenues increased by 1,223 percent. Property taxes, by contrast, increased by only 292 percent. These changes have resulted in part from actions of the state legislature, actions of local governing bodies, and the response of the tax structure to economic changes. For example, much of the large increase in income tax collections has occurred as individuals moved into higher tax brackets. The rather poor showing of sales taxes as a revenue source reflects the fact that several of the special taxes on sales, such as those on alcohol, cigarettes, and gasoline, were levied on physical quantities sold rather than as a percentage of the sales price. The decline in the importance of the property tax results from a deliberate attempt to reduce the importance of this form of taxation by increasing state aid to schools, centralizing welfare, and substituting other local taxes.

Regional Comparisons. Those who establish public policy appropriately might look not only at past history but also at practices in other states. Such a comparative examination of other states' experience might be helpful in view of the increasing economic competition among states. In this period of slow economic growth and intensifying competition, a state or locality would be unwise to impose a tax burden substantially higher than that imposed by its neighbors. At the same time, the level of expenditure should remain high enough to provide both the services demanded by expanding businesses and a quality of life attractive to potential new residents. Making comparisons, however, does not assure that what other states or localities do is right, but states can learn from the experiences of other states. One advantage of our federal form of government is that each state has the freedom to innovate and adjust to the particular circumstances of its region.

Expenditures of state and local governments in Kansas, the U.S., and selected neighboring states are shown by function in Table 3.3. Kansas total general expenditure per capita of $2,080 falls slightly below the U.S. average and exceeds that of three of the five comparison states; however, it differs significantly from Missouri, whose per capita expenditures falls considerably below those of all the other states. Function-by-function comparisons show Kansas expenditures to be near the median. Exceptions include health and hospital expenditure, which falls below that of any of the comparison states and below the national average. Welfare expenditure is lower in Kansas than in any of these states except Missouri. Variations exist, of course, in the degree to which spending is centralized within the various states. Over 40 percent of state-local direct expenditure in the United States is made by state-level governments compared to 37.5 percent in Kansas.[4]

Revenue patterns in these selected states reveal similarities, as shown in Table 3.4. The small collections from property taxes in Oklahoma constitute a striking difference, although they are offset by the much larger collections from "other taxes" in that state. Undoubtedly, these figures reflect the rather large amount Oklahoma received from the taxation of oil and gas production. As a result of the recent drastic decline in oil prices, the current

Table 3.3

State and Local Expenditures by Function, in Selected States, 1984

	Total general	Education (excludes libraries)	Public welfare	Health and hospitals	Highways	Police
Per capita expenditures						
U. S. average	$2,131	$746	$274	$197	$167	$82
KANSAS	2,080	815	194	172	236	61
Colorado	2,204	841	202	184	211	89
Iowa	2,144	844	258	218	286	59
Missouri	1,622	602	171	181	141	71
Nebraska	2,056	814	194	210	271	59
Oklahoma	1,931	767	214	205	174	58
State expenditures as a percentage of state and local expenditures						
U. S. average	40.1	27.7	76.1	46.6	59.0	14.5
KANSAS	37.5	28.1	97.6	46.5	49.5	11.3
Colorado	35.2	31.5	55.0	50.6	55.8	11.6
Iowa	41.4	31.0	89.2	44.6	51.4	15.6
Missouri	40.9	23.9	98.2	46.4	59.2	14.9
Nebraska	39.5	26.9	90.4	40.9	55.3	19.2
Oklahoma	44.6	32.5	99.2	50.6	58.8	19.6

Source: Computations based on government finance spreadsheet diskettes sup-
plied by the U.S. Advisory Commission on Intergovernmental Relations,
Washington, D.C., 1985.
Note: Only major functions are shown, although "total general" includes functions not shown separately.

picture is very different. Interestingly, Kansas receives less, per capita, from
general sales taxation than do any of the comparison states. Kansas' collections from this source also fall well below the U.S. average, but this will
probably change when the sales tax increase enacted by the 1986 Kansas
legislature becomes effective.

Comparison of the measures of centralization contained in Tables 3.3
and 3.4 indicates that these state governments have centralized revenue
more than they have centralized expenditure. This difference again reflects
the fact that these states provide grants to local governments. Kansas state
government receives only 2.1 percent of the property tax revenue but 100
percent of corporate and individual income tax revenues. This pattern is
common, except that Missouri local governments receive substantial revenues from income taxation. In past years the general sales tax was largely
utilized by state governments, but recent years have seen the rapid spread
of local sales taxes. Nationwide, states receive 83.4 percent of general sales
tax revenue, but in two neighboring states, Colorado and Oklahoma, local
use of the sales tax is more extensive.

Table 3.4
State and Local Revenues by Major Source, in Selected States, 1984

	Total general	Inter-govern-mental	Property tax	General sales and gross receipts[a]	Individual and corporate income taxes	Other taxes	Charges and miscellaneous general
Per capita revenues							
U. S. average	$2,299	$411	$408	$318	$346	$283	$532
KANSAS	2,189	329	468	248	289	255	599
Colorado	2,342	365	445	422	268	204	637
Iowa	2,137	360	493	253	316	211	504
Missouri	1,723	326	234	341	241	197	385
Nebraska	2,200	349	507	267	231	227	619
Oklahoma	2,028	331	200	267	229	463	538
State revenues as a percentage of state and local revenues							
U. S. average	61.1	84.1	4.0	83.4	91.4	83.9	41.9
KANSAS	54.4	83.5	2.1	85.9	100.0	87.1	30.5
Colorado	51.5	80.9	0.4	59.0	100.0	74.8	37.6
Iowa	59.7	84.8	0.0	100.0	100.0	95.4	39.8
Missouri	58.7	78.5	0.5	77.8	88.7	65.9	37.9
Nebraska	54.5	88.8	0.3	87.3	100.0	87.9	35.8
Oklahoma	66.2	82.5	0.0	51.8	100.0	95.0	48.9

Source: Computations based on government finance spreadsheet diskettes sup-
plied by the U.S. Advisory Commission on Intergovernmental Relations,
Washington, D.C., 1985. Prior calendar-year income used to compute fiscal
year expenditure.
[a]Does not include excise or specific sales taxes.

Past Trends and Future Decisions

The data presented above clearly show that state and local government
expenditures in Kansas have grown more rapidly than the economy as a
whole. However, data for recent years suggest we may be entering an era
in which government expenditure comprises a constant, or even declining,
percentage of personal income (see Figure 3.2).

In the 1962-84 period, revenue structure changed more fundamentally
than did the structure of expenditure. The changes in the revenue structure
resulted, in part, from deliberate decisions by state lawmakers and local
governing bodies. Much of the change came about because of interactions
among economic changes, the nature of the various revenue sources, and
administrative decisions or nondecisions. For example, the rapid growth in
the importance of income taxes has occurred largely from the high income
elasticity of that form of taxation.[5] In a time of rapidly inflating personal
income, a larger percentage of taxable income is taxed in the higher brackets of the rate schedule, and a smaller percentage is excluded from taxation
as personal exemptions. The general sales tax has an elasticity less than
one, which means that the tax yield rises less rapidly than the increase in
state personal income. Slower yet to respond to increases in personal in-

come are the selective sales taxes, such as those on cigarettes, liquor, and tobacco, which are levied on the sales of physical units (packs, bottles or gallons) rather than as a percentage of price. Without rate increases, yields from these taxes would have risen even more slowly than they did.

The decline in importance of the property tax, as well as the change in the base of that tax, which will be discussed later, results from an even more complicated set of interactions. The property tax usually functions as the "budget balancing" source of revenue for local governments. The local governing board decides upon the budget required, subtracts carry-over revenues and nontax revenues, and, based upon these figures, levies the property tax required to balance the budget. The rate to be applied is then calculated by dividing the levy by the assessed value of property in the district. In theory, the same amount of revenue will be raised whether the property in the district is assessed at the legally mandated 30 percent of market value or at some lesser value.[6] In practice, many local governing boards have been reluctant to see the property tax rate rise. This policy, combined with failure to reassess real estate as the market value increased, has resulted in property tax collections' rising far less rapidly than personal income.[7]

The rapidly increasing importance of current charges and miscellaneous revenues has resulted both from the actions of state and local policy makers to place certain programs on a totally or partially self-supporting basis, and also fortuitously from higher interest rates. Because of the cash basis law and the generally conservative approach to finance in Kansas, governments in the state often carry substantial cash balances and thus find themselves in a much better position during periods of high interest rates than do governments in states that customarily borrow in anticipation of future tax collections. Changes in the revenue received from the federal government result from changes in federal policy and for the most part are beyond the control of Kansas governments.

Is the Kansas Revenue Structure Adequate?

One cannot answer questions involving the adequacy of a revenue structure without first addressing the question, "adequate for what?" Clearly, the current structure has been providing large amounts of revenue. Whether it will provide adequate amounts in the future depends upon the level of expenditure to be financed and the response of individual revenue sources to changing economic conditions. Attempting to prescribe or recommend here what that level of expenditure should be would not be appropriate, but one must assume certain expenditure levels in order to analyze the performance of existing tax policy.

As noted above, both expenditure level and yields of the revenue structure relate closely to the level and growth of the state's economy, which is appropriately measured by Kansas personal income. Figure 3.2 shows that relative to the state's economy expenditure has leveled off in the last six years. Whether this pattern is the beginning of a long-term decline or represents a temporary pause in the upward climb cannot be determined conclusively at this time. However, the probable performance of the Kansas state and local tax structure may be projected by assuming that the present stabilization may last for some time. For purpose of the projections in this section, future state and local government expenditures are assumed to be equal to the six-year average of 15.8 percent of personal income.

Personal income in Kansas is assumed to increase at an annual rate of 6.5 percent. Although considerably lower than past growth, this figure seems appropriate in view of the lower rate of inflation and the somewhat unfavorable outlook for Kansas' major industries discussed in Chapter 1.[8] Fortunately, the assumed income growth need not be absolutely accurate. By tying both expenditure and revenue projections to personal income, we insure that under- or overestimates will parallel each other. Kansas personal income and state and local expenditures, when projected on the basis of these assumptions, are $47.1 billion and $7.4 billion, respectively, for 1990; and $64.6 billion and $10.2 for 1995.

Projections of revenue yield are most useful when the various categories of revenue are projected separately for each governmental unit and for each accounting fund. For detailed projections, all available economic data should be utilized, as well as other information about particular revenue sources, such as information about the recent sharp drop in the price of oil or the latest development involving federal aid to state and local governments. Making detailed projections is beyond the resources of this study. However, "global" projections of state and local government revenues and somewhat more detailed projections of state general fund revenues are made along with a more detailed examination of the property tax as a source of future revenue.

Since puzzling changes have occurred in the elasticities of Kansas taxes in the last few years (a matter discussed in the next section), global projections have been based on assumptions regarding the elasticity of the Kansas tax system. Tax elasticities are assumed at .7 to .85 for general sales taxes; at 1.0 to 1.5 for income taxes; and at .85 to 1.0 for other taxes. Motor vehicle taxes are assumed to range from a low annual increase of 2 percent to a high annual increase of 3 percent. Because the property tax is the "budget balancing" tax, the amounts projected for the property tax are the differences between projected expenditures and the projected yield of all other revenue sources. In addition, the following assumptions have been employed in projecting nontax revenues: 1) general revenue sharing will be eliminated, and federal assistance from other programs will remain constant; 2) current charges will increase at the same rate as personal income;

and 3) miscellaneous revenue will remain constant (this category includes interest earnings).

Table 3.5 shows the results of these projections and indicates that the present revenue system is not adequate to support the present level of expenditure[9] unless the long-term decline in the relative importance of the property tax is reversed. If the low-elasticity assumptions are correct, the property tax share of total revenue would have to rise from 21.4 percent in 1984 to 34.3 percent in 1995, which is still less than 40 percent in 1962. If the high elasticities hold, the property tax share will rise more modestly to 26.5 percent of the total.

Under the assumptions used for the high-elasticity projections, the income tax will provide a considerably higher proportion of the revenue, and as a result the role of the property tax will be smaller than under the estimates of low elasticity. Even so, the present tax system will not be able to support the assumed level of expenditure without a resurgence in the level of property taxation.

Table 3.5
Projections of Kansas State and Local Revenues,
1990 and 1995 (dollar amounts in millions)

					% of total	
	Actual	Projections		Actual	Projections	
Revenue source	1984	1990	1995	1984	1990	1995
Low elasticities						
From federal government	$ 803	$ 764	$ 764	15.0	10.3	7.5
Tax revenue:						
Property	1,141	2,101	3,495	21.4	28.2	34.3
General sales	604	789	986	11.3	10.6	9.7
Income	704	1,028	1,408	13.2	13.8	13.8
Motor fuel & vehicle	217	244	270	4.1	3.3	2.6
Other	406	550	709	7.6	7.4	6.9
Total tax revenue	3,072	4,711	6,866	57.6	63.3	67.3
Current charges	754	1,101	1,508	14.1	14.8	14.8
Miscellaneous revenue	707	871	1,064	13.2	11.7	10.4
High elasticities						
From federal government	803	764	764	15.0	10.3	7.5
Tax revenue:						
Property	1,141	1,796	2,704	21.4	24.1	26.5
General sales	604	834	1,091	11.3	11.2	10.7
Income	704	1,231	1,960	13.2	16.5	19.2
Motor fuel & vehicle	217	259	300	4.1	3.5	2.9
Other	406	592	811	7.6	8.0	8.0
Total tax revenue	3,072	4,712	6,866	57.6	63.3	67.3
Current charges	754	1,101	1,508	14.1	14.8	14.8
Miscellaneous revenue	707	871	1,064	13.2	11.7	10.4
Grand total[a]	$5,336	$7,447	$10,202	100.0	100.0	100.0

[a]Percentage total may not add to 100 due to rounding.

Although not very detailed, these projections do point up certain policy problems to be faced in the next few years. For example, if the property tax continues to decline in importance, tax-rate increases or new revenue sources will be needed. Note, however, that these are global projections for all state funds and local governments. Because monies collected for a particular level of government or for specific funds may not be transferred easily, some funds or units of government may find themselves in financial difficulty even though total revenues appear to exceed total revenue requirements. For this reason, the question of revenue adequacy cannot be separated from questions of governmental structure and organization.

Other developments are also possible. Federal revenues may increase rather than stabilize at current dollar levels. Another possibility would be an increase in earnings from current charges. A major increase might well require a shift in the present philosophy regarding charges for government services.[10]

Perhaps the greatest uncertainty revealed by this analysis pertains to the elasticity of the Kansas tax structure. Although important changes in revenue yield have been obvious for the last three or four years, the magnitude of these changes warrants closer examination.

Changing Elasticities of Kansas Taxes

The relationship between the Kansas tax structure and personal income in Kansas has undergone change in recent years. A detailed analysis of elasticities of Kansas general fund taxes reveals that there was a significant downward shift in the elasticities of almost all these taxes since 1981 (see Table 3.6). The income elasticity of the state-levied property tax on motor carriers, for example, was 1.672 for the 1977-85 period, but only .708 for the period of 1981-85. The elasticity of the individual income tax, which is the base most closely related to personal income, dropped from 1.632 in the longer period to 1.392 in the 1981-85 period. These elasticities were computed from revenue data which have been adjusted for changes in the Kansas law by Professor Darwin Daicoff.[11]

The reasons for abrupt changes in the elasticity of Kansas taxes are not at all clear. A number of factors may have affected the elasticities, but in most cases it is not possible to determine how great the effect has been.

Kansas, like many states, utilizes federal corporate and individual income tax bases as the starting point for calculation of the corresponding state taxes. In the case of the individual income tax, the federal adjusted gross income is the starting point, and, in addition, most of the itemized deductions are the same. Federal corporate income is also the starting point for the Kansas corporation income tax. In both cases, income is defined in relation to the current federal law, which means that federal changes are automatically applicable to Kansas taxes. This state policy makes compli-

Table 3.6
Elasticities of General Fund Revenues in Kansas,
Longer-Term Compared to 1981-85

Revenue source	Long-term[a]	1981-85
Property tax		
Motor carriers	1. 672[b]	0.708
Income and privilege taxes		
Individual	1.632[b]	1.392
Corporate	0.202	-0.989
Total income taxes	1.212	0.811
Financial institutions	0.002[b]	-0.628
Domestic insurance companies	-0.026	-2.870
Inheritance tax	0.981	0.020
Sales, use and excise taxes		
Retail sales	0.794	0.700
Compensating use	0.287[c]	0.243
Cigarette	-0.015	-0.379
Tobacco products	0.786	0.904
Cereal malt beverage	0.017[d]	-0.012
Liquor gallonage	0.093[d]	-0.099
Liquor enforcement	0.817[e]	-0.100
Private club	0.117	-0.080
Corporate franchise	0.844	-0.695
Severance	2.018	-0.582
Gross receipts tax		
Insurance premiums	0.893	0.936
Bingo enforcement	0.594	0.516
Miscellaneous	1.218	1.325
Total	0.933	0.558
Total less income taxes	0.738	0.351
Total less income and severance taxes	0.695	0.505
Personal income growth (annual)	9.86%	7.60%

[a]1976-85 unless indicated otherwise.
[b]Based on 1977-85.
[c]Based on 1979-85.
[d]Based on 1978-85.
[e]Based on 1976-82.

ance and administration easier, but, given the rapid changes in the federal law which have occurred recently, can result in unpredictable changes in tax yields. There were eight major federal tax bills passed in the years 1975 to 1984. The most important of these were the Economic Recovery Act of 1981, the Tax Equity and Fiscal Responsibility Act of 1982, and the Tax Reform Act of 1984.

The Economic Recovery Tax Act of 1981 replaced the depreciation schedules then in use with an accelerated cost recovery system. This change and a number of others reduced the Kansas taxable income of corporations and unincorporated businesses. Some of these changes were modified by later legislation, but a tabulation in the 1987 federal budget document shows that 1985 federal corporate tax collections will be reduced by $12.1 billion as a result of changes made in the 1981, 1982, and 1984 acts.

Changes in the federal individual income tax, including the large rate reductions, marriage penalty provisions, and changes in the treatment of tax-deferred retirement plans, have reduced federal individual income tax collections by an estimated $114.9 billion for 1985. These changes reduce the deductions that may be taken from Kansas income and increase Kansas individual tax yields. However, the retirement-plan deduction (including IRAs) reduce adjusted gross income and thus lower the Kansas income taxes.

Factors endemic to Kansas may be affecting elasticities. Minor changes in the Kansas law, such as those relating to job credits or enterprise zones, may contribute to declining elasticity.

Compliance with the tax laws may be declining. For example, there has been substantial growth in sales nationally by out-of-state mail-order firms that are beyond the reach of a sales tax administrator.

That important changes have occurred in the Kansas economy is well documented in Chapter 1. Structural changes in the Kansas economy may alter the relationship between personal income and the yield of state taxes. For example, consumption patterns may have changed in ways which reduce the yield of sales taxes. The slow growth of revenues from alcoholic beverages and cigarettes certainly reflects changing attitudes toward these products, and increased consumption of services not subject to the general sales tax may be occurring.

Whatever the reasons for the declining elasticities, they are not confined to Kansas. A recent background paper prepared by a member of the staff of the National Conference of State Legislatures reports that both the Tax Foundation and the U.S. Department of the Treasury have concluded that the elasticity of state tax revenues has fallen. The Tax Foundation reduced its estimate of the elasticity of the personal income tax from 1.7 to 1.5 and the elasticity of the sales tax from 1.1 to .9. Treasury reduced the elasticity of the state and local personal income tax from 1.6 to 1.4.[12]

Table 3.7 contains alternative projections of general fund tax revenues for the years 1990 and 1995 based on the two levels of elasticities. The low projections are based on trend lines computed from 1981-85 data; the high projections are computed from longer trends, usually 1976-85. The projections also show (bottom line of Table 3.7) the level of revenues that will be required to finance expenditures that grow at the same rate as personal income (assumed to be 6.5 percent annually).

These projected revenue requirements indicate the seriousness of the decline in elasticities. If general fund taxes grow in the next ten years at a rate consistent with that of the last ten, the current tax structure will be sufficient to finance the current level of expenditure relative to personal income. On the other hand, if the lower elasticities of the last five years

Table 3.7
Alternative Projections of General Fund Tax Revenues in Kansas, 1990 and 1995 (in millions)

	Actual 1985	1990 Low	1990 High	1995 Low	1995 High
Property tax					
Motor carriers	$ 6.6	$ 8.7	$ 9.6	$ 11.1	$ 13.1
Income and privilege taxes					
Individual	603.5	931.4	943.1	1,343.4	1,365.3
Corporation	142.0	47.9	167.1	0[d]	186.9
Financial institutions	13.9	6.6	13.1	1.4	13.6
Domestic insurance companies	.2	0[d]	.5	0[d]	.5
Inheritance tax	29.8	30.1	48.0	30.6	65.1
Sales, use and excise taxes					
Retail sales	478.7	631.5	677.7	811.5	899.4
Compensating use	68.2	73.6	75.6	84.2	88.1
Cigarette[a]	43.2	35.2	45.2	25.4	44.8
Tobacco products	1.2	1.8	1.7	2.4	2.3
Cereal malt beverage	5.1	5.0	5.1	4.9	5.2
Liquor gallonage	11.5	11.0	12.5	10.4	13.3
Liquor enforcement	17.0	18.6	24.8	19.9	31.9
Private clubs	2.2	2.1	2.4	2.0	2.6
Corporate franchise	8.0	10.7	11.5	13.8	15.5
Wheat[b]	.1	.2	.2	.2	.2
Severance	101.3	63.7	177.9	21.6	240.7
Gross receipts tax					
Insurance premiums	70.6	68.2	68.2	92.1	91.9
Bingo enforcement	.3	.4	.4	.4	.5
Miscellaneous	1.1	1.8	1.7	2.5	2.4
Total taxes	$1,604.4	$1,948.4	$2,286.3	$2,477.8	$3,083.3
Projected expenditures[c]		$2,198.2	$2,198.2	$3,011.7	$3,011.7

Source: "Low" projections are projected from 1981-85 tax collections, corrected
for rate changes. "High" projections are projected from tax collections from
a longer period (usually 1976-85).
[a]Does not include 1985 rate increase.
[b]Wheat arbitrarily projected at maximum of $200,000.
[c]Expenditures from general fund taxes are assumed to grow at 6 1/2-percent
annually from fiscal year 1985.
[d]Projected figure is negative.

continue, current taxes will fall more than $500 million short in fiscal year
1995.

These projections were made before the 1986 Kansas legislature increased the state sales tax from 3 to 4 percent. Assuming that this change
will increase the state sales tax yield by one-third,[13] this action revises the
overall picture considerably. For 1990, total tax collections will increase
from a low of $2,158.9 million (and a resulting deficit relative to expendi-
tures of $39.3 million) to a high of $2,512.2 million (and a resulting surplus
relative to expenditures of $314.0 million). The 1995 projections produce a
low of $2,749.3 in total taxes (and a deficit of $262.4 million) and a high
of $3,383.1 in total taxes (and a surplus of $371.4 million). These adjusted
data suggest that even with the sales tax increase, revenue will fall short if

the lower elasticities of the last few years continue. If the higher elasticities return, the present revenue structure should be adequate to support the assumed level of expenditure.

The Property Tax

The property tax has traditionally been the "budget balancing" revenue source for local governments. In a broader sense, the property tax is also the "budget balancing" revenue source for the entire revenue system of state and local government. Nonproperty tax revenues have been expanded in a deliberate effort to reduce the role of the property tax, but annual shortfalls in revenue often are met by increases in the property tax. For example, the annual legislative debate over school finance determines how much of local school budgets will come from nonproperty tax sources. The local school boards then utilize the property tax to finance the "residual."

The unique administrative procedures required in property taxation must be taken into account in any effort to compute the elasticity or project the future yields of the tax. Since tax rates fluctuate each year, the elasticity of the property tax may be more accurately calculated from the property tax base. The property tax base is composed of three broad classes of property: (1) real estate, (2) tangible personal property, and (3) utility property. Somewhat different assessing procedures are applied to each class. Real estate is assessed by county appraisers, but values are subject to review by the county board of equalization and the State Board of Tax Appeals. Real estate reappraisal took place in the 1960s, but most existing real estate has not been reappraised since that time.[14]

Personal property is also assessed by the county appraisers, but because personal property is mobile and has a shorter life than real estate, new lists of personal property are created annually. The Division of Property Valuation in the Kansas Department of Revenue provides guidelines for assessing many kinds of personal property and in recent years has stepped up efforts to assure county compliance with these guidelines.[15] Utility properties are assessed annually by the division.

Table 3.8 shows the changing composition of the property tax base. Real estate, especially rural real estate, has been declining as a percentage of the total tax base. Tangible personal property was becoming an increasingly important part of the total until 1980. The apparent reversal of this trend results from a change in method of collecting the property tax on automobiles. In 1979, new legislation required the tax on most automobiles be paid when the registration fee is paid. In other words, the value of these properties is no longer included on the regular assessment rolls, and thus, is not included in Table 3.8. If personal property were included, it would comprise 39.3 percent of the total in 1984. Only one other state has a higher portion of personal property in the base.

Table 3.8
Composition of Kansas Property Tax Base, 1965-84
(major classes of property as percentage of total)

Year	Real estate			Tangible personal			State assessed			Total
	Rural	Urban	Total	Rural	Urban	Total	Rural	Urban	Total	
1965	27.6	29.8	57.4	15.1	9.3	24.3	14.2	4.0	18.2	100.0
1970	28.5	31.0	59.5	13.5	9.5	22.9	13.1	4.5	17.5	100.0
1975	23.9	30.6	54.6	16.7	13.1	29.8	11.2	4.4	15.6	100.0
1980	20.1	28.4	48.5	26.4	8.0	35.2	12.0	4.2	16.3	100.0
1984	19.0	29.1	48.1	21.7	10.2	31.9	15.7	4.3	20.0	100.0

Source: Division of Property Valuation, Kansas Department of Revenue.
Note: Figures for 1980 and 1984 do not include valuation of vehicles for which
   property taxes are collected at the time of vehicle registration.

Table 3.9
Kansas Property Tax Assessments and Rates, 1965-84
(dollar amounts in millions)

Year	Total assessed value	Assessment/sales ratio		Average tax rate on	
		Rural (%)	Urban (%)	Assessed value (%)	Equalized value (%)
1965	$ 4,841.0	18.0	20.0	6.9	5.2
1970	6,080.8	18.0	21.0	8.3	6.4
1975	7,693.2	10.0	15.0	8.6	4.8
1980	11,197.0[a]	6.0	9.0	8.9	3.4
1984	12,423.1[a]	5.8	8.0	10.6	4.1

Source: Division of Property Valuation, Kansas Department of Revenue.
[a]Figures for 1980 and 1984 include valuation of automobiles on which taxes are
   collected when registration fees are paid (estimate).

The assessment/sales ratio studies conducted by the Division of Property Valuation show clearly that the failure to reappraise real property has resulted in real estate assessment far below the legally required 30 percent of market value (see Table 3.9). The percentage declined continually from 1962 until 1981, when falling farmland prices caused a slight upturn in the rural ratio. Since that time, the urban ratio has fluctuated up and then down.

No equally good method exists for determining whether tangible personal property and state-assessed property are assessed near the legally specified 30 percent of value. However, the annual updating of the assessments of this kind of property clearly has been a factor in their growing importance in relation to real estate assessment.

The assessed value of property in Kansas has grown much less rapidly than has personal income as shown by the income elasticity indexes in Table 3.10. From 1976-84, the average annual growth rate of assessed value

Table 3.10
Elasticities of the Kansas Property Tax Base, 1976-84 and 1981-84

Assessed value (1976-84)	
Real estate	.26
Tangible personal	.88
State assessed	.71
Total	.57
Equalized value (1976-84)	
Real estate	.85
Total[a]	.85
Equalized value (1981-84)	
Total[a]	.22

[a]This total includes real estate at equalized value and tangible personal and state
    assessed property at assessed value.

was 5.56 percent compared to personal income, which grew at an annual
rate of 9.7 percent. Dividing the tax growth rate by the income growth rate
yields an elasticity of .57 for the period.

Table 3.10 also shows the elasticities for the major classes of taxable
property and the elasticities resulting when real estate values are "equalized" using the assessment/sales ratio study. Tangible personal property has
the highest elasticity at .88. If real estate values are equalized at 30 percent,
using the assessment/sales ratio data, they have an elasticity of .85. The
table also provides evidence that the sharp reduction in elasticities which
occurred about 1981 in Kansas nonproperty taxes is paralleled in the property tax base. Even when equalized, the real estate base has had an elasticity
since 1981 of only .22 percent.

Nominal property tax rates have risen over the last two decades, but if
real estate had been reassessed at the legally prescribed 30 percent of value,
property tax rates would have fallen, as shown in Table 3.9. The statewide
average rate[16] rose from 6.9 percent in 1965 to 10.6 percent in 1984. If the
assessment/sales ratio studies had been used to equalize real estate at the
legally prescribed 30 percent level, the rate would have fallen from 5.2
percent to 4.1 percent in this period.

The property tax situation is currently in flux. Legislation passed in
1985 provides for reappraisal of all property by 1989. In November 1986,
the electors of Kansas will vote on a constitutional amendment to classify
property for purposes of taxation; if this amendment passes, property will
be assessed at the following percentages of value:

     1. Real property used for residential purposes,
       including multifamily residential   12%
     2. Land devoted to agricultural use, valued upon basis
       of its value in agricultural use   30%
     3. Vacant lots   12%
     4. All other urban and rural real estate   30%
     5. Mobile homes

		12%
6. Mineral leasehold interest		30%
7. Public utility tangible personal property		30%
8. Certain motor vehicles (business use)		30%
9. Commercial and industrial machinery (valued using straight-line depreciation from retail cost, seven-year life. Depreciation value never to be less than 20% of cost if machine is in use)		20%
10. Other tangible personal property		30%
11. Farm machinery, livestock, merchants' and manufacturers' inventory, household goods not used for production of income		exempt

If reappraisal is completed successfully and the constitutional amendment is adopted, large shifts in the property tax base will take place. Rough estimates of what these shifts will be on a statewide basis may be made, but the variations among individual taxing districts will be much greater. The experiences of other states clearly show that the first use of the updated values will focus much attention upon the property tax and lead to increased complaints about an already unpopular tax. These complaints can be minimized if the reappraisal is carried through and if public support can be maintained.

Tax Capacity of Kansas State and Local Governments

With respect to its adequacy, the Kansas tax structure clearly has "taken a turn for the worse" in the last five years. The elasticity of almost all state taxes and the property tax base have fallen substantially since 1981. As a result, future tax rates must be higher, or government expenditure as a percentage of personal income must decline. Even so, Kansas has not faced financial crises of the magnitude confronted by many other states. In order to place this matter in perspective, this section will analyze the tax capacity and tax effort of the governments of Kansas.

Personal income is often used as a measure of the tax capacity of a state, but it does have weaknesses. A state's ability to raise revenue is affected not only by the income of its residents, but also by business activity and wealth within the state. Tourist states, for example, are visited by non-residents who spend money and carry on activities requiring public services. Sales taxes, hotel and motel taxes, and various forms of amusement taxes can be used as sources of revenue that do not come from the personal income of the state's residents. Some states also enjoy a concentration of wealth out of proportion to the income of the state. Recent fluctuations in oil prices and the high demand for low-sulfur coal have focused attention on wealth represented by minerals and other natural resources, but real estate and other forms of wealth also are distributed unevenly.

While numerous attempts have been made to develop measures of tax capacity for state and local governments, one of the best of these is the "representative tax system" developed by the U.S. Advisory Commission on Intergovernmental Relations (ACIR). The representative tax system is designed to answer the question: "What would be the total revenue of each of the state and local governments of the fifty states if every state applied identical tax rates, in other words, national averages, to each of twenty-six commonly used tax bases?"[17] The tax bases of each state are standardized and computed from statistics from a number of sources.[18] These computed tax bases approximate the revenue potential. The tax rates to be used for each revenue source are computed by dividing the total tax base into the total revenue obtained from that tax by all states. The resulting rate multiplied by the defined tax base of each state gives the yield or "capacity" of that tax. Adding the hypothetical yields for all twenty-six taxes provides the total yield or capacity for each state.

This measure of tax capacity, as computed using the representative tax system, is relative to that of other states. Tax capacity is the estimated amount of revenue that would be collected by the state if it imposed all twenty-six taxes in the representative tax system, at the average rate.

Table 3.11 compares the 1983 tax capacity of Kansas state and local governments with the actual tax revenue from major categories of taxes. This table shows that the revenue collected from all the tax categories except the property tax is below capacity. Property tax collections, by contrast, are well above capacity. If Kansas governments had imposed all twenty-six taxes in the representative tax system at the average rate, the state would have collected $221 million more than actually was collected. A considerable shift in the sources from which the revenue came also would have taken place. One hundred eighty-four million dollars less would have been collected from property taxes, but considerably more would have been

Table 3.11
Kansas State and Local Tax Capacity and Effort, 1983
(dollar amounts in thousands)

Tax source	Tax capacity	Tax revenue	Capacity minus revenue	Tax capacity index	Tax effort index
General sales	$ 643,940	$ 548,594	$ 95,346	95.9	85.2
Total selective sales	350,964	272,880	78,084	105.2	77.8
Total license	116,814	92,574	24,240	120.6	79.2
Personal income	549,743	530,657	19,086	96.2	96.5
Corporate income	146,811	141,347	5,464	99.4	96.3
Total property	896,716	1,080,803	(184,087)	97.1	120.5
Estate and gift	28,207	27,435	722	106.1	97.3
Total severance[a]	184,650	2,339	182,311	228.5	1.3
Total	$2,917,845	$2,696,629	$221,216	102.3	92.4

Source: U.S. Advisory Commission on Intergovernmental Relations, *1983 Tax Capacity of the Fifty States, an Information Report*, M-148 (Washington, D.C., May 1986).

[a]The Kansas severance tax was not in effect in FY 1983. In FY 1984, collections from this source were $106,112,000.

collected from selective and general sales taxes. Notice that only a token amount of severance tax collections are shown. Kansas did not enact a severance tax until 1983, and fiscal year 1984 was the first full year of collections, amounting to $106 million. Note also that Kansas taxes oil and gas property as personal property.

The last two columns of Table 3.11 are indexes comparing Kansas per capita tax capacity and tax effort with the national average. Overall, Kansas tax capacity exceeds the national average by 2.3 percent, and its tax effort falls below it by 7.6 percent.

Table 3.12 reveals that the Kansas tax capacity exceeds that of three of the comparison states but falls well below that of Colorado and Oklahoma. Examination of data (not reproduced here) shows that Colorado's capacity exceeds the national average for every major tax category—sales, income, and property. Oklahoma ranks far above average in the severance category and above in property taxes, corporate income taxes, and selective sales. At this writing, however, oil prices are falling rapidly, and the Oklahoma situation may be very different now.

The tax effort indexes reveal that all the states in the comparison group, except Iowa, levy taxes which, as a percentage of capacity, are below the national average. This finding confirms the generally accepted view that states in this part of the country are not high-tax states.

Is the Kansas Revenue Structure Well Balanced?

Although concensus as to what constitutes a properly balanced tax structure is unlikely, large areas of agreement exist among those who have thoughtfully considered the matter. A paper by Robert Kleine and John Shannon delivered at the 1985 meeting of the National Tax Association provides a thoughtful statement by well-informed individuals.[19] This paper, entitled "Characteristics of a Balanced State-Local Tax System," represents a revision of earlier work by ACIR.

Table 3.12
Tax Effort and Capacity Indexes, in Selected States, 1983

	Tax capacity	Tax effort
United States	100.0	100.0
KANSAS	102.3	92.4
Colorado	122.2	79.0
Iowa	90.8	108.6
Missouri	89.2	86.9
Nebraska	100.7	94.4
Oklahoma	114.9	80.3

Source: U.S. Advisory Commission on Intergovernmental Relations, *1983 Tax Capacity of the Fifty States, an Information Report*, M-148 (Washington, D.C., May 1986).

Authors Kleine and Shannon point out that recent changes have affected the climate for state and local tax policy. Among these are the serious recessions in 1974-75 and 1980-83 and the greater demands for political accountability as evidenced by taxpayer "revolts" in several states. In addition, new and critical elements are intensified competition among the states and a renewed emphasis upon business climate. The authors identify the following factors in the evolving competitive environment:

1. International economic competition has become more intense.
2. Domestic competition has intensified. Political jurisdictions have become more aggressive in competing with other states and foreign countries for jobs.
3. The federal government has reduced its support to state and local governments, which puts pressure on states to raise more revenue. Attracting new business is seen as one way of doing so.
4. Increased competition, better communication, and transportation facilities have caused companies to become more mobile and less loyal to their home states.

The environment will become even more competitive if President Reagan's proposal to repeal federal deductibility of state and local taxes is adopted.

The authors suggest that important equity considerations, such as shielding the income of the poor, are countered by growing recognition that increased geographic mobility precludes highly progressive state or local taxes. At the same time, they believe, a wide range of exclusions, exemptions, and credits have violated the principle of equal treatment of taxpayers who have equal ability to pay. Thus, state tax reform, like proposals for federal tax reform, should be aimed at broadening the tax base to achieve lower rates. Diversification continues to be a characteristic of a good state and local tax structure, but emphasis may now be shifting from diversification of state taxes to local revenue diversification.

Characteristics of a Balanced State and Local Tax Structure

In summarizing the thinking about what constitutes a good state and local tax structure, Kleine and Shannon discuss the characteristics of individual taxes and then prepare a "report card" rating the various states. They list the following characteristics of a balanced tax system:

Personal income tax. A tax on personal income should meet the following criteria:

1. A personal income tax should provide 20 to 35 percent of all state and local tax revenue. Too heavy reliance on the personal income tax can have an adverse effect on business climate, and too little will increase the need to rely on regressive taxes with little growth potential.
2. The rates of an income tax should not be markedly higher than rates in surrounding areas.

3. A state or local income tax should offer personal exemptions or credits at least as generous as the federal income tax exemptions. Ideally, exemptions or credits should shield persons below the poverty line from paying taxes.
4. The number of deductions allowed on state income taxes should be minimized. This policy objective would simplify the income tax, make it more equitable, and be in line with federal reform efforts.
5. State and local income taxes should be indexed for inflation. This provision would prevent inflation from automatically pushing taxpayers into higher brackets and reducing the real value of personal exemptions; further, it would reduce the responsiveness of the income tax to changes in income (elasticity).
6. A state should share the proceeds of the personal income tax with local units of government or permit local income taxation with proper safeguards.

Sales tax. The general sales taxes deserve heavy weight in state and local tax structure, because they are productive, relatively stable, and exportable to nonresidents. A good sales tax should meet the following criteria:

1. A sales tax should provide 20 to 30 percent of all state-local tax revenue.
2. The sales tax rate should not be out of line with rates in surrounding states.
3. Foods, drugs, and utilities should be exempted from the sales tax, or a tax credit for the purchase of these items should be provided.
4. A sales tax should tax most services as well as goods.
5. The proceeds of the sales tax should be shared with local governments, or local governments should be allowed to levy local sales taxes subject to state-imposed safeguards.
6. A strong audit and enforcement program should be maintained to protect the integrity of the tax base.

Property tax. Although the property tax continues to be the most criticized of the major taxes of state and local governments, it will continue to be a major source of local government revenue. This revenue source is stable and productive and allows a considerable degree of local fiscal independence. In addition, the property tax reaches nonresident property owners, who make no contribution of income or sales taxes. Finally, the property tax recaptures property values created by government provision of public services. The virtues of the property tax can be maximized and its weaknesses minimized by adopting certain safeguards:

1. The property tax should provide 20 to 30 percent of all state and local tax revenue.
2. State and local government should work together to insure that the property tax burden does not become excessive. The states should finance the

nonfederal share of welfare expenditure and a major share of the cost of elementary and secondary education. The states should also share general revenue with local governments to relieve pressure on the property tax and reduce fiscal disparities between the have and have-not communities. The state can also authorize the use of local income and sales taxes, preferably piggy-backed on state taxes to reduce administrative and compliance costs.

3. States should finance a "circuit breaker" property tax relief program to shield low-income taxpayers from excessive tax burdens (this program is known as the homestead property tax refund in Kansas).

4. Property should be assessed on average no less than 80 percent of full market value (100 percent is ideal). The objective of this recommendation is to prevent low fractional assessments from providing a convenient graveyard in which assessors can "bury their mistakes." There should be a full-disclosure policy requiring that assessment/sales ratios results be available to taxpayers. This information should be allowed as evidence in taxpayer appeals.

5. Property tax laws should include a mechanism to prevent automatic, unrestrained increases in revenue from inflation-induced assessment growth. Such increases occur when property taxes are levied by rate or when public attention is focused upon the tax rate rather than the dollar levy.

6. The property tax should be administered fairly and equitably. Two measures of the quality of administration are available. The coefficient of intraarea dispersion measures the variation within a county. The median assessment level for the county and the various classes of property indicate the equality of assessment among the counties and classes of property.

Business taxes. Kleine and Shannon admit the difficulty of developing general principles that apply to business taxes, a difficulty partly caused by the confused and indeterminate distribution of the ultimate burden of business taxes. While they acknowledge that any set of principles may not be valid for a particular state, they nevertheless suggest the following as a general framework:

1. Taxes on business should be broad-based with some consideration of ability to pay. A tax based on a broad measure of economic activity, rather than on profit, could serve as the primary basis for state taxation of business firms. Money-losing or low-profit firms might gain protection by a tax credit.

2. The tax structure should apply to all forms of business and should not discriminate on the basis of the form of ownership, i.e., sole proprietorship or corporation.

3. Immediate write-off for capital investment rather than special tax inducements should be provided. "Expensing" of business capital investment for

all firms is preferable to special tax concessions that often discriminate against existing firms.

4. The number of separate taxes within a business tax system should be kept to a minimum.

5. A stable tax base should be used. This would provide a uniform flow of business tax receipts unaffected by business swings; however, as mentioned above, some safeguards should be built in to protect small, low-profit firms.

6. States should provide funding to allow local repeal of personal property taxes on inventories.

7. Rates should be moderate for unemployment insurance and workers compensation as well as for general business taxes.

Excise taxes. Excise taxes on alcohol, tobacco, and motor fuel constitute relatively minor sources of revenue for most states and have major disadvantages. They have little growth potential, fall heavily upon low-income persons, and are susceptible to tax evasions. The revenue potential of such taxes can be improved by the following steps:

1. Specific taxes on unit consumption (for example, per gallon, per pack) should be replaced by ad valorem (levied on value) taxes. State and local governments should use restraint in setting excise tax rates. Tax rates that are substantially higher than in neighboring states will encourage tax evasion.

2. When rates are increased, a portion of the proceeds should be earmarked for enforcement and audit programs. Strong programs are needed to prevent high levels of tax evasion if tax differentials are large.

Severance taxes. Severance taxes are a major source of revenue in a few energy-rich states. Such taxes are an attractive revenue source, because their payment is largely exported to other states, and natural resources cannot be moved to avoid taxes. Excessively high rates can discourage marginal exploration activities, and, as recent events have demonstrated, the yield can fluctuate greatly.

User charges. State and local governments, including those in Kansas, have increased their reliance on user charges for more than two decades. The most significant increases have been in sanitation, water revenues, special assessments, and other public utility categories. Opinion polls show that taxpayers often prefer user fees to taxes as a way of financing services. Local governments could do a better job of unbundling specific services and moving such services from general tax support to financing with user fees. Minimum levels of service could be supported with taxes, and charges could be made for higher levels of service.

Report Card on Kansas Tax Structure

It is not possible to assign numerical values to all the characteristics which make up a balanced tax system, but Kleine and Shannon have developed a "report card" that does quantify many of the characteristics

Table 3.13
Balanced Tax System Scorecard

Characteristic	Points possible	Kansas Points	Rank
Overall fiscal systems	30	23.1	14
Revenue diversification	50	39.9	23
Tax equity	35	13.0	26
Fiscal equalization	50	21.9	40
Property tax administration	35	2.5	37
Total	200	100.9	
Business climate[a]	0	-15.0	25
Grand total	200	85.9	32

Source: Robert Kleine and John Shannon, "Characteristics of a Balanced State-Local Revenue System", paper delivered at the National Tax Association Conference, Denver, 1985.
[a]Deduction up to 40 points.

they believe result in a balanced tax system. In the report card for Kansas, shown in Table 3.13, there are 200 possible points for an ideal score. Features of the tax system believed to result in a poor business climate in the state are shown as deductions from the score.

Kansas makes its best showing on the first test, overall fiscal system. This test has two parts. One part measures the progressiveness of the tax system by comparing the tax burden on taxpayers with incomes of $17,500 to $100,000. Kansas, along with seven other states, receives the maximum score of 20 points on this part. The other part of the test relates to the state share of the revenue system. Kansas receives only 3.6 points out of a possible 10, because the state raises less than the 50 percent of the state-local total.

Kansas scores 39.9 out of a possible 50 on the revenue diversification test. A perfect score on this test requires that 20-30 percent of state-local tax revenue come from the sales tax, 20-35 percent from income taxes, and 20-30 percent from property taxes. Kansas loses .6 of a point for underuse of the income tax and 9.5 points for overuse of the property tax.

Kansas scores only 13 out of a possible 35 points on the tax equity characteristic. This characteristic relates to relief for low-income people by means of the circuit breaker, homestead tax relief, or sales tax exemption or credit for food, utilities, and drugs. The authors also suggest sales taxation of services to broaden the base and make it slightly more progressive and indexation of the personal income tax. Kansas scores as follows:

	Possible	Kansas
State financed property tax relief (circuit breaker)	10.0	5.0
Sales tax exemptions or credits	10.0	5.0
Sales tax on services	5.0	3.0
Indexing of personal income tax	10.0	0.0
	35.0	13.0

The fiscal equalization test is an attempt to measure the extent to which the state aids local governments in financing certain functions. Possible points awarded and the Kansas scores are as follows:

	Possible	Kansas
Welfare, state financed	10.0	9.4
Health and hospital, state financed	10.0	5.0
Local education, state financed	20.0	7.5
General revenue sharing	10.0	.0
	50.0	21.9

Kansas receives its lowest ranking on this test. Clearly, Kansas leaves more of the financial responsibility for government in the hands of localities than the authors of the report card believe desirable.

Kansas receives its lowest absolute score on property tax administration. The score of 2.5 out of a possible 35 should come as no surprise to those who follow the Kansas property tax issue. Points are lost because assessments are not uniform, either within or among assessment districts, and therefore not in compliance with state law or the state constitution. Currently, reappraisal of property is underway, and a referendum on constitutional classification of property is on the ballot in November 1986.

The business climate test is of special importance given the current nationwide concern with economic growth. This test differs from others in that points are subtracted from a state's score for characteristics believed to indicate an adverse business climate. These deductions are based on overall tax burden, marginal income tax rate for individuals, marginal income tax rate for corporations, property tax exemption for inventories, machinery and equipment, workers compensation tax rates, unemployment insurance rates, sales tax on machinery, and worldwide unitary apportionment of corporate income. The 15 points subtracted from Kansas' score for poor business climate result from deductions of 2 points because the top marginal income tax rate is over 7 percent; 8 points because Kansas has no property tax exemption for machinery, inventories, and equipment; and 5 points because Kansas taxes sales of machinery. If the classification amendment to the state constitution passes, it will eliminate the inventory tax and reduce, but not eliminate the tax on machinery.

Policy Choices in State and Local Finance

The above analysis raises a variety of questions concerning Kansas tax policy, and these call for attention on a public agenda for Kansas. The policy choices facing Kansas in state and local finance are discussed below as follows: First, how should Kansas respond to the recent shortfalls in tax revenue relative to growth in the state's economy? Second, what direction should Kansas take concerning future reliance on the property tax? And, third, how should Kansas insure that its revenue structure promotes the economic health of the state?

Revenue Shortfalls

The preceding review of the Kansas state and local finance system reveals a large increase in expenditures and revenues since 1962. Inflation and economic growth caused a major portion of this increase; but state and local expenditures as a percentage of the personal income grew also until the trend turned slightly downward in the mid-1970s. In the last six years, expenditures stabilized around 15.8 percent of personal income. Kansas expenditures generally stayed in line with those of surrounding states and were slightly below those of the United States as a whole.

During this period, state tax rates increased somewhat, and the severance tax was added. However, much of the growth in revenue resulted from economic growth and inflation. Significant shifts in the tax structure occurred as the income tax became more important. This change was caused partly by increases in the tax rates on higher income individuals, but much of the shift resulted from the high elasticity of the income tax. Sales taxes, including the specific excise taxes, declined in relative importance; federal grants, local nonproperty taxes, and charges and miscellaneous revenues rose more rapidly than did total revenues. Property taxes became relatively less important, and property taxes as a percentage of the market value of property actually declined. In spite of this, property taxes continue to be an important part of the state and local tax structure.

Kansas escaped the severe fiscal crises and the "taxpayers revolts" that plagued many states in the 1970s. Program improvements came about without any large tax increases or large-scale borrowing programs, but, beginning about 1981, a significant shift took place. The Kansas revenue structure, formerly adequate to support expenditures at a constant or even slightly rising percentage of personal income, began to lag. Receipts fell below estimates, some tax rates were increased, collections of other taxes were sped up, and year-end balances declined.

This revenue shortfall cannot be attributed to any one, single cause. The elasticities of most of the state taxes declined substantially, partly as a result of economic changes, changes in the federal tax laws, and perhaps exemptions that have eroded the state tax bases. In addition, the growth in federal grants to state and local governments ceased, and the decline in interest rates reduced revenue from miscellaneous revenue.

More fundamental changes in the Kansas economy were occurring as described in Chapter 1. The favorable coincidences of the 1970s did not repeat themselves in the 1980s. In fact, agriculture, oil, and aircraft manufacturing, the mainstays of the Kansas economy, have all performed poorly in the 1980s. At the same time, the decline in the manufacturing sector nationally and the greater mobility of manufacturing concerns intensified the competition among the states.

The shift in the productivity of Kansas taxes also has been reflected in the revenue estimates utilized by the governor and the legislature. Prior to fiscal year 1982, the original estimates made by the concensus estimating group were always on the low side. For 1982 and all years since, the original estimates have been too high.[20]

Like the change in elasticity, fluctuating revenues and difficulties in estimating revenues are not confined to Kansas. Many states have experienced severe problems as a result of revenue shortfalls, and twenty-eight states have responded to this problem by establishing a revenue stabilization or "rainy-day" fund.[21] The absence of such a fund in Kansas reflects the fact that Kansas has not suffered financial crises, nor economic declines, as severe as many states. Also, Kansas policy makers have generally followed sound fiscal practices. There has been a strong commitment to a balanced budget, and revenue estimating has not become a source of political controversy that obscures the true fiscal condition of the state.

In sum, the revenue yield of the Kansas tax structure bears close monitoring in the immediate future to assess whether short-term trends are continuing. Further, state policy makers should consider the establishment of a rainy-day fund as partial protection against revenue shortfalls in the long term.

The Property Tax

By every comparative measure employed in this study, the property tax is overused in Kansas. The administration of the property tax scores nearly zero on the Kleine-Shannon report card. Other features of this unpopular tax cost Kansas a substantial number of points when measured against a balanced tax structure.

The Kansas legislature took major steps in 1985 to address the problems of the property tax by ordering reappraisal to be effective in 1989 and providing that a classification amendment be submitted to a public vote in November 1986. Whether or not the classification amendment passes, work on the property tax remains unfinished. Reappraisal and its implementation are massive jobs. Technical problems will be encountered, as will resistance from those who see their turf threatened and those who fear an increase in their share of the tax. The public likely will not accept the result unless an extensive educational campaign informs them about the need for the program and the process by which reappraisal is accomplished.

The classification amendment, if adopted, will change a number of the features that affect the Kansas business climate. Inventories will be exempt from taxation. Machinery, while remaining taxable, will be assessed at original cost minus a standardized depreciation factor, which will probably lower machinery assessment for most, but not all, firms. Passage of the amendment will freeze the method of machinery assessment and remove the present power of the Kansas legislature to eliminate it completely from taxation.

The classification amendment will result in taxation of business real estate at levels higher than residential property. This proposal is a compromise, accepted by most business groups as the only way to get relief from the relative overassessment of business property; it should reduce the "discrimination" against business that currently exists but will result in higher taxes than present constitutional provisions, assuming these were followed.

If reappraisal is successfully completed and the classification amendment adopted, Kansas will still be faced with the issue of future reliance on the property tax. Reducing dependence on this tax not only requires substitute revenue sources but also changes in state-local fiscal relations or even in the structure of local government in Kansas. The alternatives are three: (1) transfer local functions and responsibilities to the state; (2) provide more state financial assistance to local governments; or (3) provide local governments with more authority to levy local taxes.

The first alternative would mean a change in Kansas' tradition of strong local government.

The second alternative would raise many policy questions about formulas to be used in allocating state funds to local units and the restrictions to be imposed. Because school districts collect the largest portion of the property tax, additional state aid to schools would be a logical option but would likely intensify further the annual struggle over school funding formulas and the degree of control the state should exercise over local education. Reevaluating the disparities in educational costs between school districts of differing sizes and considering consolidations of districts or attendance centers might be necessary.

The third alternative raises the issue of local government structure. An examination of the tax capacity among counties in Kansas reveals wide differences. Certain counties would have to impose unreasonably high sales and income tax rates in order to provide significant property tax relief. With respect to smaller subdivisions, the disparities are even greater. Perhaps consolidation of functions at the county level or consolidation of smaller counties would make the local tax option workable as a means of substantially reducing the property tax burden.

Business Climate

Strategies for improving business climate fall into two broad classes. One, which might be called the "industrial-policy" approach, involves granting concessions to specific businesses, to specific classes of business, or to specific business actions or activities. Kansas already has taken actions of this type. Many local governments have utilized industrial revenue bonds and accompanying property tax exemptions to encourage the purchase or construction of specific facilities. Enterprise zones have been created and income-tax credits are given for new job creation. Successful use of such policies requires a state or local government to identify specific companies or activities that will most benefit the state's economy and direct the aid specifically to them. If successful, this policy results in maximum development at minimum cost, because tax exemptions or other concessions are not aimed at supporting economically beneficial activities that would have occurred anyway. Critics of this approach argue that governments seldom succeed particularly well in identifying the firms that have growth potential and that will contribute most to the state economy.

Another approach is to provide a climate, particularly a tax structure, conducive to growth of all business, but without specifically targeting firms or activities. This philosophy appears to lie behind Kleine and Shannon's approach. In their view, a good economic climate would be created by limiting top individual income tax rates to 7 percent and by exempting machinery and inventories from property taxation and machinery purchases from sales taxation. Confidence in the fairness and productivity of the system would be maintained by eliminating many, if not all, of the special exemptions for industrial development. Proponents see this as desirable because all businesses, including those already in the state, benefit.

In line with this latter approach consideration could be given to other options for improving business climate, such as decoupling from the federal income tax, enacting a broad-based business activities tax in lieu of the corporate income tax, or "expensing" of business capital investment, among others. Decoupling would allow the state to write its own income tax laws independently of the federal tax structure and presumably in ways more conducive to business climate.

A broad-based tax upon the activities of incorporated and unincorporated business could avoid problems with the corporate income tax, which is widely criticized by economists. The economic burden of the tax is uncertain and not necessarily based on the ability to pay. The yield fluctuates as a consequence of fluctuating profits and frequent changes in federal policy. Corporations in certain types of businesses are also highly favored under present law. Many different formulas have been suggested for such a business activities tax; frequently, they are based on measures of business activity such as sales, payrolls, and purchases. This approach would possibly provide relief provisions for businesses that have unusually bad years, but the tax would not be a tax on profits.

Kleine and Shannon suggest "expensing" of business capital investment as a means for improving business climate that is preferable to other special tax inducements. This option would allow all businesses to write-off capital investments and not discriminate against existing businesses.

Other Issues

As this conclusion is written, federal tax reform, once pronounced dead, has shown new signs of life! The final outcome cannot be predicted, but all proposals and counterproposals have involved base-broadening, which will have a major impact upon Kansas revenues. Federal action on tax reform, as well as the recent rapid changes in federal tax policy, has created uncertainty for state policy makers and emphasizes the state's dependence on the shifting political trends in Washington.

Other issues in state and local finance, often related to the major themes discussed above, will face Kansas in the years ahead. Among these are the following:

1. What percentage of total revenue should come from each of the major taxes—property, income, and sales?
2. By what criteria should tax exemptions be judged? How should low-income people be protected against unreasonable tax burdens?
3. How should financial responsibility be divided among state and local governments? Should changes be made in the organization and structure of local governments? In the way the state deals with local governments?
4. What should be the role of the "minor" taxes? Should specific unit rates be changed to ad valorem rates? To what extent should the state promote the lottery, if approved, as a revenue source?
5. Should user fees be expanded as a means of raising revenue or discouraging consumption of government services?
6. Should administrative procedures be improved to insure that the revenue due is collected and that taxpayers have confidence that others are paying their share?

Obviously, these questions are not exhaustive. Answering them would provide a good start toward defining the kind of revenue structure that would maintain a reasonable level of services, prevent undue discouragement of economic growth, and not impose unreasonable burdens on any taxpayer.

H. EDWARD FLENTJE

Capital Finance and Public Infrastructure

Is Kansas giving adequate attention to construction and maintenance of roads and highways, to development of water supply, to improvements in water quality, and to other elements of public infrastructure which are essential to economic growth? Are parks and recreational facilities and improvements in wildlife resources, those elements of public infrastructure which contribute to a high quality of life in Kansas, being properly financed? Are state facilities which provide higher education, care for the mentally ill and retarded, and other essential public services being adequately maintained and improved? These questions form the core policy issues concerning capital finance and public infrastructure in Kansas and deserve to be a part of a public agenda for Kansas.

Pat Choate and Susan Walter helped spark national attention to issues of capital finance and public infrastructure with the publication of their book, *America in Ruins*,[1] in 1981. Choate and Walter summarized the problems in this way:

> America's public facilities are wearing out faster than they are being replaced. Under the exigencies of tight budgets and inflation, the maintenance of public facilities essential to national economic renewal has been deferred. Replacement of obsolescent public works has been postponed. New construction has been canceled.
>
> The deteriorated condition of basic facilities that underpin the economy will prove a critical bottleneck to national economic renewal during this decade unless we can find ways to finance public works....
>
> Economic renewal must be the premier focus of domestic policy in this decade. Our public infrastructure is strategically bound-up in that renewal. Without attention to deterioration of that infrastructure, economic renewal will be thwarted if not impossible.

Jennifer Hartnett, research assistant in the Hugo Wall Center for Urban Studies, aided in the research for this chapter.

We have no recourse but to face the complex task at hand of rebuilding our public facilities as an essential prerequisite to economic renewal.[2]

The purpose of this chapter is to examine the issues raised by Choate and Walter as these apply to Kansas and specifically to assess public policy toward capital finance and public infrastructure in Kansas with principal attention to the role of state government. State policy toward capital finance and public infrastructure, including constitutional limitations, major statutory provisions, and court rulings, is first reviewed. The financial impact of existing public policy then is analyzed. Finally, questions about the adequacy of current policy are assessed within a framework of three major policy choices facing Kansas: first, should Kansas revise those provisions of the state constitution which limit state government's ability to undertake capital finance and respond to demands for public infrastructure? Second, should Kansas revamp current processes of capital planning and budgeting? And third, should Kansas substantially strengthen current mechanisms for capital finance and augment the resources committed to capital improvements such as new road construction, water resource development, recreational and wildlife improvements, and enhanced facilities at state institutions?

Existing Policy on Capital Finance and Public Infrastructure

Neither capital finance nor public infrastructure are terms of common usage and for this reason may not be well understood. The terms do, however, describe a broad arena of governmental responsibility—one that almost without exception affects every citizen every day, either through the pocketbook or through the provision of public services. Defining these terms should help the reader grasp the review and analysis which follows.

For the purposes of this chapter, capital finance is the method (or methods) of financing used by governments to acquire or construct public infrastructure, that is, capital assets owned by public authorities. For example, borrowing money is a common method of capital finance used by government; purchasing capital assets from current taxes is another. The former method is analogous to purchasing a home through a mortgage; the latter is similar to buying a car out of the monthly paycheck or from cash on hand.

Public infrastructure includes capital assets that have both substantial value and a useful life of several years and that are integral to the delivery of public services. Public infrastructure essential to the provision of state and local governmental services includes public roads and highways, office buildings which house public agencies, reservoirs providing water supply or flood control, computers, public parks, municipal wastewater treatment plants, and college classrooms, among others.

Constitutional Limitations

From the beginning of statehood, the Kansas constitution set severe restrictions on capital finance and limited state government's role in providing public infrastructure. Kansas joined the Union after the state debt crisis of the first half of the nineteenth century and therefore had drawn into its charter strict limitations on the ability of state government to issue public debt and a ban on state participation in internal improvements. These two features have shaped the financing of capital improvements in Kansas historically and influence public policy toward capital finance yet today. Understanding existing state policy in this area requires a review of the history, logic, and evolution of these constitutional limitations.

State Constitutional History. Public debt and U.S. government involvement with banking have been matters of controversy since the birth of the nation. Agrarian democrats were skeptical of reliance on the nation's credit for financing public improvements. This skepticism may be found in the assembled words of Thomas Jefferson:

> The same prudence, which, in private life, would forbid our paying our money for unexplained projects, forbids it in the disposition of the public moneys.... The principle of spending money to be paid by posterity, under the name of funding, is but swindling futurity on a large scale.... To preserve our independence, we must not let our rulers load us with perpetual debt. We must make our election between economy and liberty, or profusion and servitude.... I place economy among the first and most important of republican virtues, and public debts as the greatest of dangers to be feared.[3]

Andrew Jackson added another dimension to agrarian democracy's concern for public economy. During his presidency, Jackson initiated a concerted attack on "internal improvements" and ultimately made the term a part of state constitutional vocabulary of the nineteenth century. He argued vehemently against internal improvements that had from time to time found their way into appropriation bills passed by the congress. His early vetoes of localized road projects brought federal assistance for such endeavors to a halt during his presidency and for some years thereafter. To Jackson, internal improvements constituted "improvements of a local character," "subscribing to the stock in private associations," "a partnership between the Government and private companies," and "the practice of mingling the concerns of the Government with those of the States and of individuals."[4] Further, federal support of such endeavors was a dangerous practice: "The power which the General Government would acquire within the several states by becoming the principal stockholder in corporations, controlling every canal, and each 60 or 100 miles of every important road, and giving a proportionate vote in all their elections, is almost inconceivable, and in my view dangerous to the liberties of the people."[5]

Even in the face of this antagonism toward public debt, none of the twenty-six states entering the Union prior to 1840 had constitutional restrictions on state debt.[6] Indeed, few state constitutions at that time made mention of state borrowing, which was viewed as an essential power of the sovereign states. In the early 1800s, states exercised their inherent powers to borrow money and issued debt particularly after 1820 to finance improvements needed to open the new frontier. State debt was used to finance transportation links essential to commerce, such as canals, railroads, and turnpikes, and to underwrite banking institutions which sponsored such projects as well as other endeavors.

Ironically, Jackson's vehement stand against federal support of internal improvements, coupled with other precepts of Jacksonian democracy, gave added impetus to growth in state debt, which, prior to 1820, totalled less than $10 million. His emphasis on state's rights led to curtailment of federal aid for projects needed for growth on the western frontier. His undermining of the second bank of the United States eliminated a system of bank facilities as well as a key source of financing for improvements in many states. States moved with high optimism into the financial vacuum left by Jackson. Moreover, the profitability of early state projects, such as New York's underwriting of the Erie Canal, led other states to compete with grandiose plans for roads and canals which served to inflate state debts even further. By 1843, debt issued by all but a handful of the twenty-six states had mushroomed to $232 million—over twenty times the level of two decades earlier.

The depression that began in 1837 transformed the early optimism toward state debt. By 1841, nine states had defaulted on their debts; four of these repudiated all or part of their debts, and others secured downward adjustment in interest payments. An attempt to secure federal assumption of a portion of state debt was defeated in Congress. Improvement projects underway became stalled, and many remained uncompleted. To reduce their obligations, states sold a number of improvements and incurred major losses. State taxes were raised to cover the repayment of debts, and debt service became the major component of state expenditures in a number of states.

The state-debt fiasco sparked a nationwide political movement to limit state debt. Every state entering the Union from that point on would have a constitution prescribing debt limits. Of those states entering the Union before this time, all but six amended their charters to include limitations on debt.[7] This debt crisis and the political action it propelled formed the national context for the limitations written into the Kansas constitution.

The Kansas Constitution. The Kansas constitution was drafted in the Wyandotte Convention of 1859, and the framers lifted the language for the provisions limiting public debt and prohibiting internal improvements with little change from the constitutions of Wisconsin, primarily, and Iowa, secondarily.[8] These latter constitutions had been adopted in 1848 and 1846, respectively, close on the heels of the state-debt crisis. Surprisingly, debate on these two provisions was minimal. One delegate, a native of Indiana, made note of the difficulties experienced by other states, particularly Indiana, in borrowing for internal improvements. On whole, however, delegates appeared to be of one mind on public debt limits and the internal improvements prohibition and differed only on the exact language to be applied or the level of the cap on state debt. Convention floor debate on these matters likely took less than an hour.[9]

The constitutional language on public debt, adopted by the Wyandotte Convention and ultimately by the electors of the Kansas Territory, has remained unchanged now for 125 years. Indeed, no amendment to the public-debt provisions has even been proposed by the legislature in this time period. The language of the principal section (originally article XI, sec. 5) is as follows:

> For the purpose of defraying extraordinary expenses and making public improvements, the State may contract public debts; but such debts shall never, in the aggregate, exceed one million dollars, except as hereinafter provided. Every such debt shall be authorized by law for some purpose specified therein, and the vote of a majority of all the members elected to each House, to be taken by the yeas and nays, shall be necessary to the passage of such law; and every such law shall provide for levying an annual tax sufficient to pay the annual interest of such debt, and the principal thereof, when it shall become due; and shall specifically appropriate the proceeds of such taxes to the payment of such principal and interest; and such appropriation shall not be repealed nor the taxes postponed or diminished, until the interest and principal of such debt shall have been wholly paid.[10]

This section was followed by another (sec. 6): "No debt shall be contracted by the State except as herein provided, unless the proposed law for creating such debt shall first be submitted to a direct vote of the electors of the State at some general election; and...ratified by a majority of all the votes cast." In other words, debt beyond the million-dollar cap and presumably for purposes other than those prescribed must be submitted to a general-election referendum. The final section on debt (sec. 7) exempted state borrowing required "to repel invasion, suppress insurrection, or defend the State in time of war."

The constitutional language of the internal improvements prohibition was stark in comparison with the debt provisions; it said simply: "The State shall never be a party in carrying on works of internal improvement." The state-debt crisis had successfully wrought the object of Jackson's contempt, internal improvements, into Kansas constitutional history. While the term may have had clarity in the early- and middle-nineteenth century, Kansas legislators, governors, and supreme court justices would struggle with defining its content and escaping its prohibitions for the next 125 years.

Public Policy on Capital Finance and Public Infrastructure

The constitutional limitations on state debt and internal improvements have had profound impact on public policy concerning capital finance and public infrastructure in Kansas. The severity of these limits eventually motivated state lawmakers to avoid the debt mechanics of the constitution whenever possible. They have indeed devised creative means over 125 years to escape constitutional limits and adopt alternative precepts for providing capital improvements needed to achieve state purposes. In this sense, the Kansas constitution has forced lawmakers to respond to demands for public infrastructure in pieces rather than in a unified approach to meeting capital requirements. The leading precepts of capital finance that evolved in Kansas may be delineated as follows:

1. "Pay as we go;"
2. Authorize debt financing of capital improvements by local governments;
3. Pay as we go with special-purpose capital-improvement funds;
4. Authorize state agencies to undertake capital improvements with debt financing backed by anticipated revenues; and
5. Maximize federal assistance to underwrite capital improvements for state purposes.

These precepts form the tools by which state government has responded to the demands for capital improvements in Kansas. They have evolved slowly over 125 years, and their use has varied with changing economic conditions and the intensity of demands placed on state government to undertake capital improvements. An examination of these precepts of capital finance and their evolution is essential to understanding current public policy in Kansas.

Pay as We Go. Kansas began statehood facing sizeable capital requirements—the task of constructing new facilities for various state institutions coupled with debts carried over from territorial days.[11] State lawmakers met these requirements in large part through the federal lands and proceeds granted the state as part of Kansas' admission to the Union. Also, during the first decade of statehood, Kansas lawmakers read their new constitution literally and exercised its debt provisions liberally. The state's first steps in debt management, however, left much to be desired.

The first legislature under statehood began by repudiating $95,700 in debts issued by territorial officers to pay for various claims against the

Kansas Territory. The last territorial legislature had similarly repudiated these obligations but had also memorialized Congress to pay them. Congress ignored the matter, and the claimants went without compensation until 1863, when the legislature relented and issued $61,600 in twenty-year bonds to clear up the claims.[12]

Kansas' first official bond issue as a state was also mishandled and led to the impeachment of three state officers, including the state's first governor, Charles Robinson. Since Kansas' credit rating during this period was somewhat suspect, state bonds were discounted, that is, the state realized less in actual cash from the sale of bonds than the state was obligated to pay back. Being aware of this problem, the 1861 legislature authorized the governor, the auditor, and the secretary of state to negotiate a discount rate no lower than 60 percent, in other words, a rate requiring that the state receive no less than 60 percent of the face value of the bonds. A rate of 85 percent was achieved by the three state officers, but only 60 percent of the proceeds were deposited into the state treasury. Kansas' first bond scandal resulted, and the three were impeached by the lower house. The upper house convicted the auditor and the secretary of state and removed them from office but acquitted the governor.[13]

Kansas' poor credit was also amply demonstrated during this period. Most likely, the worst debt ever underwritten in the state's name were two-year bonds at 10 percent issued for military purposes in 1861. The $31,000 bonds were discounted at 40 percent of face value, and the state ended up paying $37,200 for the $12,400 received, an interest rate of 200 percent for the two-year period.

In sum, debt management during early statehood may be best described as rocky. For the first few years, tax revenues were insufficient to meet even the current expenses required to operate state government, let alone undertake needed capital improvements and help with the war effort. Therefore, in addition to taking advantage of federal land grants state lawmakers authorized debt to pay current expenses, to assist with military expenses, and to aid in the construction of the penitentiary, the state capitol, the agricultural college, the asylum for the deaf and dumb, and the insane asylum. By 1869, the state had issued $1,373,275 in bonds, $996,275 (just under the constitutional cap) for current expenses and capital improvements, and $377,000 for military purposes. The level of state debt in 1869 was $3.95 per capita, the highest per capita debt the state would incur for the next fifty years.

The million-dollar constitutional limit on debt brought state borrowing in the 1870s nearly to a standstill. At the end of the state's second decade Governor John P. St. John set forth in his biennial message to the 1881 legislative session what would become a leading precept of capital finance in Kansas: "We are creating no new debts, but pay as we go...."[14] St. John's "pay as we go" philosophy could be traced to the ideals of Jefferson and Jackson and captured the essence of constitutional antagonism toward public debt. In other words, state debt as envisioned in the constitution should be avoided if at all possible; capital improvements, indeed all necessary expenses of state government, should be paid for out of current taxes—not by borrowing money. State government should issue debt only under extraordinary conditions.[15]

St. John's "no new debts" admonition would characterize state policy for the next fifty years. Two exceptions deserve mention, although neither has had major consequences for financing capital improvements. In 1900, the state borrowed $110,000 to construct and equip a binder twine plant at the state penitentiary but paid off the obligation within two years. Then, in 1922 Kansas electors utilized the debt-referendum machinery of the state constitution for the first and last time and voted to borrow $31 million to pay a soldiers bonus for World War I veterans. No state debt guaranteed by the property tax has been issued for capital improvements since 1900. Except for the binder twine plant, no such debt has been issued since 1869, 117 years ago.

Kansas, that is, the state government of Kansas, achieved debt-free status in 1916 (see Table 4.1)—which placed Kansas in a category with five other states (Iowa, Nebraska, Oregon, South Dakota, and West Virginia) at the time.[16] State government's pay-as-we-go financing of capital improvements may have helped the state become debt-free; the key, however, was the state's avoidance of responsibility for public infrastructure other than facilities at state institutions. With constitutional encouragement, if not coercion, Kansas shifted the bulk of public responsibility for roads, water supply, sanitation, and other capital requirements to local governments—which is the next subject to be examined.

Authorize Debt Financing of Capital Improvements by Local Governments. Even prior to statehood, pioneers who came to Kansas to share in prosperity realized that the initiative for growth would reside with the local community. So spoke one territorial editor about the prospects for a local road: "If the road is to be built at all, the brunt must be borne by Leavenworth. Unless our reported wealth is fictitious there can be no doubt as to our ability to do all that will be required of us to secure this road."[17] The severe debt limits and internal improvements prohibition on state government helped assure that responsibility for the bulk of public infrastructure, roads, public buildings, water supply, parks, sanitation, and other public improvements, as well as incentives for private enterprise, would fall to local government.

In the early years of statehood, only the constitutional prohibition on internal improvements stood in the way of public enthusiasm for direct state participation in building railroads throughout Kansas. Governor Carney in

Table 4.1
Outstanding Public Debt in Kansas, 1861 to 1984

Year	Total debt (in millions)		Debt per capita		Local to state debt ratio
	State	Local	State	Local	
1861	$ .2	N.A.	$ 1.30	N.A.	N.A.
1872	1.3	$ 10.7	3.68	$ 29	8.0
1880	1.1	14.0	1.07	14	13.1
1890	.8	36.5	.56	26	45.6
1900	.7	32.4	.47	23	46.8
1913	.5	47.4	.31	28	89.6
1920	.0	72.1	.00	41	∞
1930	24.5	137.5	13.02	73	5.6
1940	14.0[a]	100.3	7.77	56	7.2
1950	5.5	110.6	2.87	58	20.1
1960	202.3	534.5	92.87	245	2.6
1970	223.6	938.3	99.42	417	4.2
1980	438.1	2,838.5	185.32	1,200	6.5
1984	356.1	5,204.1	145.35	2,124	14.6

Sources: These data were compiled from four different sources that may not have completely consistent definitions of debt; the sources are James Ernest Boyle, *The Financial History of Kansas; Summary History of Kansas Finance, 1861-1937*; Kenneth E. Beasley, *State Supervision of Municipal Debt in Kansas*; and U.S. Census.
Note: Public debt includes both guaranteed and nonguaranteed debt, although nonguaranteed debt did not appear in these figures until 1950.
[a]Estimate.

his message to the 1863 legislature urged "a general State system of rail-roads."[18] Governor Harvey similarly pleaded in 1869: "You should encourage in every judicious and proper manner the rapid construction of all these roads."[19] According to one careful student of Kansas finance, "had the constitution not expressly forbidden it, the state would have been a party in many railroad enterprises."[20]

Instead, the state chose to delegate: state lawmakers in 1865 authorized counties to subscribe for stock in and issue bonds to railroad companies and in 1866 authorized cities and counties to issue bonds for purposes of internal improvements[21]—actions the state was constitutionally precluded from taking. The Kansas Supreme Court sanctioned this move in 1871 by ruling that the internal improvements prohibition on state government did not apply to local units of government.[22] While railroads were the primary beneficiaries, local borrowing helped finance other private endeavors and construct and acquire roads, bridges, and other capital improvements. By 1872, local-government debt in Kansas had climbed to $10.7 million, eight times the level of state debt.

The rapid expansion of local debt led state lawmakers to seek a semblance of control over borrowing by cities, counties, and townships. In 1872, they passed a bond-registry law requiring local units to register their bond issues with the state auditor, to pay their debt obligations through the state treasurer, and to limit debts to legislated levels. The law failed miserably. The absence of any state capacity to review local issues allowed, even encouraged, bond frauds. The treasurer refused to act as the conduit for payment of local debts, and that feature was repealed. Local-debt limits were retained but made almost meaningless due to a multitude of exceptions and exemptions enacted by the legislature. Also passed in 1879 was a refunding law that allowed local units to refinance old debt with new debts under more liberal terms, such as extending the period over which a debt had to be repaid.[23]

Another practice of local governments during this early period was the use of debt financing to aid private industries in addition to railroads. Laws appeared on the books authorizing specific cities, counties, and townships to aid a variety of private endeavors, including woolen mills, flouring mills, starch works, prospecting for coal, oil, and gas, manufacturing enterprises, sugar mills, cheese factories, sorghum mills, and others. The courts sought to dampen local enthusiasm for such practices, indeed, held them to be illegal public aid for private purpose,[24] but these rulings were largely ignored. The legitimacy of private aid came to rest more with the absence of legal challenge and with presumed public acceptability than with court action. Indeed, early attempts of state courts to draw a distinction between public and private functions have, with time, become meaningless.[25] Today, any endeavor for which a local need is determined by an appropriate local governing body may be undertaken and underwritten with debt financing if desired.

Local borrowing for an array of public and private purposes continued unabated into the 1890s. Outstanding local debt reached an early peak of $37 million in 1892, a level nearly fifty times that of state debt. Between 1861 and 1902, local units had borrowed roughly $60 million, over one-third of which was in aid to railroads and another one-sixth assistance to private industry.[26] This generous extension of debt incurred liabilities. Kansas led the nation in defaults during this period. Seventy-seven local governments in Kansas defaulted between 1870 and 1905, one-half of these being defaults for borrowing in behalf of railroads and private enterprise.[27]

Even with all the problems and missteps, debt financing undertaken in this early period set a pattern for the division of labor between state and local government. Local initiative, motivated by the desire for growth, aided by liberal state authorizations, and sanctioned by largely favorable court rulings, made state government's role in capital finance almost inconsequential. State attention, bounded as it was by severe debt limits and a prohibition on internal improvements, focused importantly but narrowly on state facilities such as state hospitals, state colleges, the capitol, and the penitentiary. Local governments moved into the vacuum and assumed responsibility not only for stimulating economic growth but for the keystones of public infrastructure essential to growth—roads, water supply, and sewers.

The imbalance of state and local responsibility for infrastructure can be seen in the level of outstanding debt between state and local government in Kansas (see Table 4.1). The ratio between state and local debt crudely measures the extent of debt financing of capital improvements. Local-government debt has ranged from a low of 2.6 times the level of state debt (1960) to the level of infinity when state government was debt-free in 1920. In more than half the decennial measures, local to state debt is over ten to one. This same imbalance may also be seen in Kansas' share of state and local debt nationally over the past twenty-five years, as shown in Table 4.2. In 1962, Kansas' state and local shares paralleled the state proportion of national population (1.0 percent) and personal income (1.1 percent). Since 1962, local government in Kansas has taken on an increased share of local debt nationally, up to 80 percent beyond the expected proportion, while state-government debt in Kansas has fallen to one-quarter of the state's economic or demographic proportions.

State oversight of local-debt issuance has waxed and waned with changing political demands for state control over local borrowing but may be characterized as laissez faire. State statutes grant hundreds of specific authorizations for debt financing to local government. A recent study by the Government Finance Research Center described Kansas laws as "fairly flexible and relatively unrestrictive." State review of local bond issues is "largely pro forma" and focuses on procedural matters rather than the substance of a bond issue. The study concludes: "State involvement in local debt issuance is fairly minimal."[28]

Pay as We Go with Special-Purpose Capital-Improvement Funds. Pay as we go did not become capital finance policy for Kansas until after 1870. In the first decade of statehood, the initial building requirements for state institutions—for example, the state capitol, the penitentiary, the agricultural

Table 4.2
State and Local Debt in Kansas Compared to State and Local Debt in the Nation, 1962-82 (dollar amounts in millions)

	State debt			Local debt		
	Nation	Kansas	%	Nation	Kansas	%
1962	$ 22,023	$206	0.94	$ 58,799	$ 659	1.12
1967	32,472	256	0.79	81,187	758	0.93
1972	54,253	215	0.40	120,705	1,050	0.87
1977	90,200	403	0.45	169,458	1,860	1.10
1982	147,470	398	0.27	257,109	4,703	1.83

Source: U.S. Bureau of the Census [Census of Governments:] *Compendium of Government Finances.*

college, the university, and others—were met largely through the issuance of state bonds and grants of federal lands. After the state-debt cap was reached in 1869 and federal land grants were dispersed, current revenues became the principal source of funding for capital improvements. This pay-as-we-go policy placed capital improvements in competition with current operating expenses, and annual revenues became a tight lid on expenditures for capital and operating requirements of state government.

Kansas survived with a strict pay-as-we-go philosophy as long as the state faced no major demands for capital improvements. Once capital projects were desired, however, state policy makers were confronted with a choice of cutting back on some element of state operations *or* raising taxes to fund the projects *or* not moving forward with the projects. Capital improvements could easily be deferred and often were. The inability of pay as we go to provide desirable capital improvements ultimately led to its reform.

The first special-purpose capital-improvement fund was for the state capitol. In 1879, state lawmakers enacted a "special levy of taxes" to "provide for the erection and completion of the west wing of the state house."[29] For a six-year period, one-half mill out of a total of four to five mills for state purposes was levied each year and generated nearly $750 thousand for state house improvements.

The special-purpose levy was a refinement, not an abandonment, of pay as we go. State-house improvements were funded from current revenues but were insulated from competing demands for state funds. Special-fund designation protected the completion of the state house from delays or deferrals due to changing legislative priorities in the annual competition for state funds.

After completion of the state house, Kansas reverted to a pay-as-we-go policy for capital improvements. This policy remained intact for another thirty years until the state faced its most monumental capital improvement demand of the twentieth century, that of building and maintaining roads and highways. Kansas ultimately turned to a special-purpose fund to meet its obligations for roads and highways; its awkward steps around the internal improvements prohibition in the state constitution and away from a strict pay-as-we-go philosophy would delay state government's move in this direction for a number of years. Retracing these steps helps illustrate the constitutional and philosophical obstacles Kansas faces in responding to legitimate capital improvement demands.

The internal improvements prohibition in the Kansas constitution precluded state government from building roads and highways. If any doubt about the issue remained, the Kansas Supreme Court in 1871 specifically named the construction of "any roads, highways, bridges...streets, sidewalks, pavements" among other improvements as constitutionally banned from state participation.[30] The clarity of these pronouncements kept Kansas state government from assisting in the development of roads and highways for nearly sixty years, and as a result the public responsibility for road work devolved to local government in Kansas.

This pattern of local responsibility for roads prevailed nationally but soon began to change. A few states were aiding road construction before 1900.[31] By 1900, seven states were in the road and highway business; by 1909, twenty-eight states had begun state aid for roads. As a constitutional test, Kansas lawmakers in 1917 passed the state's first program of direct aid to roads, which appropriated $5,000 in general funds to aid in the improvement of county roads. Without hesitation, the Kansas Supreme Court struck down the law as unconstitutional under the internal improvements prohibition[32]—a ruling that set the stage for the first amendment to the internal improvements provision.

Kansas' first amendment to the internal improvements prohibition sought to allow state participation in road building but was, with hindsight, ill-conceived and short-sighted. Although most states had moved to a system of state highways, the amendment drafted by lawmakers in 1919 and adopted in 1920 authorized limited state aid to county roads and drew into the state constitution a rigid formula for allocating road funds. The amendment neither provided for state highways nor for a special-purpose fund to finance them.

While lawmakers struggled with the state constitution, initial state activities concerning roads were financed from state general funds on a pay-as-we-go basis. A state highway commission was established in 1917 at federal urging and was supported with general funds. State aid to county roads, once authorized in 1920, was paid for with general funds. Finally, in 1925 the enactment of a state gasoline tax was intended to put the state road program on a self-supporting basis—although draws from the state general fund continued through 1927.[33] Demands for road and highway improvements clearly exceeded the state's ability to meet even its limited obligation from current revenues.

Demands for more active state participation in roads and a stable funding base shortly led state policy makers back to revising the restrictive language of the amended internal improvement provision. In 1928, legislators drafted carefully worded amendments that first authorized state government to "adopt, construct, reconstruct, and maintain a state system of highways" and, second, gave state government the power to "levy special taxes, for road and highway purposes, on motor vehicles and motor fuels."[34] Kansas electors adopted both amendments by more than a three-to-one margin.

Providing an exemption from the internal improvements prohibition and creating a special-purpose fund quickly made roads and highways state government's principal contribution to public infrastructure in Kansas.

Whereas state participation in roads and highways prior to 1917 was nil, state government spent nearly $20 million, or 60 percent of the entire state budget, on building and maintaining roads and highways in 1930. Roads and highways had moved from nothing to three-fifths of state expenditures in thirteen years. Except for changes in tax rates, which have risen to meet growing demands for road and highway improvements, the basic program set in place over fifty years ago remains intact today.

Since 1930, two additional special-purpose capital-improvement funds have been established—both authorized under constitutional amendments. Both funds are supported through a continuing levy on all real property in Kansas. The Educational Building Fund was enacted in 1941 for the "construction, reconstruction, equipment, and repair of buildings and grounds" at state educational institutions under the control of the Board of Regents. The State Institutions Building Fund enacted in 1953 provides for similar capital improvements at state institutions "caring for persons who are mentally ill, retarded, visually handicapped,...children who are deprived, wayward, miscreant, delinquent,...juvenile offenders," and others in need of care. Tax rates for these two building funds have been revised by legislative action from time to time but have generally stabilized since 1965 at 1 mill for regents institutions and .5 mill for other state institutions. In 1985, these rates generated $12 million for capital improvements at regents institutions and $6 million for capital improvements at other state institutions.

An examination of the deliberations leading to the creation of the Educational Building Fund provides some insight into the rationale of special-purpose capital-improvement funds and the arguments against them. At the urging of the Board of Regents, Governor Payne Ratner recommended the establishment of the Educational Building Fund in his message to the 1941 legislative session because of the "lack of an orderly building program."[35] The pay-as-we-go philosophy had placed a moratorium on facility improvements at state colleges and, according to Ratner, a building fund supported by a dedicated revenue source would insure "long range planning" and "sound economy," and "prevent the constant competitive bidding between schools for legislative attention to building needs."[36] Legislative opposition to Ratner's recommendation focused mainly on the enactment of a new tax but also railed against the concept of an earmarked revenue fund. Argued one state senator: "I am not in favor of creating a fund in advance for the pressure groups to clamor for....I want to...pay when it is necessary for what we need and can afford—but not pay in advance for something not needed now."[37] Said another lawmaker: "I claim that when a public spending body is given a certain sum each year, that body will see that such sum is spent."[38] The capital-improvement fund passed both houses by a two to one margin.

The special-purpose building funds have provided a steady but flexible source of capital finance. Today, they assure that no less than $18 million will be expended annually on new or improved facilities at state institutions. The legislature may, within parameters, vary the purpose of the funds or on an annual basis adjust the level of revenues available. For example, when students swamped state college campuses during the 1950s and 1960s a portion of the Educational Building Fund was diverted to expansion of student dormitories. The level of funds has been adjusted in response to changing capital requirements or to changes in policy. For example, in 1965, when state policy was revised to move mentally ill persons from state into local facilities, lawmakers reduced the levy for the State Institutions Building Fund from .75 to .50 mills.

While these two major building funds were established under the authority of specific constitutional amendments, the legislature may, as demands arise, enact special-purpose capital-improvement funds statutorily, as was done to complete the state capitol in the late 1800s. Most recently, lawmakers created a Correctional Institutions Building Fund and intermittently levied a property tax to support the fund.

Authorize State Agencies to Undertake Capital Improvements with Debt Financing Backed by Anticipated Revenues. For seventy years, the Kansas constitution's restrictive debt limits and lawmakers' "no new debts" policy kept state government largely debt-free, and with a few minor exceptions the state avoided debt financing of capital improvements. Kansas first departed from its historic antagonism to debt in the 1930s and has since steadily expanded authorization for debt financing of capital improvements by state agencies. This shift in course toward debt financing was charted by state lawmakers and has been repeatedly sanctioned in state courts. The history of Kansas' move into debt financing of capital improvements is largely one of court rulings that have freed the state from constitutional debt limitations. Through improvisation by the legislature and a friendly judiciary, the teeth in the state constitution's debt limits have been extracted.

Kansas took its first step toward a form of revenue debt financing of capital improvements with encouragement from the federal government during the depths of the great depression. The 1933 special session of the Kansas legislature ironically had as its major occupation the impeachment of the state auditor and the attorney general in the "great Kansas bond scandal" (that arose from the appalling lack of state supervision over local, not state, debt issues).[39] During this session, Governor Alf Landon urged that state laws be placed "in harmony with the national program" on the condition that "effective safeguards to control public borrowing" were made.[40] In response, lawmakers authorized the state highway commission to enter into thirty-year loans (termed "revenue anticipation warrants" in the act) from the federal government for the purpose of "construction, improvement, reconstruction, and maintenance of public highways and bridges" and to pay these loans "solely from revenues accruing to the highway fund."[41] Lawmakers took pains to explain in the act that their authorization for borrowing did "not constitute an indebtedness of the state within the meaning of any constitutional provision or limitation."

Upon challenge by the attorney general, the Kansas Supreme Court agreed with lawmakers and permanently bent open, at least partially, constitutional bars on debt financing.[42] Using somewhat strained logic, the court first ruled that "[w]arrants are not bonds," since highway bonds were presumably banned by the 1928 constitutional amendment exempting highways from the internal improvements prohibition. Second, and more importantly, the court ruled that state debt limits applied only to "debts to be paid by a general property tax."[43] The court reasoned that since property was the only source of taxation when the constitution was written in 1859, constitutional debt provisions were intended to limit only those debts backed by the property tax. Presumably, then, the state could contract any debt not paid by the property tax. By narrowly interpreting the constitutional concept of state debt, the court opened not a crack but a gaping hole in the state constitution's debt limits.

Ironically, a few weeks later the Kansas Supreme Court seemed to bring the state-debt limits back to life.[44] In this instance, the court reviewed an appeal similar in its major features to the case concerning highways. The 1933 special session had also authorized the Forestry, Fish, and Game Commission to borrow federal funds for the purpose of making public improvements and to repay the debt from license fees collected by the commission. In this case, the court made no note of the earlier case and ruled the authorization to be in violation of the state constitution's debt limits.

In expanding the realm of debt financing available to the state, future courts would choose to follow and expand upon the precedent in *State, ex rel., vs. State Highway Commission* and at the same time ignore the Forestry, Fish, and Game Commission case. In 1949, for example, the Kansas Supreme Court sanctioned debt financing of student dormitories by the Board of Regents. Such debt, the Court ruled, does not "pledge the faith and credit of the state," could not "be paid directly or indirectly from the proceeds of any tax levy," but was "payable solely and only from the revenue and income derived from the operation of a certain dormitory or dormitories and the facilities of the college."[45] Further, the court reasoned, even if debt financing of dormitories constituted a state debt, it was not debt backed by a property tax and therefore was not limited by the state constitution.

In 1953, the court further augmented avenues of debt financing available to the state. In *State, ex rel., vs. Kansas Armory Board*,[46] the court ruled valid the issuance of revenue bonds used to construct and remodel national guard armories throughout the state, even though repayment of this obligation depended on annual legislative appropriations for building rentals.

Although these rents would be drawn from the general tax funds of the state, the court judged the bonds free of state-debt limits, since they would be "paid by other than a tax on any property."[47]

With the armory decision, the once-potent debt limits in the Kansas constitution had been rendered toothless. By defining state debt to be only that debt backed by the property tax, the judiciary had narrowed the constitutional meaning of debt by tying it to a revenue source that largely had been abandoned by state government. In 1953, for example, the property tax was but one of twenty-four taxes being imposed by the state and was generating less than 5 percent of the state's total tax revenue. In addition, the state secured revenues from a variety of fees and charges, such as tuition, student fees, hunting licenses, and state park fees, among others. With the court's blessing, state lawmakers were freed from constitutional debt limits to undertake debt financing of capital improvements that could be paid for from revenues anticipated from any one of twenty-three state taxes or an even larger number of fees and charges collected by the state.

State lawmakers have acted upon the authority granted by early court rulings and steadily expanded debt financing of capital improvements to achieve a variety of state purposes, such as higher education, road building, park and wildlife development, among others. Dozens of statutory authorizations allow debt financing of state facilities. Through such financing, the state has built dormitories, a state office building, student unions, athletic facilities, classrooms, campus housing, libraries, parking facilities, state freeways, a fish hatchery, and a turnpike, among other projects, and has purchased computers, telephones, a dormitory, state office buildings, and other capital assets. Legislative authorization to undertake other capital projects, such as a Southeast Kansas toll road and resort facilities at state parks, also has been enacted but never exercised.

Under this new authority, revenue debt in Kansas leaped from almost nothing in 1950 to over $200 million in 1962, and to roughly $400 million in 1982 as shown in Table 4.2. Even with this dramatic move into debt financing of capital improvements, however, Kansas has had, during this same period, a steadily decreasing share of the total debt issued by state governments nationally. For example, while Kansas' share of the nation's population and personal income was 1.0 percent and 1.1 percent respectively, in 1980, the state's share of state debt nationally dropped from .94 percent in 1962 to .27 percent in 1982. In sum, other states in the aggregate have used debt financing much more extensively than Kansas has over the past twenty to thirty years.

In addition to the vehicle of revenue bonds for debt financing, state lawmakers have more recently entered into less-common, long-term financial obligations in order to undertake capital improvements or acquire capital assets. These obligations illustrate the flexibility now available to and being exercised by state government in applying the state's credit. In addition to securing road improvements and office facilities, state credit is being used to acquire water supply and to rehabilitate railroads within the state.

The 1958 amendment to the internal improvements prohibition allowed state government to participate in water-resource development for the first time in state history. Shortly thereafter, state lawmakers gave assurances that the state would share in the costs of constructing certain federal reservoirs being planned in Kansas. By 1977, state officials had reached agreements with the federal government to repay a minimum of $25 million with options of up to $69 million for water storage in nine federal reservoirs. These agreements are essentially fifty-year, low-interest federal loans. To date, the state has paid over $15 million on these loans, $10 million of which has come from general funds of the state and the balance being revenues from the sale of water stored for the state. Financing mechanisms are being put in place to underwrite the state's liability in these reservoirs through revenues from water users and eventually to repay all past draws against the state's general funds.

State lawmakers created a new mechanism for debt financing of state facilities in 1982. Prior to that time revenue bonds had become the common vehicle for debt financing of state buildings. In that year, the secretary of administration was authorized to borrow within certain limits from the state's idle funds to purchase a state office building (the Santa Fe building). In this instance, the state loaned itself $11.2 million with certain terms for repayment, one being that the loan would be repaid from revenues charged for use of the office building. The same mechanism was used again in 1984 to construct a new state printing plant. In this case, the $3.9-million loan is to be repaid from charges for state printing services.

In 1983, state lawmakers departed substantially from past practice in the use of state credit and conditionally guaranteed up to 50 percent of a federal loan for railroad acquisition and rehabilitation. Specifically, the secretary of transportation was authorized to receive from the federal government and pass on to the Mid-States Port Authority (a creature of the state) an $18-million loan, $12 million for the purchase of 300 miles of the Rock Island railroad in North-Central Kansas and $6 million for rehabilitation of the railway. In acting on this authority, the secretary reached agreement with the federal government to pay up to one-half of any losses to the federal government in the event of a default on the loan by Mid-States Port Authority. No understanding was arrived at as to the source of funds that would be drawn upon to pay such a default.

One question left unanswered by Kansas' entry into debt financing is whether indeed the debts being incurred are guaranteed by the taxing power of the state. Most authorizations for debt financing enacted by the legislature assure that "the faith and credit of the state" is not pledged; nor are constitutional provisions on indebtedness violated. In fact, however, a number of authorizations pledge revenues from major tax funds of the state, such as the state highway fund or the state freeway fund. Other enactments authorize debt, the repayment of which is dependent on state appropriations, often from general tax funds, as in the armory case or in the lease-purchase of equipment. In this instance, the legislature must appropriate the funds required or renege on commitments made some years in the past and default on the debt. In the case of college dormitories, lawmakers diverted monies from the Educational Building Fund, a total of roughly $15 million from 1955 through 1968, to help subsidize what were intended to be self-liquidating, revenue-debt projects. Since the state has not defaulted on any debt in recent years, the issue of guaranteed payment has not been tested. State lawmakers have taken whatever actions were necessary to meet the financial requirements of past debt out of a sense of moral, if not legal, obligation.

Maximize Federal Assistance to Underwrite Capital Improvements for State Purposes. Kansas historically has sought to maximize federal assistance available for capital improvements. Literally at the dawn of statehood, federal grants of land and land proceeds were committed to the construction of facilities at state institutions, particularly state colleges. In the twentieth century, federal assistance to roads and highways began in the 1920s and continues at a high level today. During the depression, Kansas officials took exceptional steps to place state laws in harmony with federal programs and receive federal assistance. Construction of federal water projects in Kansas began in earnest in the 1940s, and since 1958, the State of Kansas has agreed to financial participation in the construction of federal reservoirs. Federal general revenue sharing began in the early 1970s and was committed by Kansas lawmakers largely to capital improvements. Federal assistance for wastewater treatment also started in the 1970s and was passed through the state to local government in Kansas.

By 1985, the federal government was spending $30 billion nationally to construct, maintain, and operate public infrastructure. The real value of federal outlays for infrastructure grew by 24 percent in the 1960s and by 46 percent in the 1970s but has declined by 13 percent from 1980 to 1985. The real value of federal assistance for highways and water-resource development, two components of infrastructure of primary interest to Kansas state government, declined from roughly $22 billion in 1965 to $17 billion in 1985 (1985 dollars), a drop of 23 percent. In 1985, half of the roughly $4 billion for water-resource development will be spent on operations, operating federal reservoirs, for example, rather than on capital projects.[48]

Federal assistance available for capital improvements has, in real-dollar terms, stabilized or is on the decline. Federal aid for state highways, the one stable source of assistance for the last twenty-five years, has shown a steady increase for the period from $51.2 million in 1960 to $189.3 million in 1985 but in terms of 1985 dollars has declined slightly. Federal general revenue sharing provided Kansas state government with $170 million from 1973 through 1981, roughly $20 million annually for eight-and-one-half years, and state lawmakers allocated most of these funds to capital improvements at state universities. This program was eliminated for state governments in 1981. Federal assistance through the land and water conservation fund has provided $38 million to outdoor recreation improvements in Kansas since the program's inception in 1965. For Kansas, this program reached a peak of $4.3 million in 1977 but has dropped to one-tenth that level for the current year. Federal assistance for wastewater treatment, which Kansas state government passes on to local units without state financial participation, has declined nationally from $5 billion in 1980 to $3 billion in 1985 (in current dollars). The current administration in Washington, as well as members of Congress, has called for the complete phase-out of the wastewater treatment program by 1990. Water-resource development by the federal government has been on the decline in real terms since its peak in the 1960s. Although these expenditures are not channelled through state government, the state has benefited from numerous federal water projects and participated financially in the construction of nine federal reservoirs in Kansas. Since 1976, no new federal water-resources projects have been authorized. In sum, except for highways, the federal government does not appear to be a promising source of funds for infrastructure over the next decade.

Financial Impact of Existing Policy

Given the constitutional limitations on capital finance and public infrastructure and policy precepts which have evolved in response to public demands for capital improvements, what has been the financial impact of current public policy in terms of expenditures for capital improvements? Is state government providing an adequate level of financing for public infrastructure?

In actual dollars, total expenditures on capital improvements by Kansas state government have increased steadily over the last twenty-five years, as shown in Figure 4.1. Capital improvement expenditures, excluding certain debt-service payments, certain capital leases and purchases, outlays on capital equipment, and capital improvements at the turnpike, grew from $69.3 million in 1960 to $295.8 million in 1985. The bulge in expenditures from 1977 through 1981 may be explained in part by the issuance of $144 million in freeway bonds from 1976 through 1979, an increase in state highway user fees in 1976, and the availability of federal revenue sharing in this period and its elimination after 1980. The 1984-85 bulge may be explained by an increase in federal gas taxes in 1982 and another increase in state highway user fees in 1983.

While the growth in capital expenditures based on actual dollars is impressive, capital expenditures, when adjusted for the increased costs of capital construction, have declined generally over the past twenty-two years (see Figure 4.1 also). Adjusted-dollar expenditures in Figure 4.1 have been adjusted by a construction price index for state and local government to the real value of 1985 dollars.[49] Based on these adjustments, the real value of capital improvement expenditures by state government has fallen. In ten of

Figure 4.1
Capital Improvement Expenditures from All Funds,
Actual and Adjusted Dollars, 1960-85 (in millions)

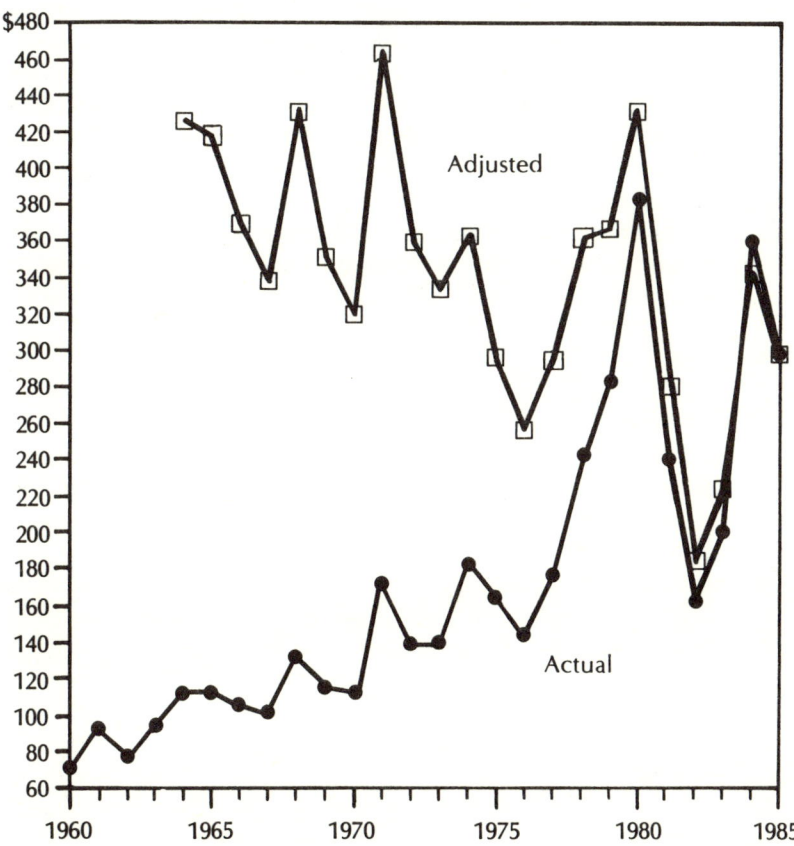

Source: *Governor's Budget Report,* FY 1962-FY 1987.
Note: In adjusted dollars, 1985 = 100.

the past eleven years (1975-85), the real value of capital improvements has dropped below the average of the prior eleven-year period (1964-74). In terms of real value, average capital improvement expenditures since 1974 have dropped 25 percent below the level of the prior eleven years (1964-74). This decline may be explained by the sizeable capital requirements of the earlier period, such as completing the interstate system, but such expenditures presumably would be offset by similar expenses in the latter period, as well as by the requirement to maintain a capital stock of substantially increased value.

Capital improvement expenditures of Kansas state government also has not kept up with growth in overall state expenditures or with personal income in Kansas, as shown in Figures 4.2 and 4.3. As a percentage of state expenditures, capital improvement expenditures have fallen from a high of 25 percent twenty to twenty-five years ago to a low of 8 percent in 1982. State response to other public demands on state resources, such as educational programs, social services, welfare, and health care, has reduced consistently and dramatically the share that capital improvements have had of the state budget. Capital improvement expenditures also have decreased as a portion of Kansas personal income from a high of over 1.9 percent in

Figure 4.2
Capital Improvement Expenditures as a Percentage
of State Expenditures from All Funds, 1960-85

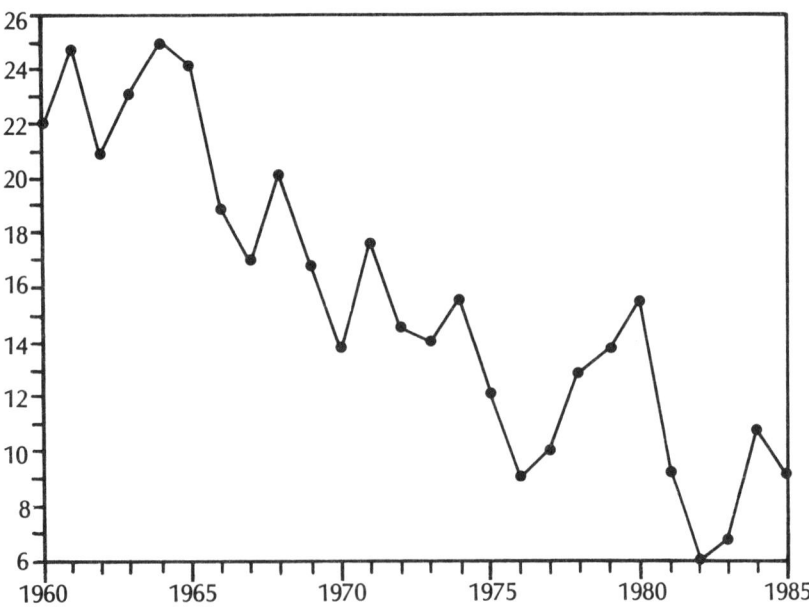

Figure 4.3
Capital Improvement Expenditures from All Funds as a Percentage of Kansas Personal Income, 1962-85

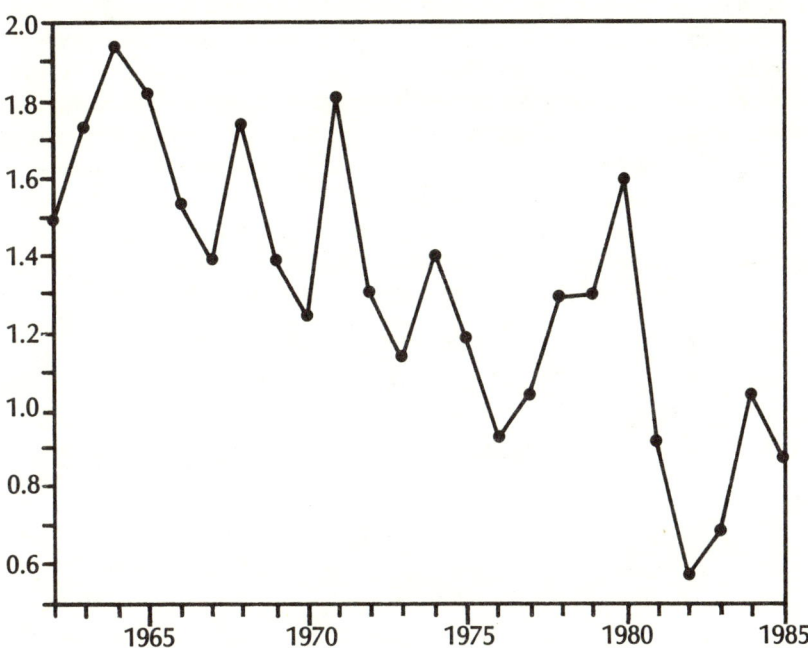

1964 to a low of under 0.8 percent in 1982. On average, capital expenditures as a percentage of personal income have fallen from nearly 1.6 percent prior to 1975 (1962-74) to less than 1.1 percent from 1975 to 1985. In actual dollars, this .5 percent drop may be translated into a loss of $172 million in capital improvements for 1985.

In sum, while capital improvement expenditures have grown significantly in actual dollars over the last twenty to twenty-five years, these expenditures have fallen steadily in terms of increases in construction costs, growth in overall state expenditures, and the rise in personal income. These consistent and marked patterns of decline raise questions as to the adequacy of existing public policy concerning capital finance and public infrastructure and suggest that state government should examine alternatives for improvement.

Policy Choices in Capital Finance and Public Infrastructure

The review of existing policy concerning capital finance and public infrastructure in Kansas and an assessment of its financial impact raise three fundamental issues concerning the adequacy of current public policy. First, are those provisions in the Kansas constitution which guide and limit capital finance adequate for the future? Even for the immediate future? Will the constitution allow state lawmakers to respond to new public demands for capital improvements in areas of state responsibility? Second, are state government's procedures for planning and budgeting capital improvements adequate for the future? Does the state have the capacity to identify new demands for capital improvements, assess their value in achieving state purposes, and set priorities among them for funding? Third, is the current level of funding for capital improvements adequate? Are current means of capital finance adequate for the future?

Revise Constitutional Provisions Concerning Capital Finance and Public Infrastructure

Should Kansas eliminate the internal improvements prohibition and reinstitute debt limitations on state government that are reasonable and responsive to economic change, yet hold state lawmakers accountable when using the state's credit?

The restrictive state-debt provisions and the prohibition on internal improvements in the Kansas constitution originally were lifted from states whose constitutions were written in the 1840s at the height of a national phobia concerning state debt and debt financing of internal improvements. Over the course of state history, these constitutional restrictions have deterred state action in providing public infrastructure essential to economic growth. For example, Kansas has had to go through the cumbersome process of constitutional revision in order to assist in areas of public infrastructure so basic as the development of roads and water resources and therefore has simply lagged behind other states in responding to demands for capital improvements in areas of compelling need. In road building, Kansas trailed most other states by ten years and a few by over twenty years in making a commitment to constructing and maintaining state highways. Argument could be made that Kansas' late entry into road work helped cause a patchwork of county roads throughout the state and contributed to the state's eventual acceptance of far too many of these local roads as state highways.

The difficulty of crafting constitutional amendments that meet the test of time also has delayed Kansas' response to demands for public infrastructure. Two of the four amendments to the internal improvements provision may in retrospect be described as time-bound, that is, out-of-date soon after their adoption. The roads amendment of 1920, for example, was obsolete almost from the time of its adoption and had to be abandoned completely and replaced eight years later. The 1980 amendment requiring federal assistance for the state to act on certain improvements became quickly dated as a new administration in Washington charted the decline of federal initiative in domestic assistance. Changes in the 1980 amendment are now being called for and under consideration.

Second, Kansas state government continues to be precluded from important areas of public infrastructure, although exactly what is prohibited remains open to question. Determination of what constitutes a prohibited "internal improvement" resides with state courts, or ultimately with four justices of the Kansas Supreme Court, when a complainant challenges legislative action under the constitutional prohibition. Based on past legal opinions, state government likely could not initiate direct assistance to airports, housing, railway rehabilitation, and certain forms of public transportation—in the absence of federal assistance. Since "internal improvements" as a term has fallen from current usage, courts would have to research the period of the 1830s and 1840s or earlier to determine the original meaning of the term. Kansas may be faced with a future situation in which state lawmakers are reading the speeches of Andrew Jackson to assess whether a new technology of public infrastructure, such as road building at the turn of the century, is a prohibited internal improvement.

The constitutional limitation on state government's ability to undertake certain capital improvements has effectively pushed the bulk of public responsibility for infrastructure onto local government in Kansas, a situation that has deterred the development of capital improvement projects that are regional in nature, that is, beyond the scope of one local jurisdiction but not of compelling statewide importance. For example, a major recreational improvement, such as resort facilities at a state park or a recreational corridor on a major river, would draw from a market area substantial distances beyond the boundaries of a single local government yet not from the state as a whole. A major new freeway, such as the long-discussed road from Wichita into Southeast Kansas, would have profound economic impact in the region but clearly less significance statewide. Governments at both state and local levels share an interest in undertaking such improvements, but neither level can justify sole responsibility for the project.

Also, when the principal initiative for infrastructure lies with local government, the development of public infrastructure will be more uneven across the state. Those communities advantaged by wealth, growth, and a capacity for foresight will be more able to identify and act on demands for capital improvements. In contrast, those communities struggling against long-term, adverse economic and demographic trends will be disadvantaged. Further, a community with inadequate infrastructure may be foreclosing opportunities for future economic growth—a situation which ultimately affects the economy of the state as a whole.

In contrast to the internal improvement prohibition, the state-debt limits in the Kansas constitution have been rendered meaningless through judicial interpretation. Since 1953, state government has used a variety of debt-financing mechanisms in order to undertake capital improvements or acquire capital assets, and each legislature now may enter into debt financing largely as it sees fit. Except for the exclusion of property tax debt, there are no constitutional limits on the level of debt, the level of debt service, the length of financial obligations, and the methods of repayment. Debt may be incurred against the major tax funds of the state for any period of time desired. Future legislatures may choose not to appropriate funds for debt repayment and thereby default on past debts, but to date the financial obligations entered into by past legislatures have been honored.

The absence of effective constitutional guidelines for debt financing increases the likelihood of debt defaults in the future. In addition, as the level of debt financing by state government expands, the number of purposes for which debt financing is used increases, and as the variety of debt mechanisms grows, the possibility that a future legislature will renege on past debts also rises. State lawmakers have avoided this situation to date by taking a relatively conservative posture on the use of debt financing.

The absence of effective constitutional guidelines on debt also creates a diffuse approach to debt financing by state lawmakers. Authority for debt financing is decentralized in a number of state agencies for a variety of state purposes. A diverse set of revenue sources is pledged for debt repayment. A comprehensive accounting of these debts and the liabilities incurred by them is neither required nor readily available. The lack of current information on the state's debt status does not, of course, contribute to informed decision making in the use of debt financing.

The lack of effective constitutional provisions concerning state debt coupled with the growth of debt financing makes the state susceptible to a demagogic attack on the issue. Kansas has moved into extensive debt financing without major difficulty. The first problems with state debt, if and when they do occur, will likely spark a reaction to current practice and possibly demands for a reinstatement of stringent debt limits on state government. The adoption of reasonable debt provisions in advance of any problems may foreclose such a possibility.

Revamp Capital Planning and Budgeting

Should Kansas revamp state processes for capital planning and budgeting, augment the expertise on capital finance available to the governor and the legislature, and assure that state lawmakers receive consistent, current information on the state's capital assets and liabilities and on capital expenditures?

With a few important exceptions, the quality of capital planning and budgeting in Kansas falls short of best practice in other states. Both the governor and the legislature lack information and expertise on capital finance that would be essential to improve the quality of decision making concerning capital improvements. In the absence of essential supports for capital planning and budgeting, political considerations dominate many aspects of decision making, that is, decisions are arrived at by agreement among those who have influence.

A political approach to determining which capital projects move forward and which do not works but has drawbacks. First, the process works better for some state purposes than for others. Those state purposes that have the backing of influential, well-organized interests, such as university facilities and road improvements, are advantaged. Expertise and information promoting such facilities are much better developed. Other state purposes, such as correctional facilities, recreational improvements, or general state offices, are disadvantaged. Expertise and information in support of these facilities is consistently lacking. Facilities serving other state purposes fall in between these extremes. Also, more politically attractive improvements, such as construction of a new building, take precedence over equally important yet less palatable capital expenditures on such items as preventive maintenance or rehabilitation of facilities.

Second, inadequate and inconsistent capital planning and budgeting weaken the claim capital improvements have on a fair share of the state's resources. In the absence of effective capital planning and budgeting, requests for the construction, acquisition, maintenance, and improvement of capital assets compete poorly with demands for improvements in state operations. Poorly planned capital facilities make easy targets for elimination or postponement, in order that current demands for improved teacher salaries, social services, health care, and other state programs may be met. As shown above, state expenditures for capital improvements have not kept pace with the increased costs of capital construction, the growth in overall state expenditures, or the rise in personal income; indeed, capital expenditures consistently and dramatically have fallen relative to these indices.

The lack of expertise in capital finance also likely increases the costs of raising funds for capital improvements—although this would be difficult to document without additional study. Without expertise, the state is less well equipped to negotiate lower interest rates and lower underwriting costs for packaging and marketing state debts.

The adequacy of current procedures for capital planning and budgeting may be understood better by examining best practice gleaned from other states. Over the past few years, the Council of State Planning Agencies has sponsored a series of studies aimed at helping state governments respond to problems of infrastructure.[50] According to Vaughan and Pollard, who focus attention primarily on planning and budgeting of capital improvements, the ideal planning process should

1. assess the impact of social and economic change on demand for facilities;
2. inventory current capital assets and facilities;
3. conduct ongoing assessment of the condition and utilization of existing assets and facilities, for example, how facilities are valued or depreciated; and
4. provide advice to decision makers on whether to replace, rehabilitate, maintain, or abandon facilities.

The ideal capital budgeting process should

1. be coordinated with capital planning;
2. assess capital projects for operating-budget impact, both short-term and long-term;
3. set priorities for competing projects using, for example, project evaluation, cost-benefit analysis, needs assessment, appraisal of net present value, and funding availability; and
4. evaluate alternative sources of funding, for example, federal, local, private, or other.

In examining capital planning and budgeting in Kansas against best practice, state government comes up short overall. Current procedures do not consistently provide the governor or the legislature with the information outlined above. While Kansas falls short of having a consistent, government-wide approach to capital planning and budgeting, certain agencies do exemplary work in this area. The Kansas Water Office, for example, has underway a planning process for water resources that likely will serve as a model for other states. The Kansas Department of Transportation has in place a carefully conceived process for setting priorities among state high-way segments that require preservation or modernization and budgeting available funds.

A critical deficiency in overall capital planning and budgeting is the absence of information on capital finance, specifically concerning the capital assets and liabilities of state government and the extent of state expenditures for capital improvements. Improvement in these processes would require relevant, up-to-date data that are not now part of standard budgetary information nor of financial reporting by state government. Three important examples of this void include

1. Failure to distinguish in either budgeting or financial reporting between capital leases and other lease expenditures. As a result, major expenditures for the acquisition or improvement of capital assets are not recorded, and a complete accounting of capital expenditures is not easily available.
2. Failure to recognize and report on the value and depreciation of capital assets. The absence of consistent valuation measures withholds information concerning the status of state government's capital stock, its overall value, useful life, salvage value, and obsolescence.

3. Inconsistent reporting of long-term obligations of the state. This informational void keeps state policy makers unaware of certain financial obligations of the state and the extent to which these obligations pledge future revenues, either taxes or other revenues.

In addition to these major deficiencies is other inconsistent or nonexistent reporting on capital finance in areas such as contingent capital liabilities, debt-service expenditures, expenditures for preventive maintenance, operating costs of capital improvements, and capital improvements made from state assistance to local units of government, among others.

The principal reason behind the uneven quality in capital planning and budgeting and the gaps in essential information concerning capital finance is that no authority, including the governor and the legislature, requires any better. No organizational entity other than the legislature and possibly the governor has the authority to take the steps required to bring capital planning and budgeting in Kansas more in line with best practice in other states. Capital improvements are currently considered as an appendage to the review of operating budget requests, but the Division of the Budget has limited authority to revamp the process. The Division of Accounts and Reports also would have limited authority to require the reporting of certain financial information on capital assets and liabilities. Legislative staff involved in fiscal analysis depend largely on information provided by executive staff or by state agencies directly. None of these agencies likely would have the staff necessary to make major improvements in the process, nor would such steps be initiated without clear support for such action from the governor and the legislature.

A modest departure in improving capital planning and budgeting in Kansas could be taken by simply augmenting the authority and staff of existing agencies with responsibility for capital budgeting, finance, and financial reporting. Clearly defined authority supported by staff competent in matters of capital planning, budgeting, and finance likely would put in motion immediate and ongoing improvements in the quality of the process. A bolder initiative would be for state lawmakers to create a capital budget and an independent agency with authority and expertise for reviewing capital plans and budgets and for overseeing the capital assets of the state. Authority for financing capital improvements also could be lodged with this agency. Both executive and legislative officials logically would participate in the governance of this independent agency and its staff.

Revamping capital planning and budgeting in Kansas would require additional expenditures, but these would be minimal in terms of the value and ongoing investments in capital assets being made by governments in Kansas. National estimates place the current value of capital stock owned by state and local governments in Kansas at $16.1 billion.[51] The state's share of this figure is not known but could be as much as 20 percent, or even higher. State government spends annually over $300 million on capital improvements, debt service, and the acquisition of capital equipment. Outstanding debt of state government ranges at $400 million and more. Spending $1 to $2 million to assure that the capital assets of the state are well tended, that capital investments are well planned and budgeted, and that state debts are well managed would likely be a sound expenditure over the long term.

Expand State's Investment in Public Infrastructure

Should Kansas raise the level of investment in state infrastructure that aids economic growth, specifically in state highways, water-resource development, recreation and wildlife improvement, and state agency facilities?

A number of national studies have concluded that the level of investment in public infrastructure has become seriously deficient and that this deficiency hinders economic growth.[52] The question of whether the nation or state government in Kansas is adequately replacing obsolescent or deteriorating infrastructure or providing new infrastructure for growth may not be answered definitely. How much capital investment is enough ultimately becomes a policy choice facing Kansas. In the absence of a definitive answer, the following considerations impinge on the issue:

1. State expenditures on capital improvements have declined consistently and dramatically relative to construction costs, overall state expenditures, and personal income over the past twenty to twenty-five years. In addition, Kansas' effort in capital investment falls substantially below various national projections of infrastructure needs.
2. With respect to highways, preservation and modernization of existing roads require virtually all available funds. The $320 million bond program for state freeways has been exhausted. Federal assistance for highways, while stable or increasing in actual dollars for the past twenty-five years, has not kept up with the cost of construction. State-highway user fees also are declining relative to costs. Requests for $700 million in system-expansion projects presently are backlogged.
3. Federal assistance for purposes other than highways is being substantially reduced. Revenue sharing for state government has been eliminated. Funding for outdoor recreation stands at one-tenth of earlier levels. Major federal water projects are on hold. Proposals for further reductions are under consideration. Federal assistance for capital improvements directed to state purposes represents a particularly vulnerable target for actions aimed at reducing the federal deficit.
4. Capital improvement requests of other state agencies are backlogged:

   - Recreational improvements, both new parks, such as one proposed at Hillsdale Reservoir, and enhancement of existing park facilities, are

being postponed. State agency officials identify improvement needs of $5 million annually.
- Resort facilities at state parks have not moved forward for some years.
- Wildlife improvements, such as minimum streamflow and protection of wetlands and riparian areas, are being postponed. State agency officials identify improvement needs of $11 to $13 million annually.
- Preventive maintenance at state universities, state office facilities, and state institutions is being reduced.
- New correctional facilities have been stalled.

State government's historic policy of pay as we go has deterred state investment in public infrastructure and deserves careful reexamination. Pay as we go conflicts with a leading principle of capital finance, which is, pay as we use. In other words, those who benefit from a public facility should pay for its development and operation, and the amount paid should be tied to the level of use. In Kansas, one-half to three-fourths of capital expenditures (the exact amount is indeterminable with existing budgetary information or financial reporting) violate a pay-as-we-use philosophy. Under dominant Kansas practice, current taxpayers and use-fee payers bear the burden of making capital improvements for others who will benefit from the improvements ten, twenty, or more years into the future. As a result, current policy creates inequities as to who pays for capital improvements and places a questionable restraint on the level of capital investment to be undertaken in any one year.

Kansas could move away from pay as we go toward pay as we use by amortizing the costs of capital projects over the life of a project, in other words, extending the state's use of debt financing for capital improvements. This shift would not only begin to rectify financing inequities but also would allow the state to move ahead with backlogged projects and avoid the increased costs of construction due to project deferral. In the past twenty-five years, construction costs for state and local government have nearly quadrupled. One dollar spent on capital construction in 1960 has a value of twenty-five cents today. With expanded debt financing, state government could initiate projects earlier, benefit from their completion, and offset future interest costs with lower construction expense.

Relative to other states, the credit of the State of Kansas is not overextended. Per capita debt in Kansas is one-fourth the level of state debt nationally. Kansas could expand debt financing by over $1.1 billion and still fall below average state debt per capita. While increased use of state credit is an attractive alternative for moving expeditiously on backlogged capital projects, such action is not advisable without strengthening state capacity in terms of improved information and expertise on capital finance.

Beyond extending debt financing, other options for expanding revenues for capital improvements are available. Increased user fees would be one option compatible with financing capital improvements over a project's life.

The building funds have been a stable source of capital investment, and consideration could be given to increasing revenues flowing into these funds and possibly consolidating the two funds into one capital-development fund for state facilities. A drawback of the building fund includes continued reliance on the property tax, a revenue source that has not kept pace with the costs of construction. Another option deserving consideration is dedicating a small portion of the general fund to capital improvement purposes. This alternative would give recognition to the general interest of the state in preserving and modernizing the infrastructure yet also would allow lawmakers the flexibility to adjust the level of capital expenditures in response to changing demands.

Finally, expansion of state investment in public infrastructure would not be advisable without parallel steps toward improving capital planning and budgeting and the quality of expertise and information on capital finance. Kansas responsibility for public infrastructure divides reasonably well in to water resources, state highways, and state facilities. The authority and staffing of agencies responsible for coordinating these areas should be strengthened in order that they may perform the following assignments:

1. develop standards for inventorying, valuing, and depreciating public infrastructure and report annually to the governor and the legislature on these matters;
2. develop standards for budgeting and financial reporting of capital expenditures that are consistent across state agencies and over time;
3. provide technical assistance on capital planning conducted by state agencies and review capital improvement plans prepared by state agencies;
4. develop analytical methods for setting priorities among capital projects, including assessments of benefits against costs, net present value, and opportunity costs, among other techniques;
5. recommend annual budgets for capital improvements and specific alternatives concerning the source of financing;
6. issue debt for financing capital improvements within parameters of purpose and debt levels set by law; and
7. manage debts issues to the economic benefit of the agency and the state.

In sum, Kansas faces policy choices concerning constitutional revision, the adequacy of capital planning and budgeting, and the proper level of investment in public infrastructure. These policy choices in capital finance and public infrastructure deserve a place on the public agenda of Kansas. How these public policy issues are eventually resolved will determine the future status of Kansas' roads and highways, parks and recreational areas, wildlife resources, water supply and quality, and facilities at state institutions.

5   *HERMAN D. LUJAN*

Educational Governance and Finance

Education in Kansas, as in most states, is comprised of three tiers: elementary and secondary education, postsecondary community and vocational education, and higher education. A variety of institutions is found within these tiers, especially at the postsecondary level. Community colleges, vocational institutes, public state and municipal universities, private universities, and technical institutes all provide educational opportunities to the Kansas populace beyond the high school level.

Both the governance and financing of this educational system reflect the breadth of constituencies and interests served by the institutions involved. As currently organized, elementary and secondary education functions under an elected ten-member State Board of Education and an appointed commissioner of education. This board also administers state schools for the visually handicapped and state-supported schools at seven institutions under the Department of Social and Rehabilitation Services. Additionally, the board supervises locally elected boards that govern Kansas community colleges, local proprietary schools and boards, and community college boards. Accordingly, the state board has a span of control extending from the elementary and secondary tier into the postsecondary tier.

By contrast, public higher education functions under a single Board of Regents. The regents oversee regional state universities at Fort Hays, Pittsburg, and Emporia, Wichita State University, Kansas State University, and the University of Kansas. In addition, the Kansas Technical Institute also falls under regental control. All private colleges and universities as well as Washburn University are independent of state governance.

Education constitutes a key segment of the public agenda in Kansas. State taxes currently provide over $1 billion annually for educational purposes; local taxpayers fund another $700 million; and students contribute over $100 million. The magnitude of this annual investment prompts questions as to whether Kansas is receiving full value on its investment in education. What should Kansans expect for this level of expenditure in education? Are all educational purposes receiving adequate attention? Is the state's financial effort adequate or inadequate to address future educational demands? Are there too many or too few schools? How does Kansas assure that these questions are being addressed?

This chapter focuses on education and key policy choices concerning education in Kansas. In exploring this subject, issues of educational governance and finance interact and form the core of this review.

Educational Governance

The demands being placed upon education in the next decade or two will be markedly different than those of past years. Education will be expected to serve a changing clientele, play a more vital role in the economic, social, and cultural well-being of the state, and aid Kansas in its competition with other states. These changing demands and expectations will affect educational governance and ultimately finance.

The Demographic Setting

The demography of America is changing rapidly as a result of birth rates and immigration. Once a haven for the oppressed of Europe, America is now a haven for the world, especially the Third World. As people of color join the stream of American immigrants, birth rates are undergoing dramatic shifts. From 1946 to 1964, birth rates rose rapidly, then fell until 1980, when a new upswing occurred. This new crest reflects the coming of age of the so-called "baby boom" of 17 million Americans born during the 1946-64 growth period, some of whom are having their own children, although in a more delayed pattern than their parents because of changes in gender roles and cultural mores.[1] As a result, except for a few fast-growing communities, the number of school-age children will be on the decline throughout the 1980s.

This drop in the youth cohort is accompanied by a basic change in the composition of that cohort. While births among whites are down (1.7 children per female), they are up among Blacks at 2.4 and Mexican-Americans at 2.9. Whereas the average age for whites is 31 years, for Blacks it is 25 and for Hispanics, 22.[2] School enrollments of minority youth are rising throughout the U.S., although the distribution varies significantly by region. Table 5.1 reflects these data for Kansas and surrounding states. While minority enrollment in Kansas is one-half the national average, Kansas ranks second among the plains states in minority enrollment but only above Nebraska and Iowa among surrounding states.

The increase in Hispanic youth, resulting both from high birth rates and immigration, has produced specific educational consequences of

Table 5.1
Percentage of Minority Public School Enrollment in Selected States, Fall 1980

	% of total enrollment
Kansas	12.7
Colorado	22.1
Iowa	4.1
Missouri	14.8
Nebraska	10.5
Oklahoma	20.8
U. S.	26.7

Source: Harold L. Hodgkinson, *Guess Who's Coming to College*, January 1983.

note—namely, demands for bilingual educational services. This need is complicated by the rapid rise in the number of Asian inmigrants who are foreign born (60 percent) and bilingual and already make heavy use of programs offering English as a second language. Because Asians as a group proceed disproportionately into the educational system, their needs, both in terms of strengths (higher scores on mathematics) and weaknesses (linguistic skills), pose important programmatic issues for education.

Given the trends for the 1980s, primary educational demands for the 1990s will be felt by middle-aged baby boomers adapting to a changing technological and economic world and minority youth preparing for major roles in the twenty-first century. Moreover, differing educational preparedness and needs of these two groups will affect educational programs at every level, practices, costs, and systems of delivery for the next twenty years.

Changing patterns of family life represent another important dimension of demographic impact. Census data indicate that 59 percent of those born in 1983 will live with only one parent and that out of 100 born in that year only forty-one will reach age eighteen in a two-parent, undivorced family.[3] Currently, 12 percent of babies are born out of wedlock, one-half of these born to teenage mothers, regardless of ethnic group. Moreover, many of these mothers, while unmarried teenagers, have more than one child. This problem seriously affects Kansas, for as noted below in Chapter 6, Kansas ranks high nationally in the percentage of births out of wedlock. Because teenagers are more likely to have premature babies, this group is also more likely to have offspring in need of special educational programs.

In addition, poverty clearly has a heavy impact on children. In 1983, for example, children comprised 40 percent (14 million) of those in poverty.[4] Of these 14 million, 50 percent live in female-headed, single-family households. The combination of partially educated, teenaged females heading households in poverty-ridden, bilingual-language settings holds serious implications for education at all levels. Preparation at home bears consequences for learning at school.

In short, what the educational system nationally will be seeing is an increasingly poor, more ethnically diverse and multilingual, less-traditionally prepared youth cohort with educational demands requiring adjustments at all educational levels.

For Kansas, the picture differs somewhat. Urban concentration, poverty, and ethnic and multilingual diversity are relatively muted in comparison to many other states. Moreover, Kansas ranks eighth among the fifty states in the percentage of the school-age population that completes high school. This ranking coupled with the open entry available beyond high school places Kansas among the more accessible and successful educational systems in the country. This condition, however, should not divert awareness of these trends. For example, growth in the Kansas City metropolitan area and Wichita contains the forces of urbanization alluded to above. Urban poverty, ethnic diversity, and central-city schools do exist, and the suburban phenomenon, for example in Johnson County, of a relatively homogeneous and affluent pattern of growth will not shield Kansas from social and economic forces found in metropolitan areas throughout the U.S.

In sum, education in Kansas will experience demographic forces now at work in the nation. These forces, while not as potent in Kansas as in other parts of the country, will require response and adaptation from the educational system. Entering the system will be:[5]

1. More children from poverty households;
2. More children from single-parent households, often headed by teenagers;
3. More children from minority cultures;
4. More children in need of different or special educational programs;
5. More linguistically diverse children; and
6. In general, fewer children.

This changing constituency will occupy education for at least the next twenty years. Services will have to be geared to a student cohort without traditional backgrounds or preparation. Education will have to respond to fundamental shifts in aptitude and proficiency among different cultural and age groups. Enrollment will be declining, and colleges will be called on to serve an older clientele. These conditions raise important policy issues about educational offerings, and place demands on governance at all levels of education in Kansas.

The Economic Setting

While education serves the mind, it also fuels the economy. Skills and talents, once developed, become the basis for economic growth and development. As noted in Chapter 1, in the early 1980s, while the rest of the nation was exceeding 1979 levels of employment, Kansas achieved that milestone only in the second half of 1984. The rate of business formation in Kansas lags behind the national rate and considerably behind that of the surrounding states to the south and west. Kansas faces the likelihood of a continued depression in agriculture and mining, modest growth in aviation, and generally constrained development, all of these reflecting the decline in its core industries.

Largely as a result of economic change, the state's population is declining from 2.27 percent of the U.S. population at the turn of the century to a projected .93 percent at the turn of the next century. With this rate of loss, Kansas has one of the slowest-growing populations in the country. Outmigration further exacerbates this demographic condition. From 1980 to 1984, the annual net outmigration for Kansas was 6,000 persons, most of whom were young adults and those with education and skills. The loss of young people magnifies aging of the Kansas population to the point that Kansas now ranks ninth among the states in the number of residents over 65 years of age. Although Kansas educates well, other states gain from Kansas' investment in education. Therefore, a crucial issue for Kansas is maintaining a quality educational system and retaining the products of that excellence to improve the socioeconomic composition of the state.

The state's transition from the traditional, largely agricultural economy will depend upon a number of factors. Land remains reasonably priced in the state. Basic transportation is present but currently in a deteriorating condition. Kansas has a productive and well-educated work force, a central location, state fiscal stability, reasonable and diverse taxes, and local communities with a history of and an interest in economic growth. These factors set the stage for defining the relationship between education and economic growth in the state.

Educationally, these trends, along with the broader framework of national trends, call attention to two factors: the need for job-specific training to meet local demand and the need for enhancing the Kansas economy. Nationally, the most rapidly growing jobs include data-processing-machine mechanics, paralegal personnel, computer analysts, computer operators, and service-industry jobs ranging from food preparation to employment counseling and tax preparation.[6] To these should be added others that reflect local and regional community needs in agriculture and that reflect a transition in emphasis from food production to food processing and marketing. Because job training lies largely within the purview of the community colleges and the vocational-technical schools, educational programs designed to meet this need are primarily their responsibility.

Broad job skills that meet the talent requirements necessary to develop the Kansas economy are numerous and varied. Nationally, these skills include evaluation and analysis, critical thinking, general and technical problem-solving, organizational and reference skills, adaptability to new ideas, and communication skills. These abilities evolve as a result of advanced study, and therefore nurturing them is the responsibility of the regional and research universities.

The development of such skills has particular relevance for research dealing with the nature of the economic transition the Kansas economy is experiencing, especially in the agricultural and mineral industries. For example, the need to supplement food production with product marketing would appear to be crucial for economic growth in Kansas. Clearly, the state must commit to a twofold, major educational agenda that focuses first on specific research designed to identify essential means by which the Kansas economy can retrofit itself to changing national and international market forces and, second, on educational offerings that will create and hone skills necessary for understanding and working with such market trends. Both this research and the development of research skills will place demands on the state's institutions of higher education.

The Policy Setting

The demands of a changing constituency and for a more vital role for education in the economy will require effective educational governance particularly at the state level. At the policy level, Kansas most nearly resembles other states in its approach to the governance of basic education. The State Board of Education sets standards, and the state funding program serves to equalize basic offerings among the many school districts. In that regard, the state legislature exercises its responsibility for state basic education in three ways: administratively through local school boards and districts, financially through the school-equalization program, and qualitatively through the State Board of Education. By these means, the 306 school districts are coordinated and assisted such as to assure one of the better graduation rates in the country from public common schools.

Among the distinctions from other states worth noting is the election of the State Board of Education. In many states, the board is appointed. Appointment has the advantage of enhancing professionalism at the policy level and of making more attractive the appointment of substantively knowledgeable board membership while minimizing the political nature of the governing process. As school districts face financial austerity and increased competition from other sectors for limited state funds, the value of an appointed board lies in its ability to generate a substantive case for legislative action. The drawback, however, is the loss of political muscle gained by electoral choice. For Kansas, a basic policy issue appears to be responding to funding reductions while maintaining a quality of basic education that currently exceeds the national average. In the competition over funds these cuts will produce, an elected state board may have difficulty in facing the broad substantive decisions involved because of political pressures and contraints. Board selection could, therefore, be an issue worthy of consideration.

At the postsecondary, two-year education level, coordination is a major problem, with program authority divided between two state boards, the Board of Education and the Board of Regents. Like most of the states, Kansas places most vocational and technical education under the State Board of Education. Unlike most states, however, a major provider of this service is placed under the Board of Regents. When other factors compound this confusing situation, policy direction becomes clouded, the quality of services inhibited, and access for students to the training they need seriously complicated, if not impaired. Nine area vocational schools, for example, fall under the control of local boards that offer secondary curricula. Five vocational-technical schools fall under boards of control (Beloit, Coffeyville, Goodland, Newton, and Johnson County), and two community colleges (Cowley and Pratt) include a vocational-technical school. Finally, nineteen community colleges offer college preparatory and career-related education.

This pluralistic picture reflects the fundamental policy dilemma Kansas faces: how can lower-division, college-level education, basic technical education, and vocational education be coherently provided at the postsecondary level?

This policy issue, while obvious in most aspects, is particularly difficult because the American tradition has treated academic and technical, two-year education essentially as a matter of vocational education and thereby avoided the basic question of what should constitute postsecondary, but not university, education. Since vocational education typically is viewed as an extension of the high school experience and since high schools offer vocational education, the relegation of its governance to state boards of education that supervise secondary schools seems appropriate. The problem is that high schools provide both precareer and college preparatory training. Meanwhile, community colleges provide posthigh school academic training and offer posthigh school career training along with other technical and vocational institutions—all in a two-year setting or less. From this perspective, postsecondary training can be seen as a discrete but contiguous posthigh school process, with job training and lower-division academic training as its two primary ingredients. If viewed in this way, the anomaly of having two-year academic and vocational-technical education split between the State Board of Education and the State Board of Regents becomes apparent. Thus, at the policy level, this stepchild dilemma is an essential policy matter that should be addressed. This issue cannot be resolved without defining the role of vocational-technical education more clearly, particularly with respect to the economy of communities and the state as a whole, and clarifying the relationships of area vocational schools and community colleges.

State universities in Kansas have existed in a more coherent policy setting, with the Board of Regents as a statewide governing body. Unlike many of its state peers, a consolidated approach to higher education policy in Kansas has long been in place, minimizing the political competition among regents and their institutions common in many states. In this centralized setting, competition is contained within the board structure, allowing higher education to compete against other educational segments in a more unified manner. The tradeoff, however, is a leveling effect in which top institutions advance more slowly than their peers and smaller institutions do better than they might on their own.

Nationwide, the governance of higher education has become a pressing issue because of the primacy of the states in providing for and funding higher education.[7] During the 1960s and 1970s, higher education was expanding rapidly, and the fundamental governance issues involved planning, program review, and the administration of the various sectors of higher education. Thus, states made changes in the structure and governance of higher education, moving toward the formation of coordinating boards, in part to deal with the competition between separate boards of regents or boards at separate levels (e.g., state colleges and universities) where such levels existed. Seven states strengthened coordinating boards already in existence, two replaced coordinating boards with statewide governing boards, and three modified and strengthened existing entities peculiar to their local situations.[8] In the early 1980s, Florida, Minnesota, North Carolina, and Tennessee reorganized vocational-technical education; Pennsylvania consolidated the governance of higher education; Rhode Island abandoned a single governing board for a board at each of the three levels of education; Connecticut strengthened its coordinating board; Massachusetts created a new statewide board to replace all existing agencies and boards; and Colorado and Washington created new coordinating boards with more authority.[9]

By the mid-1980s, because of crises in financing higher education, states have turned their attention from higher education coordination to higher education coordination and finance. As federal support declines while inflation continues, states are generally faced with maintaining and improving higher education at the same time resources decline and demands for funding increase. Universities are also being expected to contribute in new ways to economic growth and the cultural well-being of their regions. These growing demands bring to the surface underlying issues of governance:[10]

1. Duplication in high-cost graduate and professional programs.
2. Conflict between institutions.

3. Legislative or executive reaction to intense institutional lobbying.
4. Dissatisfaction with the existing governance structure.
5. Perceived weakness in the quality of educational leadership.

As elsewhere, these issues have emerged recently in Kansas.

The duplication of high-cost graduate and professional programs is worrisome and evidences itself in the issue of the future relationship between Washburn University and the state. The issue of duplication also emerges in the aspirations for graduate and professional offerings at Wichita State University. Presently, the latter issue has been contained by the program-approval powers of the Board of Regents. Recent attempts by the board, however, to eliminate graduate programs and consolidate professional education for teachers illustrate the limitations of existing governance.

Conflict between institutions has flared in Kansas, most significantly in the case of medical education in the Wichita area, which was resolved by regental action involving Kansas University Medical School and Wichita State University. This kind of conflict currently exists in two other important cases. One involves the continued community interest in Wichita as a site for graduate and professional study and the desire on the part of the Washburn University Regents to have Washburn placed entirely and independently within the state system under the Kansas Board of Regents. The latter issue has become polarized in the legislature and prompted gubernatorial pronouncements that Washburn, if admitted, should be part of the University of Kansas. The issue currently stands unresolved in the public arena, carries a high profile, and seriously challenges current governance arrangements while enhancing political involvement in the governance of higher education.

Reaction to intense institutional lobbying also manifests itself in the case of the Washburn issue. The Topeka delegation in the legislature, sensitive to local interests, has pressed for the inclusion of Washburn in the regental system as a freestanding, separate institution. Moreover, Washburn has allied with the nineteen community colleges receiving state support on a credit hour basis. The potential voting block involving Topeka legislators and those from community college districts reflects, even in theory, the potential intensity of the lobby to support the Washburn proposal. That intensity emerged in legislative debates over out-district tuition to community colleges for services to out-of-district students and included a payment to Washburn University for its vocational offerings. While clear merits attach to all sides of this issue, the politicizing of the question serves as a poignant example of higher education lobbying, as well as the inability of current governance to give direction to the resolution of these issues.

Concern over the efficacy of the existing higher education governing structure is linked to lobbying and reveals itself in the ongoing debate over graduate and professional study at Wichita State and recent gubernatorial comments on the need to end turf and funding wars among the six state universities. The governor called for a master plan to provide vision for all of higher education and end annual contention over funding, institutional lobbying for those resources, and perceived duplication in offerings. The call for a master plan clearly expresses reservations on the part of the chief executive about the capacity of the current governing structure both to provide staff analyses essential to guide effective policy and funding decisions in the state house and advocacy for the institutions.

With regard to effective educational leadership in Kansas, the turf wars, coupled with intense institutional rivalry over diminishing state funds at a time of retrenchment and transition, all point to the difficult dilemma posed for the regents within the current governing structure. The regents come from the areas and represent the interests of the six institutions. Through their budgetary authority, they serve as advocates for the regental institutions. In so doing, they must, with difficulty, try to make an objective case for higher education overall while advocating the special interests of their respective regental institutions. To do both well is not easy; to maintain credibility, especially in times of fierce competition over shrinking resources, is harder still. This conflict becomes most apparent when political leaders call for the need to clarify the roles and missions for each of the several institutions. While clearly a matter of regental purview, this issue remains incompletely attained in sixty-one years of regental governance.

As these issues indicate, higher education in Kansas currently faces a number of significant policy choices that bear upon the governance structure and its capacity for handling those issues, difficult and political as they may be. These current concerns rise against a backdrop of fiscal shortfalls that blur the good record of the current governing body and the general quality of Kansas higher education. This record notwithstanding, the need to address these policy concerns, both in the present and in the near future, remains.

Educational Finance In Kansas

Responding to new demands from a changing clientele and expectations that education contribute more directly to the economic well-being of Kansas will require a sound financial base. The magnitude and diversity of education in Kansas has produced a complex plan of educational finance. Revenue sources and allocation procedures vary by tier and by type of institution. Understanding the complexities of educational finance uncover issues facing Kansas in this area.

Financing Elementary and Secondary Education

The common schools in Kansas are financed by a mixture of local, state, and federal revenues. Local revenues provide the bulk of support, supplemented substantially by state funds and further augmented by program-specific federal funds. Since this study focuses on the role of state government, a review of the level of state support for education is essential and can best be accomplished through a review of Kansas financing in comparison with that of selected states and with national trends.

The level of revenue support for Kansas appears in Table 5.2. Revenues available to elementary and secondary education in Kansas were estimated at over $1.5 billion for 1984, an increase of 93.5 percent over 1976. State aid to elementary and secondary education in Kansas increased from $306.6 million in 1976 to $681.3 million in 1984, an increase of 122.2 percent. In the same period, local and other aid increased from $352.3 to $761.5 million, an increase of 116.2 percent. Federal assistance fell from $90.4 to $68.9 million in this period, a drop of 23.7 percent.The share state revenues provide of total school revenues increased from 1976 to 1984 school by 4.2 percent (from 40.9 percent to 45.1 percent), the local share increased by 3.4 percent (from 47.0 percent to 50.4 percent), and the federal share decreased by 7.5 percent (from 12.1 percent to 4.6 percent).

These trends indicate that state revenue has provided the primary support for the stability that exists in the funding of the common schools, which is in keeping with the philosophy that underpins the Kansas School Equalization Act. That act generally provides each school district a budget floor of 105 percent of the median budget per pupil. In this way, the state

Table 5.2

Sources of Revenue for Elementary and Secondary Education in Kansas, 1976-84 (dollar amounts in millions)

	Local[a]	State	Federal	Total	Local[a] (%)	State (%)	Federal (%)
1976	$352.3	$306.6	$90.4	$ 749.2	47.0	40.9	12.1
1977	340.8	363.9	97.1	801.8	42.5	45.4	12.1
1978	449.0	379.0	50.0	869.0	50.6	43.6	5.8
1979	517.5	450.0	72.1	1,039.6	49.8	43.3	6.9
1980	541.5	498.9	70.4	1,110.8	48.8	44.9	6.3
1981	674.9	538.8	65.9	1,279.7	52.7	42.1	5.2
1982	704.4	574.0	68.2	1,346.6	52.3	42.6	5.1
1983	735.7	619.9	68.9	1,424.5	51.6	43.5	4.8
1984[b]	761.5	681.3	68.9	1,511.7	50.4	45.1	4.6

Source: National Education Association, *Estimates of School Statistics*, 1976-
        1985.
[a] Local and other.
[b] Estimated.

regulates budget escalation while equalizing state funding in recognition of the varying revenue capacities of different districts.

In addition to equalization aid, all districts receive funds from an income-tax rebate. State aid for transportation also is provided, based on the number of pupils living 2.5 miles or more from the school they attend. Moreover, the state assists in a variety of special programs, including special education, education of the deaf-blind and the severely handicapped, vocational education, bilingual education, basic adult education, driver education, and food assistance, among others. Finally, schools receive 3.5 percent of severance tax receipts for oil, gas, coal, or salt properties in their districts.

The state-level effort in Kansas can be better understood if compared to sister states in the surrounding area, as shown in Figure 5.1. While Kansas provided 45.1 percent of common-school funding in 1984, Nebraska provided 28.1 percent, Missouri 37.2 percent, Colorado 40.2 percent, Iowa 42.0 percent, and Oklahoma 61.4 percent. All surrounding states increased the state contribution to school finance in the period, which reflects a national trend. Only Oklahoma, with its oil-rich revenues, exceeded Kansas in effort. Kansas falls below the national average of 49.0 percent but exceeds all but one of its neighboring states and stands out as a leader among the plains states in state support of the common schools.

In Kansas, the contribution of the federal government in financing schools has decreased dramatically, federal funds dropping from 12.1 percent of revenue receipts in 1976 to 4.6 percent by 1984. The decline in federal financing of schools occurred in the U.S. as a whole and in all of the comparison states except for Iowa, which experienced a slight increase. The decline in federal revenues most likely reflects other demands on the federal treasury and declining federal assistance. The mood of the current administration and Congress provides little hope for a reversal of this trend.

Financing Community Colleges

The nineteen Kansas community colleges offer up to two years of comprehensive education beyond the high school. Their curricula vary and either parallel college or university curricula or are vocational, technical, or adult and continuing education in nature. Community colleges operate locally and regionally and offer quality, low-cost education to Kansas residents.

Community colleges are governed by local boards of trustees but are certified by the State Board of Education. Consequently, their financing is a mix of local and state revenues.

The staple in community college funding is the ad valorem tax at the local level. Local taxes are supplemented by state financing based on credit hours, out-district aid from the state and pertinent counties based on student

Figure 5.1
**State Contribution to Revenues for Elementary and Secondary
Education in Selected States, 1976-84 (%)**

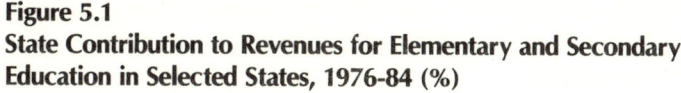

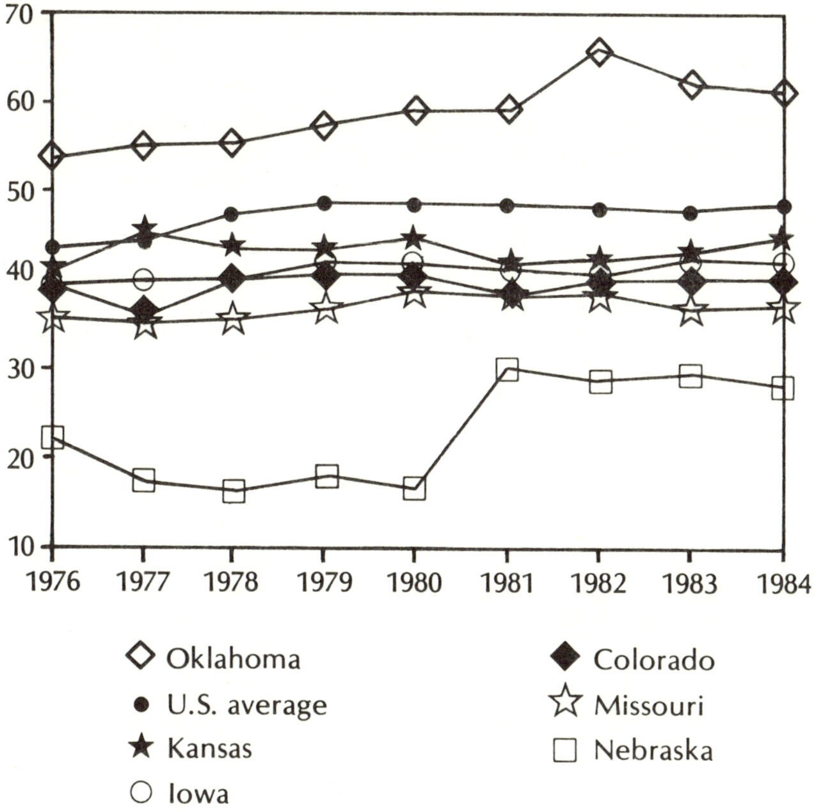

◇ Oklahoma   ◆ Colorado

● U.S. average   ☆ Missouri

★ Kansas   □ Nebraska

○ Iowa

enrollees from outside of the community college district, tuition, and a variety of federal sources, including vocational education, adult basic education, and job training through the Job Training Partnership Act. The funding from the primary revenue sources is shown in Table 5.3. As these data show, the local property tax provides the majority of support for community colleges in Kansas, a sum of $44.6 million in 1984, which comprised 59.4 percent of operating revenues, up from 50.1 percent in 1979. Between 1979 and 1984, the state share of community college aid fell from 38.4 to 32.5 percent; the share composed of revenues from tuition declined from 9.3 to 6.3 percent; and the federal share dropped from 2.3 to 1.8 percent.

Community colleges, therefore, rely on the property tax supplemented by state aid. Tuition provides revenue at a very modest level, as does the

Table 5.3
Sources of Revenue for Community Colleges in Kansas, 1979-84
(dollar amounts in millions)

	Local	State	Tuition	Federal	Local (%)	State (%)	Tuition (%)	Federal (%)
1979	$21.7	$16.6	$4.0	$1.0	50.1	38.4	9.3	2.3
1980	24.2	19.7	3.9	1.1	49.5	40.3	8.0	2.2
1981	30.5	20.7	3.7	1.2	54.3	36.9	6.6	2.2
1982	33.4	21.7	3.9	1.2	55.5	36.0	6.5	2.0
1983	41.5	23.3	4.1	1.3	59.1	33.2	5.8	1.9
1984	44.6	24.4	4.7	1.3	59.4	32.5	6.3	1.8

Source: Compiled by Kansas State Department of Education.
Note: Figures include only revenues for operating expenses.

federal government. While this mix of funding sources has sustained community-based postsecondary education in Kansas, shrinking assistance from
sources other than the local property tax poses a potentially serious problem
for community colleges in the future.

The narrowing base of support becomes especially significant as the
demand for education in an increasingly technological society grows. Community colleges and other providers of technical education play an important role in offering vital job-related training and education. Such skills are
essential to the adaptation and development of local economies to changing
trends and forces. Although increasingly important to businesses, their funding from a number of sources has not kept up with the cost of living and
poses a serious educational and economic issue for Kansas communities,
as well as the state as a whole.

Financing Public Colleges and Universities

The number of annual full-time students attending public colleges and
universities in Kansas, in other words, regents institutions, community colleges, and Washburn, has increased by 4,300 from 1977 to 1984, an increase of 5 percent (see Table 5.4). This increase occurred while the number
of high school graduates in Kansas, the primary source of entering freshman
at public colleges and universities, dropped 20 percent. As a result, Kansas
ranks fifth nationally in the number of full-time students per high school
graduate. This ranking means that Kansas provides an attractive, accessible
opportunity for higher education given the number of students available for
university enrollment.

While the number of full-time students increased by 5 percent from
1977 to 1984, state appropriations for public colleges and universities in
this period increased from $192.3 million to $329.1 million, an increase of
71 percent. This rate of increase matches almost precisely growth in the

Table 5.4
Full-time Students and State and Local Appropriations for Public Colleges and Universities in Kansas, 1977-84 (dollar amounts in millions)

Year	Students	Appropriations
1977	86,710	$192.3
1979	87,216	245.7
1980	89,991	271.0
1981	90,814	287.2
1982	91,735	299.3
1983	91,689	300.7
1984	91,022	329.1

Source: U.S. Department of Education, National Institute of Education, *How States Compare in Financing Higher Education, 1984-1985: Estimates for Public Instiutions*, May 1985.

Table 5.5
State and Local Appropriations for Public Colleges and Universities, as a Percentage of State and Local Revenue, and Per Full-time Student, in Selected States, 1984

State	Appropriations as % of revenues	Appropriations per student	
		1984[a]	% change 1977-84[b]
Kansas	10.7	$3,173	-1.6
Colorado	7.7	2,424	1.9
Iowa	9.6	3,352	-11.2
Missouri	8.1	2,959	-16.0
Nebraska	7.9	2,646	-16.8
Oklahoma	8.6	2,839	15.2
U. S.	8.9	3,467	-1.6

Source: U.S. Department of Education, National Institute of Education, *How States Compare in Financing Higher Education, 1984-1985: Estimates for Public Institutions*, May 1985.
[a] Figures include only appropriations for operating expenses.
[b] In constant dollars.

cost of living in this period. In other words, an additional 4,300 students were served without real-dollar increases in appropriation.

The percentage of public funds that are used to support public colleges and universities indicates the priority of education beyond the high school compared with the funding of other services of state and local governments generally. As shown in Table 5.5, Kansas places a high value on financing public higher education. In 1984, 10.7 percent of state and local tax revenues were appropriated for current educational operating expenses of public colleges and universities. Kansas ranks above the national average, higher than all of the comparison states, and sixteenth nationally on this measure.

In terms of appropriations per full-time student, Kansas falls in the middle range, appropriating $3,173 per student and ranking thirty-first nationally. Of the surrounding states, however, only Iowa provides more financial support, $3,352 per student. When 1977 and 1984 are compared in constant dollars, the appropriations per student for Kansas decreased by 1.6 percent, with Oklahoma and Colorado the only comparison states experiencing an increase. Iowa, Missouri, and Nebraska all underwent substantial decreases in per-student appropriations based on real dollars.

The financing of public higher education also relies, in addition to appropriations, on tuition dollars. States vary in the importance they place on student tuition as a funding source. Table 5.6 provides three measures of tuition: 1) tuition revenues of public colleges and universities per full-time students; 2) percentage change in tuition per student in constant dollars; and 3) a ratio of state and local appropriations for public colleges and universities plus tuition revenue to the same appropriations exclusive of tuition.

Tuition revenue per student in Kansas is $923, which is 12.5 percent below the national average and ranks Kansas thirty-sixth among the states.

Table 5.6
Tuition Per Full-time Student, Tuition Revenue Relative to State and Local Appropriations for Public Colleges and Universities, and Tuition Per Student Relative to Disposable Personal Income Per Capita, in Selected States, 1984

	Tuition per student[a]		Tuition measure[c]	Tuition index[d]
	Actual	% change[b] 1977-84		
Kansas	$ 923	-11.2	1.29	84
Colorado	1,622	49.7	1.67	142
Iowa	1,398	7.0	1.42	145
Missouri	1,178	8.1	1.40	119
Nebraska	1,066	-7.6	1.38	100
Oklahoma	650	-14.1	1.23	67
U. S.	1,055	12.1	1.30	100

Source: U.S. Department of Education, National Institute of Education, *How States Compare in Financing Higher Education, 1984-1985: Estimates for Public Institutions*, May 1985.
[a] Tuition revenues of public colleges and universities per annual full-time students.
[b] In constant dollars.
[c] This measure is defined as the ratio of state and local appropriations for public colleges and universities plus student tuition revenue to state and local appropriations exclusive of tuition; it suggests the importance of tuition as a funding source relative to state and local appropriations.
[d] A fifty-state index of tuition per student relative to disposable personal income per capita.

Of the neighboring states, only Oklahoma has lower tuition. When converted to constant dollars, tuition per student for the past seven years has actually decreased in Kansas by 11.2 percent. Colorado, Iowa, and Missouri experienced an increase in tuition dollars, when inflation is taken into account. Nebraska dropped by 7.6 percent, and Oklahoma fell by 14.1 percent.

In examining tuition revenues relative to state and local appropriations, Kansas ranks slightly below the national average. On this measure, higher ratios indicate a greater proportion of tuition dollars in the funding package and may also show a large number of out-of-state students paying nonresident tuition. Again, all neighboring states, except Oklahoma, rely on tuition revenues more than Kansas does.

Table 5.6 also shows an index based upon tuition revenues per student relative to personal disposable income per capita. This index measures tuition relative to residents' ability to pay. Kansas again ranks thirty-sixth nationally with only Oklahoma, among the comparison states, ranking lower. This measure suggests that Kansas students could afford to pay more in tuition given their personal income.

In sum, the solid financial base that Kansas has evolved has paid off for the state in the form of a well-educated and highly-skilled work force. For example, 80.5 percent of school age population graduate from high school, ranking the state eighth nationally on retention.[11] Kansas also ranks fifth nationally in the proportion of high school graduates who go to public colleges and universities in the state indicating that Kansas provides attractive and accessible opportunities beyond high school.[12] The key financial challenge facing Kansas is maintaining educational quality at a time of declining enrollments. The critical issue for state government is continuing a stable financial base for all levels of education while responding to new educational demands.

Policy Choices in Educational Governance and Finance

The policy choices posed here are not intended to be exhaustive but are provided as options to promote discussion of the governance and financial issues raised by this analysis. In the course of their consideration, other ideas could emerge as alternatives to those examined in the context of this chapter.

Governance of Education beyond High School

Educational governance beyond high school constitutes a major challenge facing Kansas. Education at the postsecondary and higher education levels lacks effective coordination. No authority at the state level is articulating a strategic vision of what role these critical segments of education can and should be playing in the economy and in the state's future.

The role of vocational education in the educational system poses certain policy questions. Currently, vocational education at the postsecondary level falls under the supervision of the State Board of Education, except for the Kansas Technical Institute in Salina and the Vocational-Technical Institute at Pittsburg State University. These latter institutions are governed by the Board of Regents. Thus, two separate entities coordinate the actions of vocational education. The Board of Education exerts some control over vocational and vocational-technical schools, but they are governed by local school districts, community college boards, or area boards. Although postsecondary vocational schools are governed locally, they receive no local tax support for program operations and, with the decline in federal funds, are primarily dependent upon the state for funding. Of concern is whether or not they receive enough direction from the state, and whether they respond to the current needs of the community and the state for vocational education.

Community college curricula are usually considered to be college-paralleled with an emphasis on vocational, technical, adult, continuing, and general education. Community colleges also provide some college-preparatory instruction and therefore are a multifaceted segment of the Kansas educational system.

Community colleges have district-wide taxing authority and fall under the authority of local boards of trustees. They are, however, supervised by the State Board of Education. Because of this dependency on district-wide taxing authority, some thought should be given to the governance of the community colleges. Coordination seems to be the necessary policy ingredient in such a consideration, along with some attention to the regional aspects of postsecondary education.

In summary, then, a key policy choice is the coordination and governance of postsecondary education, including community colleges, vocational schools, and vocational-technical schools, all of which provide, among other things, vocational and job-related education and training.

Kansas could allow the governance of the various sectors of postsecondary education to remain as they presently stand, that is, distributed between the State Board of Education and the Board of Regents, with area boards in certain instances involving area vocational education and local boards as in the case of community colleges. This option would leave the postsecondary tier unintegrated, thereby maximizing area and local involvement in postsecondary governance, but current ambiguities regarding technical education and vocational training would continue.

An alternative to the present structure would be to create a State Board of Postsecondary Education appointed subject to legislative approval consistent with the appointment of such boards generally. Headed by an appointed director or other designated chief executive officer, the board would coordinate the community colleges, area vocational schools, vocational-technical schools, and technical institutes.

The experience of coordinating boards in other states as well as the State Board of Education and the Board of Regents could serve as guides for enabling legislation. At minimum, the new board would establish standards, coordinate curriculum, degrees, and programs, and oversee state funding and assistance in accordance with legislative guidelines or instruction. Specifically, the board could be charged with the following assignments:

1. Identify postsecondary educational needs, including lower-division college instruction, vocational education, and technical education.
2. Approve and apply a state plan for postsecondary education.
3. Set tuition and fee guidelines for postsecondary education.
4. Distribute federal and other state-administered funds.
5. Set standards for degrees and other certification applicable in postsecondary education.
6. Establish enrollment and transfer guidelines.
7. Approve and authorize new programs.
8. Develop and recommend capital and operations budgets for postsecondary education.
9. Approve new institutions, mergers, or eliminations.
10. Oversee financial equity and arbitrate issues relating to out-district funding and revenues.
11. Approve and monitor off-campus activities and programs.
12. Undertake and monitor relations with the State Board of Education and the Board of Regents as appropriate.
13. Coordinate relationships with counties and other area or local units involved in postsecondary education.
14. Oversee and establish such area and local boards as may be appropriate for community college, area vocational, and technical education in the state.
15. Assure program access and improve the quality of postsecondary education.

This option would allow for the integration of postsecondary education, clarify relationships with the secondary schools in vocational education, and facilitate the offerings of both vocational and technical education in a more coherent fashion. In addition, this option would also combine these offerings with those of the community colleges to assure coordinated programs and curricula at the postsecondary level. This board would provide a statewide setting for addressing out-district issues and assure access, financial equity, and educational quality in postsecondary education.

With respect to higher education, as well as all education beyond high school, key policy issues relate to the coordination of higher education and to higher education's contributions to the economy of Kansas:

1. The scope and mission of Wichita State University need definition. As an urban university in the state's largest city, WSU has a unique urban and industrial base, and the development of advanced degrees within that setting should be addressed.

2. A comprehensive plan for higher education would appear appropriate. Each institution within the regental system plays a unique role and serves particular constituencies with its programs. A comprehensive plan would allow for clarification of the roles of the vocational schools, the community colleges, and the state universities and of relationships with private colleges and universities. Such a plan also would help to clarify the roles of the regental institutions. Because in Kansas no single state agency is responsible for comprehensive planning, the potential for a coordinating board to carry out this function is an appropriate subject for discussion. A number of states have higher education coordinating boards that perform planning and assessment functions but leave the authority for operation of the system to existing governing boards.

3. Private higher education plays a significant role in Kansas through twenty-two private colleges, and the state's interest in these institutions deserves further definition. One college, St. John's College of Winfield, is closing its doors this year because of debt problems and declining enrollment. A reduction in federal financial aid will further threaten these schools in the immediate future.

   At issue is how private colleges can survive financially and what their role should be in the system of higher education. The private colleges could potentially play a leading role in maintaining a balance between the demands for highly technological training in present-day society and the continuing importance of the development of the liberal arts generally. Moreover, the private colleges could deal with the ethical and value dimensions of education, which often conflict with the mission of public institutions. Requests by the Independent College Association to the legislature for an increase in tuition grant money likely will continue in the face of a less-than-optimistic economy. If the state is to become more active in coordinating higher education, then the role foreseen for private institutions in the total Kansas educational system must be clarified.

4. By some means, Washburn University must be coordinated with the balance of higher education in Kansas. Whether Washburn is to be brought under the governance of the Kansas Board of Regents is an issue that will continue to confront Kansans. The board already governs six universities, and the addition of Washburn to the system raises long-term financial questions that would imply further stretching of scarce dollars among seven, rather than six, institutions. However, the state and local taxpayers currently spend millions of dollars to support Washburn.

5. Institutions of higher education contribute to economic and cultural well-being of Kansas in a number of ways. They train talented individuals to support the economy, provide research and other kinds of support to the business sector, and act as cultural centers in their regions. A vision of higher education's role in the social and economic future of Kansas needs

formulation and direction.

In this regard, colleges and universities should explore their opportunities to provide support to the business sector, including small business and agribusiness. Such support might mean developing a curriculum that responds to the skill requirements of local businesses. Efforts at off-campus extended education clearly should be explored, particularly with the current revolution in telecommunication techniques. In addition, local business, local educational institutions, and government need to become partners in research and development. Coordinating research and development efforts not only would share the costs of program development but also would pool ideas.

Actions of the 1986 legislature provide a framework for the contributions of state universities to the economy of Kansas. Other states are experimenting with diverse programs to enhance the universities' role in economic development. Many possibilities exist for furthering economic development via the state educational system, and these should be systematically explored.

These issues point out the need for a coordinated approach to higher education, and to that end Kansas could retain the Board of Regents as the sole governing body charged with planning, program review, budget review, and other governing powers, and charge the board with the responsibility to resolve current, specific issues involving graduate and professional degrees at Wichita State University, the future status of Washburn University, and the development of appropriate educational responses to the economic development needs of the various regions of the state. This option would continue governance as it stands and require that the regents resolve the politically and educationally difficult issues and continue to be responsible for educational planning and for clarifying the missions and roles of the several regental institutions.

As an alternative, Kansas could establish a Higher Education Coordinating Board to plan, collect information, provide analyses, conduct program reviews of new and existing programs and provide these as appropriate to the governor and the legislature, review budget proposals, coordinate the use of uniform procedures for budgetary and other reporting requirements, coordinate relationships with the private four-year institutions, and conduct similar activities for the postsecondary sector in the event that a State Board of Postsecondary Education is established. The membership of the coordinating board would be appointed according to procedures governing the appointment of comparable boards and would be administered by a director or other designated executive officer.

As one of its first assignments, this board could develop a master plan for higher education which would include study of the issue of graduate and professional study at Wichita State University (including the appropriateness of graduate and professional study in the applied sciences), the future status of Washburn University, and appropriate educational responses to the economic development of various areas of the state.

If a State Board of Postsecondary Education were adopted, the coordinating board would develop an appropriate master plan for adoption by the Board of Postsecondary Education and in that effort address the roles of community colleges, area vocational and vocational-technical schools, and technical institutes. It would consider the special role of the Kansas Technical Institute (including its transfer from the Board of Regents) and advise and coordinate technical offerings at Pittsburg State University. In accordance with that plan, the coordinating board would conduct program and budget reviews, establish uniform reporting procedures, collect systematic information and data, and conduct such intensive studies as might be required by the governor, the legislature, and the State Board of Postsecondary Education.

Specifically, the coordinating board would have the following responsibilities:

1. Planning duties
   - Develop role and mission statements for institutions.
   - Identify the state's educational goals, objectives, and priorities for higher and postsecondary education.
   - Prepare a comprehensive master plan discussing needs, trends, enrollments, continuing education, adult education, vocational and technical needs, public service, and other special requirements.
   - Review, evaluate, and comment on operating and capital budgets.
   - Recommend legislation.
   - Recommend financial-aid programs and approaches.
   - Prepare recommendations for program and institutional eliminations, mergers, and new programs or institutions.
2. Program responsibilities
   - Approve new degree programs.
   - Assess and review program modifications.
   - Evaluate existing programs periodically.
   - Assess and review off-campus programs.
   - Adopt guidelines for consortia or joint programs.
3. Coordinating duties
   - Promote interinstitutional cooperation.
   - Recommend minimum admission standards and enrollment policies.
   - Establish guidelines for student transfer.
   - Review and monitor compensation and employment policies.
   - Arbitrate disputes.
   - Establish data and reporting standards and procedures.
   - Monitor activities for compliance with state law.

A coordinating agency could provide a statewide and systemic perspective on the issues facing both higher education and postsecondary education. Such a coordinating board would offer the governor, the legislature, and the governing boards outside planning and analytic assistance and provide a third-party view on programs and budgets, within the framework of an approved state master plan. The fact that such a plan remains incomplete in higher education underscores the need for it, especially in light of the financial difficulties facing the Kansas economy and current federal cutbacks. The board also would be able to offer a substantive point of view on the difficult issue of new graduate-level degrees at Wichita State, the future role of Washburn with regard to state higher education, and technical education in Salina and Pittsburgh and could comment on the merits of each case, leaving the difficult policy choices where they properly lie, in the governing boards and in the executive and legislative branches.

This approach would also allow the Board of Regents and the proposed State Board of Postsecondary Education (if adopted) to act as advocate with regard to the interests of their educational sectors and the institutions they govern. The conflict between the roles of analyst and advocate has posed difficulties for the Board of Regents, for example, in resolving current issues involving institutional interests, rivalries, and the clarification of roles and missions.

We should note that where such boards exist, their contribution in planning, program review, and evaluative studies is enhanced by their playing a substantial role in budget review. This review role, rather than preemptive of the regental role, is typically complementary to it, providing the governor and the legislature with a referent perspective for responding to regental requests and regental advocacy of the interests and needs of higher education. Significantly, the role of such a board at the postsecondary level would vary to the extent that local and area funding comprise important segments of postsecondary funding. In this latter case, the coordinating board would serve as a key resource for the State Board of Postsecondary Education in responding to area and local interests.

Governance of Elementary and Secondary Education

The governance of elementary and secondary schools falls under the purview of the State Board of Education and its ten elected members. The governance of the common schools is a matter of long tradition and poses no monumental policy issues. However, the question of whether such boards should be appointed or elected generates ongoing debate. Election does overtly politicize the governance of basic education. By contrast, appointment could, but might not necessarily, result in a membership based on civic leadership and substantive knowledge of the field of education, in which case statesmanship could replace partisanship in state governance of the public schools.

In recognition of the good record of Kansas in basic education, Kansas could continue the present method of selection of State Board of Education membership by election. This option enhances local and area involvement in the state board by requiring election of members from across the state; it relies on a professional staff for expertise and keeps professionalism within the framework of responsibility to an elected board.

As an alternative, Kansas could consider appointing the membership of the State Board of Education, selection to occur in a manner consistent with the selection of members to other comparable state boards and commissions. This option has the potential for appointment based on expertise and civic leadership with concurrence by legislative approval, thereby assuring that elected representatives review the credentials of and approve appointees. Appointment would minimize the direct partisanship central to selection by election.

Finance of Elementary and Secondary Education

At the elementary and secondary level, four central conditions characterize educational finance in Kansas.

1. State aid to elementary and secondary education in Kansas increased from $306.6 million in 1976 to $681.3 million in 1984, an increase of 122.2 percent. In this period the state share of elementary and secondary finance grew from 40.9 to 45.1 percent, which reflects substantial state investment in elementary and secondary education, and implies that stability of such support forms the current critical financial issue, especially in view of the modest Kansas potential for increased tax revenue and shifts in other sources of revenue such as federal funding.
2. From 1976 to 1984, the percentage of school revenues from local funds in Kansas grew to 50.4 percent, a share higher than the United States as a whole. Kansas ranks lower in the percentage of revenues coming from local funds than do her sister states of Nebraska, Missouri, Colorado, and Iowa.
3. From 1976 to 1984, federal funds dropped 23.7 percent to only 4.6 percent of total school revenue. Current federal cutbacks, while they will affect elementary and secondary funding, should not be critical.

In Kansas, the state economy within the framework of the existing tax structure offers little immediate hope for new resources, given other competing interests at the state level. Because the funds needed involve matters of both local and state benefit, an approach to providing them should be sensitive to the broad effects that would accrue. For this reason, new, rather than existing, resources should be used to provide the funds that are necessary.

Because basic education serves the broadest citizenry, its support, if new revenues are desired, should come from a broadly based tax source. In that regard, a surcharge on the individual income tax could provide one source of new revenue. Moreover, such a device could be specified by local option, thereby allowing local initiative. If new sources are desired, however, their effects on the existing equalization program are important since such a policy could result in significant advantage for wealthier districts over districts economically less-well-off in the state. Finally, with the state already providing 45.1 percent of support, the issue of the extent of state support beyond this level requires consideration.

Given these concerns and constraints, Kansas could pursue several options in elementary and secondary school finance:

1. *Make no changes in current policy and retain the distribution of funds in accordance with the state equalization program, thereby requiring districts to absorb reductions within current funding formulae and ceilings.* This option would have the effect of requiring local districts to adjust to funding reductions and would probably inhibit efforts at new programs in the immediate future.

2. *Raise the level of state support from 45.1 percent to a ceiling of 50 percent, with no other changes in the state equalization program, allowing new revenues so derived to cover reductions to the extent possible.* This option would have the effect of placing a ceiling on state support within the state equalization program and providing state absorption of current cutbacks, but would require local responsibility for future reductions.

3. *Place a surcharge, to be determined by legislative action, on the individual income tax dedicated to support of basic education, proceeds to be collected by the state and distributed through the state equalization program to local districts.* This option would have the effect of using a broad tax for the benefit of basic education, but would require state initiative and responsibility for the levying, collection, and distribution of the tax and its revenues.

4. *Authorize a local-option surcharge to the individual income tax to provide revenues to cover reductions, proceeds to be distributed through the state equalization program as an increment to local districts.* This alternative would allow a broad-based tax to serve as the revenue source for funding reductions and other needs, requiring, however, that the state collect and disburse the revenues within the equalization formulae.

5. *Authorize a local-option surcharge to the individual income tax, whose revenues, if in excess of the equalization program allotment by more than a percentage to be designated by the legislature, would have such excess funds paid into the equalization program for redistribution to support new education programs or maintain quality programs.* This option would allow local determination of new revenues and their use in a manner designed not to undermine the intent of the state equalization program.

Finance of Community Colleges

At the community college level, the basic financial issues are these:

1. The local property tax provides the majority of support for community colleges in Kansas, a sum of $44.6 million in 1984, which comprised 59.4 percent of operating revenues, up from 50.1 percent in 1979.
2. Between 1979 and 1984, the state share of community college aid fell from 38.4 to 32.5 percent; the share composed of revenues from tuition declined from 9.3 to 6.3 percent; and the federal share dropped from 2.3 to 1.8 percent.
3. Stable sources of funding must be found that will compensate for reductions in these funding sources. A level of tuition must be set that is appropriate relative to other costs and to the need for improved services.

A funding approach should address the need for a coordinated, statewide program of vocational education, but also recognize that benefits accrue locally and regionally. Moreover, vocational and technical education, particularly given its job-training and career-specific effects, is of special benefit to the business sector. Given these interests, Kansas could consider the following options:

1. *Allow the ad valorem tax to remain the basic revenue source, with no changes in the manner or level of state support.* This option would require local and area absorption of federal reductions and possible increases in fees and would relieve the state of expanded responsibility.

2. *Shift financial responsibility to the state level, the amount to be determined by the legislature, to support lower-division academic, vocational, and technical instruction in community colleges, area vocational schools, and technical institutes and schools.* This option would provide additional state revenues for two-year academic, vocational, and technical education and assumes continuance of the ad valorem tax. Distribution of the added revenue is important, and should be fashioned in a way to assure that statewide needs for job-related training are efficiently met.

3. *Authorize local revenue options other than the property tax, including increased user fees, a business-activities tax, or other local sources.* Additional revenues would be paid as an increment to out-of-area payments already made. This option would allow local and area jurisdictions to provide additional funds for community colleges, area vocational schools, and vocational-technical schools; it also assumes continuance of the ad valorem tax and would leave to local units the manner of revenue distribution.

Finance of Higher Education

With regard to higher education, the following factors are central:

1. Kansas places a high value on education beyond high school, using 10.7 percent of tax revenues for public colleges and universities and thereby ranking sixteenth nationally on this factor.

2. Students in Kansas rank thirty-sixth nationally in dollars spent for tuition; the contribution of tuition to the revenues of public colleges and universities declined 11.2 percent in constant dollars from 1977 to 1984; and the ratio of dollars spent to personal disposable income indicates that Kansans could afford to pay more for tuition.

The basic financial issue facing Kansas is the need to maintain a high-quality system of higher education in the face of a decreasing number of high school graduates.

Kansas exceeds the national average with regard to its collective financial actions in support of public higher education. When tuition is compared to personal disposable income, however, Kansas ranks thirty-sixth among the fifty states, indicating that Kansans could afford to pay more tuition to improve higher education. Given the current status of financing higher education, Kansas could consider the following options:

1. *Make no change in the existing approach to financing higher education, leaving the Board of Regents to recommend levels of support and approaches required to absorb reductions in federal support.* This option would require program reductions in accord with regental policy as federal support diminishes; further, it would have significant impact on the research institutions, and serious educational and economic consequences on all institutions.

2. *Authorize the Board of Regents to increase tuition up to a ceiling of one-third of the cost of education at regental institutions, allowing this authority to be exercised annually as part of the state budgetary process.* This option would have the effect of requiring the regents to explain use of the ceiling authority within the budget-justification process and to do so for the purpose of cushioning federal or other reductions and for program improvements in the pursuit of quality. A tuition increase would allow new revenues without placing further burden on the state general revenues.

In summary, this report has considered governance and financial issues facing the three tiers of education in Kansas—basic education, postsecondary education, and higher education. While the issues discussed are not exhaustive, they include a number of significant concerns that Kansas faces. These are complex issues, and their place on the public agenda for education reflects the need for a careful review of them and of other, related issues not addressed here.

To facilitate that consideration, a series of options is offered here in an attempt to focus public discussion and to develop a coherent and statewide perspective on the financial and governance needs of each sector of Kansas education. These options call attention to the need for funding alternatives that will buffer impending federal cutbacks while allowing for new programs or activities essential to maintaining the quality of Kansas education and to address the needs of its changing demography and an economy in transition. These options underscore the need for better coordination, especially in postsecondary and higher education, and for the integrity of the postsecondary sector.

6   *MAURICE J. PENNER*

Better Health for Kansans

Good health is basic to human happiness: "If you have your health, you have everything." Americans value health. Eighty-one percent of the respondents to a 1981 Gallup poll found "good physical health" cited as very important; only "a good family life" scored higher at 82 percent.

To a large extent, health is a direct result of how we live. Well over half of today's health-care costs could be eliminated by preventive actions, such as changing high-risk lifestyles. Even healthy people have to pay—in added costs for health insurance, tax-supported medical services for the indigent, and productivity lost to death and disease.

This chapter examines five significant health problems for Kansas: lack of prenatal care, undetected health impairments in young children, teenage pregnancy, unhealthy adult behaviors leading to premature death and disability, and unnecessary placement in nursing homes. These problems are largely preventable and are analyzed in terms of incidence, severity, history, current policy in Kansas, and likely federal action. Policy choices selected on the basis of feasibility and likely success as preventive measures are then discussed in terms of potential impact, cost, and drawbacks. These choices do not exhaust the possibilities and are intended to promote discussion on potential solutions.

Health, Public and Personal Responsibility

At the beginning of this century, infections from the environment and inadequate nutrition caused the most serious and prevalent diseases. Since then, sanitation, water purification, immunizations, and improved diets have advanced America's health. Dr. S.J. Crumbine, executive secretary of the Kansas State Board of Health from 1904 to 1923, worked for many of these improvements. He reduced the spread of disease by prohibiting common drinking cups in all public buildings, trains, and soda fountains, and by banning roller towels from public washrooms. He successfully achieved passage of an antidumping law that improved the purity of Kansas' rivers and streams.[1]

Dr. Crumbine's work improved health. Further progress came with technological advances in the diagnosis and treatment of disease, in other words, "sickness care." However, half of these diseases could have been avoided by lifestyle decisions and better access to preventive health care.

The cost of sickness care has jumped dramatically since 1950. Nationally, actual expenditures on health care increased thirty times over from 1950 to 1984. Relative to economic growth, U.S. health expenditures have increased from 4.4 percent of gross national product in 1950 to 9.4 percent in 1984 (see Figure 6.1). In 1984, Kansans spent $3.1 billion, 9.5 percent of Kansas personal income, on health care, a figure which translates into $1,265 spent by every Kansas resident on health.

The reasons for cost increases include general price inflation, an aging and growing population, and increased use and intensity of medical technology. While inflation and population growth are not easily influenced, the use of medical technology may be reduced by preventive actions. Even small improvements through preventive work could substantially reduce public expenditures on sickness care, lower health-insurance costs, and augment the personal income of Kansans now being spent on treating preventable ills.

Today's major causes of death and disability have changed to chronic disease and automobile accidents. Both can be reduced by changes in lifestyle, such as ending tobacco use and wearing car safety belts.[2] However, these are personal decisions. Liberals and conservatives disagree about whether the state should seek to influence such behavior. To liberals, the evidence and potential benefits justify governmental incentives for healthy changes in behavior. While conservatives acknowledge the individual's responsibility and society's burden for these choices, several have argued for limiting government's role to education about the consequences from these behaviors.[3]

The young and the old face other difficulties. Infant deaths have not fallen as sharply in the U.S. and Kansas as in other industrialized nations, due largely to high rates of teenage pregnancy and lack of prenatal care. To worsen matters, the percentage of unmarried teenage mothers continues to increase, resulting in diminished opportunities for mother and increased child and governmental welfare expenditures. Again, the role for the state may be controversial. Actions to reduce teenage pregnancy may conflict with the wishes of some families to avoid discussion or action on sexual matters outside of the family. The failure to act, however, may result in perpetuating welfare dependency. Also, the children of teenage mothers more often suffer abuse or death than children of older mothers.[4]

The aged are living longer but require assistance in daily activities, especially in the last six years of life. In 1982, sixty-five-year-olds could expect two more years of life than their counterparts in 1960.[5] If friends or

Figure 6.1
National Health Expenditures, Total and Total as a Percentage
of Gross National Product, 1950-1984 (dollar amounts in billions)

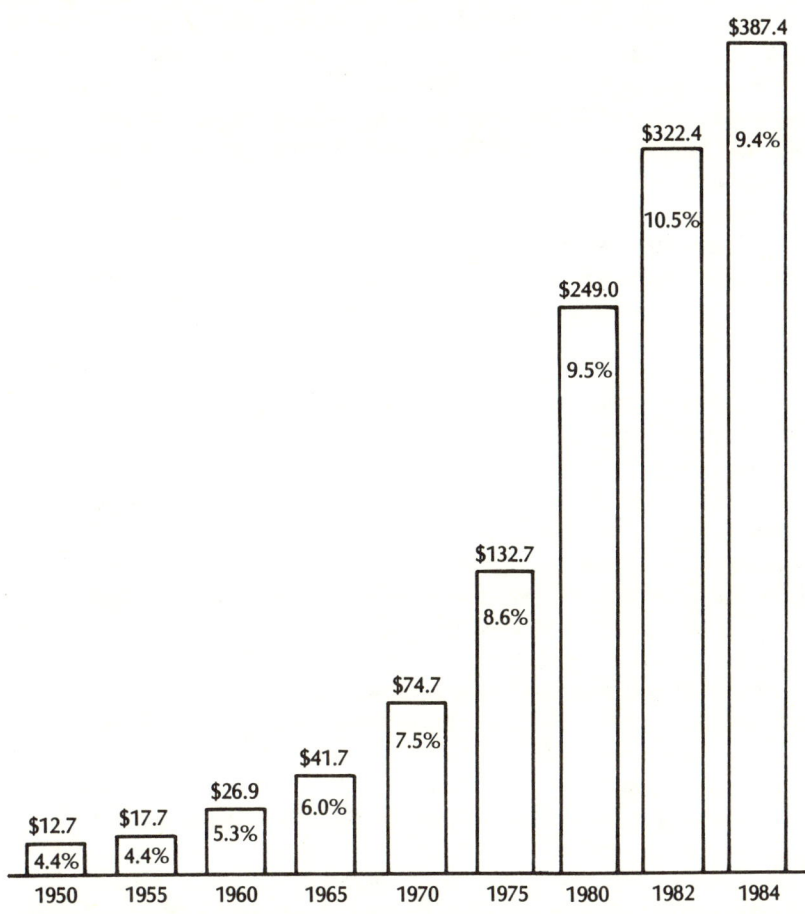

Source: Kansas Department of Health and Environment.

family members cannot provide this care, it must be purchased, obtained from publicly supported home-care programs, or provided in a nursing home. For twenty-five years, the number of Kansans of very advanced age has been increasing rapidly. The supply of free or low-cost home care has not kept pace with the demand, because of increased need and lack of public funding. Many elderly cannot afford home care and have no family nearby or able to supply all the needed help. Researchers have found that about one-fourth of all nursing-home placements could have been post-poned, if not prevented, had affordable home care been available.[6]

Nursing-home costs are staggering. Within six months of admission, most Kansas nursing-home residents have spent all their savings. Their bills are then paid through state and federal assistance (i.e., medicaid), which is costly for taxpayers and demeaning for the resident. In some cases, couples divorce to prevent one's cost for care from impoverishing the other. While medicaid provides home care for its frailest clients, many low-income persons are ineligible; later, they will qualify, after paying for a few months of care in a nursing home. Here the issue is whether the state should assume more financial responsibility for the home care of low-income persons. While medicaid costs for nursing homes can be reduced by increased state support for home care, overall governmental expenditures may increase, depending on how such programs are structured.

Prenatal Care

An infant's chance of being born healthy largely depends on adequate prenatal care. Infant mortality and low-birth-weight risk doubles where care is lacking, as often occurs for young or poor mothers. Low birth-weight is associated with infant death, mental retardation, health impairments, and extremely high costs for hospital care. For every low-birth-weight infant who dies, at least one other survives with a significant handicap. Increasing the number of mothers who receive adequate services during pregnancy would lead to better health outcomes and lower costs for hospital and institutional care.[7]

In 1983, 85 percent of Kansas newborns received adequate prenatal care, according to the Kansas Department of Health and Environment (see Map 6.1). Fifteen percent did not receive adequate care. The department measured adequacy from birth-certificate data regarding when care began, the number of prenatal care visits, and gestational age of the infant at birth (i.e., prematurity). Needed services include physician and nurse monitoring of maternal and fetal well-being, access to nutrition and social-work support when needed, and identification of maternal-risk factors on pregnancy outcome, such as substance abuse and cigarette smoking during pregnancy. First-time parents also need education on how to care for their babies.

Poverty and teenage pregnancy are frequently linked to inadequate care. In 1983, 34 percent of Kansas teenage mothers received inadequate care, double the rate for older mothers; one out of eight Kansas births is to a teenage mother.[8] Rates are similar for poor mothers.

The infant-mortality rate is another measure for adequacy of care. The Kansas infant-mortality rate has been steadily declining since 1920, when 71 out of 1,000 infants died before their first birthday. In 1973, Kansas had the fourth-lowest rate in the nation at 15.5 per 1,000; by 1984, infant deaths

Map 6.1
Percentage of Pregnant Women Receiving Adequate Prenatal Care in Kansas, 1983.

Percent Adequate Care

42.1 70.0 80.0 90.0 93.5

Source: Office of Information Systems and Computing,
Kansas Department of Health and Environment.

had fallen to 8.7 per 1,000. However, other states have improved even more, and Kansas now ranks eighth nationally. Despite this improvement, infant deaths are much more frequent among those not receiving adequate care. In 1983, there were 18.6 deaths per 1,000 for these underserved infants.[9]

Most of the decline in infant mortality is due to increased survival of low-birth-weight infants in neonatal intensive-care units. A baby weighing less than two-and-one-half pounds now survives more often, because of technological advances made in treatment for these infants. However, the incidence of low-birth-weight babies has fallen only slightly, and marked improvements in infant mortality and morbidity will not occur without additional declines.

Problems related to geographic location in the state also persist, especially in Southwest Kansas (see Map 6.1). Access to obstetrical care in rural and poverty areas has deteriorated with the soaring costs for malpractice insurance. Low medicaid reimbursement for physician prenatal care also contributes to this problem. Geary County in northeastern Kansas has the state's highest birth rate but has no physician who will accept medicaid patients for obstetrical care.

The Kansas Department of Health and Environment has estimated the state's costs for inadequate prenatal care at over $5 million for babies born in 1983.[10] This figure includes $3.25 million in preventable short-term hospitalization charges, often in high-cost neonatal intensive-care units. Medicaid clients comprise nearly one-sixth of the infants receiving this care, at a cost of $15,000 per case, and medicaid pays for nearly 200 of these cases each year. At least half are preventable through adequate care and compliance with doctor's orders.

Economic, educational, and social factors result in a lack of prenatal care. Young and poor mothers often lack insurance coverage and may not know about or qualify for medicaid or other public-health programs. Knowledge about the need for professional care, early in the pregnancy, is not widespread among this group. For social reasons, these mothers may engage in "denial" of the pregnancy, if unhappy about it; they also may feel uncomfortable in medical settings such as the doctor's office or public-health clinics. Many prenatal programs for the poor have employed outreach workers to convince pregnant girls and women to make needed visits.[11]

Assessment of Current Policy

Local health departments offer prenatal care, outreach services, counseling, advice on nutrition, and follow-up visits for high-risk pregnant women (young and low-income) and their children. In addition to federal funds that are matched by local health departments, the state will provide

$600,000 for these programs in 1986, up from $105,000 in prior years. Kansas also appropriated $854,000 in general aid to local health departments for 1986. The Kansas Department of Health and Environment has notified local health departments of a likely 13-percent reduction in federal funds for these programs in 1987, because of Gramm-Rudman budget-deficit measures.

Medicaid clients can receive prenatal care from a physician; however, some also receive counseling, nutritional education, and assistance from health-department programs. Those above medicaid income guidelines, those who are eligible but have not applied for medicaid or to health departments, and those without health-insurance coverage are not helped under existing policy.[12]

Pregnant women ineligible for government programs sometimes can obtain prenatal care at hospital-based clinics. The client's ability to pay determines the fee charged. A few Kansas hospitals, largely in urban areas, offer such services; the economic pressures of cost containment, increased competition, and malpractice-insurance increases may reduce the number of these clinics.

Kansas has no state policy requiring schools to refer pregnant students for prenatal care and counseling, nor to follow up and remind them to use these services. Also, Kansas has no requirement for education on the need for prenatal care. A few schools provide this information in family-life or parenting courses.

The medicaid program reimburses physicians up to $111 for prenatal care, an amount far below the customary charge. This payment will be doubled in 1986 and should increase physician acceptance of medicaid clients. In several areas of Kansas, no physician provides obstetrical services, due to sharp rises in malpractice insurance and difficulties in recruiting physicians to areas without hospitals or other physicians.

Medicaid refers its clients to physicians for prenatal services but does not monitor to see if needed visits are made or doctor's orders are followed. Of nearly 8,000 babies born each year to medicaid clients, one-third do not meet recommended guidelines on the number of physician visits, and 10 percent are of low birth-weight, compared to 6 percent for all Kansas births.[13]

Policy Choices

Increase State Financial Support for Prenatal Care. Kansas could choose a policy that no pregnant women be denied prenatal care for financial reasons. This policy would require additional state funding for physician services and local health department programs, which was increased $500,000 by the 1986 Kansas legislature. If the federal government cuts funds for these programs, more additional state funds would be needed to maintain services at current levels. Funding this expansion could be difficult given the limits of current revenues and competition with other state priorities.

In addition to expansion of these public programs, consideration should be given to the role of hospital-based and other private clinics that provide prenatal care and charge only what the mother can afford to pay. Public prenatal programs already serve the very low-income, notwithstanding federal cutbacks. Needed are low-cost services for those above medicaid income-eligibility limits and without private-insurance coverage.

Adopt Statewide School Policies for Pregnant Students. Kansas schools could be required to refer all pregnant students, as well as recent exstudents, for prenatal care and counseling and to follow up periodically and assure that care is sought and is being provided. Because of the wide variation in school-district health services, schools might need to work out arrangements with the public health department or other health organizations. In some cases, this requirement would add to costs for schools or health departments and generate requests for modest increases in state funding.

Kansas schools also could be required to offer information on the need for prenatal care and parenting education. Most health-education experts believe such a requirement is best made part of a comprehensive, coordinated health-education program, an issue discussed later in this chapter.

Expand Use of Nurse Practitioners and Physician Assistants. Prenatal-care services could be increased in rural areas through expanded use of nurse practitioners and physician assistants as professional caregivers in local health departments. Their malpractice insurance and salaries cost far less than do those of physicians. Research has demonstrated their effectiveness in providing prenatal care and in screening those needing immediate attention from a physician.[14] However, they, like physicians, might be difficult to recruit in rural areas.

Require Case Management for Pregnant Medicaid Clients. The Department of Social and Rehabilitation Services could be required to establish case-management procedures for all pregnant medicaid clients. A monitoring system could remind pregnant clients of the need for a prenatal visit, check to determine if an appointment is made and kept, and query clients on compliance with doctor's orders. This requirement would add to the costs of administering medicaid but might substantially reduce expenditures for neonatal intensive care and for hospitalization of low-birth-weight infants.

Medicaid could also pilot-test an incentive system for clients to make needed visits and comply with doctor's orders. A small cash bonus paid to clients for these desired behaviors might increase prenatal-care quality and reduce the incidence of low birth-weights among Kansas medicaid clients.

Child Health

Early-childhood health problems can interfere with a child's school performance if not detected and treated before learning and development are affected. For example, difficulty in seeing at near-point (hyperopia) will cause a child to fatigue easily from reading and perform poorly in school. Because the child unknowingly corrects for this dysfunction, neither child nor parent suspect a vision problem. Hyperopia may not be diagnosed unless the parent takes the child to an optometrist or ophthalmologist or the child attends a school that does comprehensive vision screening.

Before school age, children need to be assessed regularly for growth and development, vision, hearing, and other impairments. If health problems are not detected and treated, the child may begin school with an undetected handicap and leave before graduation. Evidence from two states that require preschool health examinations (California and Minnesota) shows that one-third to one-half of the school population have health impairments that were unknown prior to being uncovered in these examinations.[15] A five-city study of school-age children found 38 percent had not seen a doctor in the past year; and 26 percent did not have a family doctor.[16]

Health impairments of children are frequently not detected for a number of reasons. First, many parents do not see a need for preventive checks for seemingly healthy children. If parents visit their doctor only for suspected problems, preventive care for the child follows the same pattern. Also, preventive visits are usually not covered by insurance and require extra time and effort. Even with no cost to the parent, such as medicaid's early and periodic screening program for children, most parents do not take advantage of this free and heavily promoted service.[17]

As a child grows, healthful behaviors come under the child's control and are more subject to the influence of the school and peer group in addition to the family. Each child faces personal decisions concerning smoking, alcohol, drugs, seat-belt use, diet, stress, and exercise. A study of self-reported health behaviors by Kansas children offers insight into these decisions. Among thirteen- and fourteen-year-old boys, 19 percent regularly use tobacco, 16 percent use alcohol, and 56 percent do not eat enough fruits and vegetables.[18] One-third of U.S. children are overweight and, if present trends continue, one-half will have seriously elevated cholesterol levels when they reach middle age.

While health habits begin in childhood, they may be influenced by the school. For example, dental education on how and why to brush teeth has been shown to improve technique and frequency. A landmark study of the effectiveness of school health education found that comprehensive kindergarten through 12th grade (K-12) programs improve health knowledge and change health attitudes and behavior in desired directions. Of the seventh-graders in these K-12 programs, 7.7 percent were cigarette smokers versus

12.7 percent for those in a comparison group. Tobacco-use decisions are especially significant. Not only does tobacco use pose the single greatest risk for future adult health, tobacco decisions heavily influence future decisions about the use of drugs and alcohol.[19]

While educators agree on the importance of good health habits, they disagree on the time schools should spend on it. Classroom time spent for health education may conflict with time for music, art, history, and basic skills. Should it be the school's purpose to teach children to become healthy adults? Or should this function remain with the family and peer group, where healthful outcomes are somewhat less certain?

Assessment of Current Policy

Kansas requires school districts to offer free preschool health assessments to receive federal funds for special education. These assessments, known as "Count Your Kid In" health checks, must be publicized by the school district. Some districts offer these check-ups in one location, one time per year, and meet the minimum requirement. Others offer them throughout the district and school year; in addition, many will make assessments upon parental request.

Kansas requires proof of immunizations for school entrance but does not set other requirements for assessing the health of new students. Preschool examinations are required in half of Kansas' school districts and are sometimes offered during "kindergarten round-ups." However, 82 percent are performed by the family's doctor and at the parent's expense; school and public-health nurses assess the remainder in school districts that require health assessments.[20]

All Kansas schools must do vision and hearing screening at specified intervals. The quality of these tests varies, because methods are determined locally. For example, some districts test vision for nearsightedness but not for other problems. As a result, reading-related vision impairments may not be detected for several years, if at all. Hearing tests may not be performed in soundproof areas because of the acoustical condition of most schools. Undetected hearing problems can lead to educational and behavioral difficulties.

As of 1982, twenty-four states required that all students receive some health education, generally a nonelective course, prior to graduation.[21] Kansas does not have this requirement. As a result, important health matters are not discussed in some schools. For example, drug and alcohol education is one of the most popular areas in school health education; but a 1983 survey of Kansas schools found only 28 percent of the elementary schools had any type of educational program for substance abuse.

Kansas does require all schools to have "a program in health and hygiene." School programs vary considerably in comprehensiveness and in the proportion of students who benefit. A comprehensive program usually includes information on nutrition, disease control, dental health, alcohol, tobacco, and drug abuse, parenting and sex education, safety, first aid, mental health, and community health. Learning objectives that are part of a comprehensive plan are established for each grade. The Kansas Department of Education has prepared a model health curriculum as a guide for Kansas schools.

Regarding tobacco, Kansas has no state policy prohibiting its use by students on school premises. A Kansas Department of Health and Environment survey found some Kansas schools permit student use of tobacco at school. In Kansas, the purchase of tobacco by persons under age eighteen is illegal; however, vending-machine sales and weak enforcement have resulted in the availability of tobacco to minors.

Policy Choices

Increase the Number of Young Children Receiving Health Assessments. Kansas could increase the number of young children receiving health assessments. The state could require school districts to offer "Count Your Kid In" examinations several times during the year and in several locations or make these more accessible by informing parents that an assessment can be made by appointment at the parents' and school's convenience. This requirement would add to local school costs, but children would benefit from earlier detection and treatment for health impairments.

Health assessments also could be required for all new school entrants. Over half of Kansas' schools already have this requirement. The costs for this measure could be borne by parents who wished to pay the family doctor for a preventive visit; school nurses could assess remaining children. Where school nurses were unable to perform these checks, local health departments could assist. Because of the additional staff time required, schools and health departments would likely request state financial assistance to fulfill this mandate. Parents might have to pay for required assessments, where schools did not offer them. This proposal could include a waiver for those parents objecting on religious grounds.

Upgrade School Vision and Hearing Standards. The Kansas Department of Health and Environment has developed guidelines for vision screening in the schools. Similar guidelines are being discussed for hearing tests. Kansas could require all schools to follow these guidelines. This requirement would result in some districts' purchasing additional screening equipment, using central screening sites, and adding staff time for training and for performing these lengthier tests. The major benefit would be better educational performance by students whose vision and hearing impairments otherwise would have resulted in reading retardation and other learning and behavior problems.

Require K-12 Health Education in all Kansas Schools. Kansas could mandate health education, that is, require all schools to provide K-12 health education and to coordinate the different health programs now being offered, such as programs on drug and alcohol abuse, parenting, and nutrition. Another approach would be to test students on health knowledge at periodic intervals, as in the Kansas competency-based educational program. Michigan does testing for required health education. Such testing would give local school-district personnel and voters information on the health competency of their students but would not mandate health education for Kansas schools. Educators could focus on health matters of local concern; however, some districts might neglect sex education if it were not mandated. The major benefit of either a mandate or testing would be a renewed focus on health education that should result in better health outcomes. The major drawback would be competition between health and other subjects and the necessity for in-service health-education training for many teachers.

Prohibit Use of Tobacco in School Buildings. Kansas could prohibit use of tobacco in school buildings. This prohibition would cause adjustment problems for teachers, students, and staff and require staff time to enforce the ban. The major benefits would be bringing school policies into conformance with existing law and discouraging this risk behavior.

Teenage Pregnancy

Teenage pregnancy is both a health problem and a social problem. Not only are teens socially unprepared to assume the responsibilities of parenthood, they are far less likely to receive adequate prenatal care, a situation which has severe consequences for the infant. Teen mothers are usually unmarried, and those who are married experience marriages three times less stable than those of older brides, largely because 80 percent of these marriages were motivated by pregnancy. Early motherhood also results in more children. The public pays for the consequences of teen motherhood in the form of increased expenditures for aid to dependent children and medicaid programs, reduced tax revenues from lowered lifetime earnings, and social costs, because these children are far more likely to be abused and institutionalized. An Urban Institute study estimated that one-fourth of U.S. welfare expenditures, five years from now, could be eliminated if teenage pregnancies were cut in half.[22] U.S. taxpayers spend $8.6 billion to support teen mothers and their children.

More than 1 million teenage pregnancies occur in the U.S. each year. Fifty percent of teen girls are sexually active; four of every ten fourteen-year-old girls will become pregnant before they turn twenty. Having a baby before age eighteen reduces the mother's chance of graduating from high school by one-half and results in lowered job opportunities and earnings.

During 1983 in Kansas, 7,000 known pregnancies resulted in 5,015 births. Teenagers have a third of Kansas abortions. Forty-two percent of

Kansas teen mothers were unmarried, up from 23 percent in 1970. One of every eight Kansas births is to a teenage mother, double the rate for most industrialized nations and higher than the U.S. average. One-third of Kansas' teenage mothers do not receive adequate prenatal care, a situation that triples the chance for death or disability.[23]

Teenage mothers are frequently daughters of teenage mothers; this role-modeling has been cited as a major cause for the incidence of teen motherhood. Studies have found that about half of teen pregnancies may be intended by the mothers—to produce their own object of affection, to cement a deteriorating relationship, and to show they are grown-up and should be treated like adults.

Other reasons include earlier and higher rates of teen sexual activity and lack of contraceptive use and knowledge. A Kansas study explains the causes of teenage pregnancy as follows:

> Physical Changes. Teens are experiencing a growth spurt second only to infancy. Puberty commences making them very aware of their bodily changes as well as causing them to feel helpless and vulnerable. At this time, girls have a very fragile self-esteem.
> Emotional Changes. The teenager is striving for emotional autonomy.
> Intellectual Changes. Teens are concrete rather than abstract thinkers. They do not plan ahead or think of the consequences of their actions.
> Vulnerability. Teens suffer from two forms of egocentricity: 1) they want to be like everyone else, 2) they have their own personal fable: 'I am invincible, I am immune, I cannot get pregnant.'[24]

The entertainment media contributes to the increase in teen sexual activity. Television viewers see as many as 9,000 scenes of suggested sexual intercourse and sexual innuendo each year. The consequences are seldom discussed by the media; nor is information provided on where to obtain contraceptives or counseling. A majority of Kansas schools avoid the issue. A 1986 survey of Kansas schools found that less than half offer any program in sex education even though school principals do see a need for concerted school action.

European teens are similar to U.S. teens in sexual activity; however, their pregnancy and abortion rates are far lower because they learn where to obtain family planning and to discuss the importance of contraception, personal responsibility, and sexuality.[25] Studies on the effectiveness of sex education report that information alone does not result in reducing teen sexual activity or pregnancy. However, school programs that increase the availability of contraceptives have reduced teen pregnancy rates by as much as 40 percent. Access can be increased in several ways, such as informing students where contraceptives can be obtained or dispensing contraceptives at school-based adolescent health clinics. The latter approach is effective even where parental consent is required.

Public opinion favors increased sex education and contraceptive availability for teens, according to a 1986 Gallup Poll; however, several groups have fought these measures, citing them as sanctions for teenage sex. They believe that advertising the availability of contraceptives gives teenagers a double message: "Teen sex is wrong, but here's where you go to avoid the consequences." However, researchers have never found that sex education or contraceptive availability leads to increases in teen sexual activity.[26]

Assessment of Current Policy

The federal assistance Kansas receives for family planning requires that these services be made available regardless of the client's age. The Reagan administration has attempted to mandate that parents be notified when minor children seek these services. Critics of this proposal state that parental notification requirements would have a chilling effect; as many as one-fourth of those teens now receiving contraceptives would not seek them if their parents were informed. In Kansas, the state's two most-populous counties prohibit their health departments from dispensing contraceptives to minors without parental approval. Fear of liability suits from parents has been cited as one reason for this policy. Since federal regulations prohibit such age discrimination in federally-funded family planning programs, Kansas has allocated some of its federal funds to private organizations that do not discriminate on the basis of age.

Teenage parents must take legal responsibility for their offspring under Kansas law but often cannot provide financial support for their children. The state's child-support program attempts to collect support from all fathers, but, because teen fathers rarely have regular wages or attachable assets, collection efforts seldom succeed while the fathers are teenagers. Later, the father may be required to pay support, but follow-through seldom occurs without the active intervention of the mother.

Parents of teen parents are not responsible for grandchild support under Kansas law; however, the teen mother's parents often provide support and shelter. In 1985, Wisconsin enacted a law requiring parents of teen parents to take financial responsibility for their grandchildren, until their children reach age eighteen and assume this obligation.[27] This measure should increase the amount of financial support from the father's parents and provide continuity for the teen father to eventually assume this support.

Kansas has no policy that attempts to counteract media influence regarding the encouragement of sexual activity. Several states, for example Michigan, New York, and Wisconsin, have recently begun media campaigns that explain the consequences of teenage sex, as well as the need for and availability of family-planning services. Several states also require sex education in the schools. Kansas has no policy requiring sex education, and most schools do not offer it.

Federal regulations require that the aid-to-dependent-children program offer family planning services to all clients. About 10 percent of female clients aged 15-30, a group that has a high pregnancy rate, use these services. Federal funds pay for 90 percent of the costs for these services.[28]

Policy Choices

Require Grandparent Support for Children of Minors. Kansas could require that parents be held legally responsible for the financial support of their minor children's children, and then transfer legal responsibility to their children when those children reach age eighteen. This measure would give parents financial incentives for more closely monitoring their children's behavior and would shift public financial support and mother's parents' child-support costs to all responsible parties. The drawbacks would include the lack of an impact on poor parents, such as welfare clients, who have no attachable income or assets, and the difficulty many parents experience in achieving effective control over their teenagers. Parents caught in these circumstances would view this law as unfair.

Counteract Media Romanticization of Teen Sex. Kansas could mount a media campaign to counteract the media's romanticization of teenage sex. Such a campaign could draw attention to the consequences of teenage sex, such as pregnancy, sexual diseases, cervical cancer, and the emotional and financial responsibilities of parenthood that often lead to child abuse, and could provide information about where to obtain counseling and family-planning services. The costs for this campaign could be funded through increased taxes on the entertainment media, such as cable television and rental and sale of videotapes. The benefits would be unknown, because similar programs have not yet been evaluated; however, if these messages increased teen knowledge on the availability of contraceptives, this effort likely would reduce teen pregnancy.

Require Sex Education in Kansas Schools. Kansas schools could be required to provide sex education as part of comprehensive health education. The benefits and drawbacks of a K-12 health-education requirement have been discussed above. A sex-education mandate would ensure provision to teens of needed information and would probably reduce teen pregnancies if knowledge of contraceptive availability were enhanced by these programs. The drawback would be that some parents would object to such programs as an intrusion on the family's authority.

Increase Awareness of Family Planning for Teens on Welfare. The Department of Social and Rehabilitation Services could be required to counsel teens currently on welfare or in state custody about family-planning needs. This measure would add to the agency's administrative costs; but savings

would offset costs if those counseled and referred for family planning sub-
sequently had fewer teenage pregnancies. Consideration should also be
given to pilot-testing the use of cash awards for those teenage females on
welfare who do not become pregnant. Since most teens on welfare are
children of teenage mothers, the offer of a strong incentive would be needed
to overcome the effects of role modeling on this high-risk group. Experi-
mentation with amount and frequency of awards would determine if this
option were cost effective. Counseling and career planning should also be
offered to explain the benefits of postponing pregnancy. However, some
would object to paying persons for behavior that should occur for moral,
rather than financial, reasons.

High-Risk Adult Behavior

Unhealthy behavior or lifestyle contribute to one-half of the deaths in
the U.S. Heart disease, cancer, stroke, and accidents account for 76 percent
of U.S. deaths.[29] In 1981, 66 percent of all Kansas deaths were from the
first three in this list.[30] Smoking, considered to be the most damaging lifestyle choice, is implicated in 75 percent of all lung cancers as well as other
cancers, heart disease, emphysema, retarded fetal growth, infant mortality,
spontaneous abortions, and other health problems. The real costs for smoking include added health-care expenditures, absenteeism, and lost productivity from illness and death, costs estimated to exceed $27 billion in the
U.S. each year. Because 30 percent of Kansas men and 20 percent of the
women smoke, the cost for Kansans exceeds $250 million a year.

Other unhealthy adult behaviors include drug and alcohol abuse, poor
dietary habits, lack of exercise, nonuse of seat belts, and poor stress management.[31] A 1977 Kansas survey estimates the state has 142,000 problem
drinkers. A national study found 10 percent of adults were moderately
overweight, and another 12 percent were obese. Two-thirds of U.S. adults
have no regular exercise program. Poor diet and lack of exercise increase
the risk of heart disease, hypertension, diabetes, and stroke. As much as
one month of life is lost for each pound an individual weighs that is ten
pounds over ideal weight. Fewer than 15 percent of Americans regularly
use seat belts, except in states with mandatory seat-belt laws, where 40 to
50 percent regularly "buckle-up." Nonuse of seat belts doubles the risk of
death.

The recent focus on individual responsibility for health began with a
1974 Canadian government report, "A New Perspective on the Health of
Canadians." The report discussed the major causes of death (which are
essentially the same in the U.S. and Canada) and identified the underlying
causes as lifestyle decisions. Official reaction took the form of reports and
legislation in Great Britain, Sweden, and the U.S. In 1976, Congress passed
the National Health Information and Health Promotion Act. The Secretary

of Health and Human Services was empowered to "undertake and support necessary activities and programs...to increase the application and use of health knowledge, skills, and practices by the general population in its pattern of daily living."[32]

In 1979, Kansas developed its own health-promotion program, Project PLUS (program to lower utilization of services), which was designed to be implemented by business and industry. The program assists businesses in setting up programs at the work site. This approach was considered promising, since most adults work and can be reached through the work place. Employers were likely to save health-care and production costs, enabling them to offer health promotion to employees. Studies on these programs find some evidence for employer-cost savings, often exceeding employers' costs for health promotion. However, since few studies use experimental designs, they are not conclusive. Of additional interest is whether work-site programs can increase the proportion of adults who change their behavior in healthful ways. A recent study on Johnson and Johnson employees found work-site programs increased the percentage who regularly exercise from 7 percent to 20 percent for women, and 19 percent to 30 percent for men.

Over the past decade, many employers, especially large employers, have added health promotion as an employee benefit. A 1983 study of large Kansas City-area firms found two-thirds had at least one type of health-promotion component.[33] Services can include health assessment, risk appraisal, counseling, exercise, smoking cessation, alcohol and drug abuse treatment, and hypertension screening and treatment. While large employers frequently offer health promotion, small ones generally do not, because of high start-up costs and lack of facilities and space.

Assessment of Current Policy

One mechanism for promoting healthy behavior is health-insurance incentives, such as a discount for nonsmoking. In Kansas, nonsmokers can receive discounts for home, auto, and life insurance, and in a few individual health policies. Most health insurance, however, is obtained through employer groups, and Kansas group health policies do not currently have a nonsmoker discount. Such discounts are offered in Blue Cross/Blue Shield plans in the states of Idaho, Minnesota, Oregon, and Virginia. A Health Insurance Association of America study found 20 percent of the responding companies offered nonsmoker discounts with cost savings of 6 to 10 percent.[34] Kansas Blue Cross/Blue Shield has been asked to offer these discounts in the state-employees health insurance plan but has declined, citing as its reason the fear that employees would lie about their smoking in order to receive the discount. Since insurance companies use the number of smokers in estimating the plan's payments for medical care and premiums for this coverage, underestimating the number of smokers could result in a loss for the insurance company.

The state's health-promotion program, Project PLUS, provides assistance to businesses who wish to establish health programs at the work site. The necessary professional personnel are provided through the Kansas Department of Health and Environment. Due to the geographic difficulties of operating a statewide program from Topeka, departmental staff also have trained local health-department workers in how to plan and implement work-site programs. However, local health departments are largely funded through property taxes, which have not kept pace with inflation; and their federal and state funds must be dedicated to specific programs. As a result, local health departments do not have staff to devote to health promotion. Cutbacks of 13 percent in federal funds for local health will worsen this situation.

In 1986, the Kansas legislature enacted a mandatory seat-belt law. Twenty-two states have similar laws; front-seat occupants must be "buckled-up" or face a fine. In spite of widespread nonuse of seat belts, many car occupants will obey a seat-belt law. In states with this law, compliance averages 50 percent, versus 10 to 15 percent in other states.

Policy Choices

Increase the Use of Nonsmoker Discounts. Kansas could increase the availability of nonsmoker discounts in group health plans by requiring health insurance companies to offer this feature to employers. This measure would allow employers to decide, as they usually pay for much, if not all, of the premium. Hopefully, most employers would decide to offer the discounts and require smoking employees to pay more for their health insurance than nonsmokers. Not only would smoking be further discouraged, nonsmokers and the employer would no longer be subsidizing additional health costs for smoking workers. The discount would encourage some smokers to quit; however, most would not find the additional insurance costs great enough to dissuade them, as evidenced from the effects of increased tobacco taxes on cigarette consumption. A few employees would lie about tobacco use in order to receive the discount, but they might be too few to affect projected benefit payments; moreover, those who hide their smoking might also smoke less than before.

Provide Financial Assistance for Health Promotion at Work Sites. Kansas could provide financial assistance to local health departments offering health-promotion programs to small employers. School and senior-citizen programs also could be included, since health promotion has been shown to benefit the old as well as the young. Services could include health assessment and risk-factor appraisal, shared use of community and school exercise facilities, and drug and alcohol treatment. Funding the costs for these efforts would be difficult given current economic projections for Kansas and planned federal cutbacks. An alternative approach would be to provide tax incentives to employers offering health promotion, although targeting these for small employers might be difficult.

Unnecessary Placement in Nursing Homes

Hardly anyone wants to be confined in a nursing home, with the consequent loss of independence, privacy, and home life. Nursing-home placement occurs when activities of daily living, such as dressing, washing, and eating, cannot be performed without help and when this aid is not practical, available, or affordable at home. The elderly are especially affected, and over one in eight needs some help to manage in the home. This proportion increases to one in four for those over age 75, and to one in two for those over age 85. Their needs for home care are often not covered by medicaid, medicare, or private insurance.[35]

Almost 150,000 Kansans are over age 75, and this segment has been growing rapidly. Between 1960 and 1980, the size of this age group increased 47 percent compared to 8.5 percent for the total state population. This age group is at greater risk of having to go to a nursing home because of failing health; also, one-third reside alone and frequently are poor.

Although care at home is generally provided by family or friends, family may not always reside nearby or have time to provide all the needed help. However, contrary to popular myth, families provide the overwhelming amount of home care for the elderly; they seek out nursing homes for their loved ones only when care becomes an insurmountable problem, such as with a bedfast and incontinent person.

Studies find 10 to 40 percent of new nursing-home residents could have postponed, if not prevented, placement had affordable home care been available or known about. These services include home health care, personal care, housekeeping, home-delivered meals, grocery shopping, transportation for medical treatment, and other aids. Home-care services are generally available in Kansas cities, but they may not be affordable for those not on medicaid. In rural areas, a few of these services can be purchased, and availability has been improving as a result of early hospital discharges. Medicare's prospective-reimbursement system pays hospitals a flat rate for each case; hospitals thus are encouraged to provide home health and personal care so that patients can convalesce at home. Additionally, many elderly persons and their caregivers do not know about home-care services; they believe there is no alternative to a nursing home.[36]

Home-care services are provided by family, friends, volunteers, private individuals and businesses, and by publicly subsidized programs. Medicare will pay for home health and personal care, if there is a documented need for skilled nursing in the home, not just help in bathing and dressing. Medicaid in Kansas provides many home aids for its clients, if they are found to be at immediate risk for nursing-home placement and meet income guidelines; single persons must receive less than $400 in income per month. Federal regulations require that medicaid home assistance cost less than an intermediate-care nursing home, which is about $30 per day.

The Kansas Department of Social and Rehabilitation Services provides housekeeping assistance for those in need and without a caregiver at home. The income guidelines are less stringent than for medicaid, but there are waiting lists throughout the state. Area agencies on aging administer several home-care programs, including home-delivered meals, transportation for medical treatment, and home health, homemaker, and personal care. Again, there are waiting lists for almost all services. Funding for these services comes from federal and state funds that are administered by the Kansas Department of Aging; additionally, sixty-five counties also have property-tax levies for aging that are frequently used for home care.

The lack of affordable home care can result in overuse of nursing homes. In the fall of 1985, 21,516 Kansans over age sixty-five, 6.9 percent of this age group, resided in nursing homes.[37] This percentage is significantly higher than the national average of 5 percent and may reflect the lack of affordable home care. A report from St. John's Hospital of Leavenworth, Kansas, supports this theory. Their social-services department reviewed the records for the 131 patients who were discharged to nursing homes between 1983 and 1985. Fifty percent were judged able to have returned home "with some extra assistance with personal care and homemaking." Because medicare's prospective-reimbursement system financially rewards hospitals that shorten stays to periods for needed acute care, some of these persons "would not have required long term support but rather needed a longer recuperation period than was allowed by Medicare."[38] Massachusetts, New York, and Pennsylvania, which have extensively subsidized home care for low-income persons, have 4.7 to 6.1 percent of their elderly in nursing homes.[39]

Assessment of Current Policy

Kansas requires that all medicaid admissions to nursing homes be reviewed before placement in a care home. These reviews can be obtained for persons not assisted by medicaid; however, few have been requested. Most Kansans do not enter nursing homes as medicaid clients; however, they become clients after exhausting their assets to pay for nursing-home care, generally within six months. Half of Kansas nursing-home residents have their care paid for by medicaid and constitute the single largest expense for medicaid in Kansas.

No state policy guarantees home care to those without caregivers or ineligible for medicaid's home-care program. Federal, state, and county funds are used for home care; however, these have not been sufficient to meet demand. A planned reduction of 25 percent in federal funds will further reduce the supply of subsidized home assistance. County-funded home assistance increasingly requires client payments, based on income. Federal regulations under the Older Americans Act forbid this practice in their programs; similarly, income-eligibility limits cannot be set in these programs.

Home and nursing-home care are rarely covered by private insurance. However, a new insurance product does reimburse for some of this care. Long-term-care insurance plans are now being reviewed by the Kansas Insurance Department for marketing in the state. The plans have limits on coverage, such as a deductible, copayments, excluded diseases, and maximum payouts. Senior-citizen organizations are also planning to sell policies to their members. The features and exclusions are confusing and require explanation. Widespread use of long-term-care insurance could benefit individuals and government. Because only one in four sixty-five-year-olds will ever reside in a nursing home, insurance allows the aged to share the risk for this catastrophic event and reduces future medicaid costs. However, policies with too many restrictions will give the elderly false assurance about being protected from catastrophic nursing-home costs.

Volunteers care for elderly Kansans and will be increasingly needed as the state's population ages. Several state agencies use federal and state resources to establish, train, and maintain volunteers. Recruitment and training require staff time, additional transportation expense, and other costs, but resources are severely limited due to fiscal constraints on federal and state governments.

Policy Choices

Require Preadmission Screening for Nursing-Home Placement. Kansas could require preadmission screening and a discussion of home-care options before a patient consented to placement in a nursing home. Learning about home-care alternatives should result in postponement and prevention of some nursing-home stays. This measure should not block admission for those wanting it, nor delay it in cases where immediate care is clearly needed. The costs for screening would average $30 to $50 per admission and could be borne by the individual or the state. Some persons would not like this additional requirement and might fear screening could block admission, even if told otherwise. If screenings were performed by nursing homes or providers of home-care services, there would be potential conflicts of interest regarding recommendations for community or nursing-home care.

Increase State Financial Support for Home Care. Kansas could increase state financial support for those unable to purchase needed care. The Kansas Department on Aging has proposed providing aid to local home-care programs that charge clients based on their ability to pay. Program costs and savings in nursing-home care would depend on how home-care programs were structured. Programs that limited subsidies to those who requested admission to a nursing home would result in an overall reduction in governmental costs, largely in medicaid savings for nursing-home care. Here, no money would be spent on home care unless it appeared to result in postponement of institutionalization. However, persons needing but unable to afford home care would not receive help, until they applied to be admitted to a nursing home.

A more generous but costly policy would be to combine the previous approach with additional state support for home-care services that charge clients based on ability to pay. Medicaid savings from the previous approach could be used in part to fund this effort. The most generous approach would be an entitlement to home care, with client charges based on income, such as in Massachusetts. Massachusetts has two-and-a-half times Kansas' elderly population, and this program cost $90 million in 1985.

Another approach would be to aid caregivers with a state tax credit. The credit could pay for home care while the caregiver is at work and be a small reimbursement for their time and effort. However, a tax credit would not help those without caregivers, who are at greatest risk for premature placement in care homes.

Require the Insurance Department to Offer Forums on Long-Term-Care Insurance. Kansas could increase public awareness and information about the availability of long-term-care insurance by requiring the Insurance Department to hold public forums on this subject. Because these insurance plans are complex, objective, consumer-oriented information is needed to help the elderly make informed decisions. An alternative, which was under consideration by the 1986 Kansas legislature, would be to require all medicare supplement policies to cover community and some nursing-home costs. The major benefit of this proposal would be to provide far more coverage for the majority of elderly that purchase supplemental medicare insurance and thereby sharply reduce medicaid costs. However, additional premium costs would reduce the use of medicare supplements, which cover most medical care not reimbursed by medicare.

Increase the Use of Volunteer and Low-Cost Caregivers. Kansas could use more resources to increase the number of volunteer and "low-cost" caregivers. Funding could be provided for area agencies on aging to set up "volunteer banks." Here, volunteers "earn" future hours of home care for themselves or their families with a record kept of their savings. The state could pay low-income, able-bodied elderly to care for those at risk for institutionalization; a federal law allows these persons to be paid two-thirds of the minimum wage without counting this income against social security and food stamps. Kansas could expand its employment exchanges for seniors wanting to provide home care for others; often, they charge less than younger workers. School programs could also focus on providing volunteers for snow-shoveling and other chores.

A variety of approaches could be tried. All options attempt to increase the quantity of volunteer or low-cost providers, make alternatives to nursing-home care more attractive, and reduce demand for tax-supported home-care programs. However, increased volunteerism would not eliminate the need for additional public resources. Also, more nursing-home beds will be needed to keep pace with increases in the number of aged persons.

Conclusion

Poverty presents a significant obstacle to preventive health care. Low-income persons cannot afford preventive care and often do not understand its value. They concentrate on the present. Lack of hope and low self-esteem combine to devalue the future and the worth of preventive actions. Eliminating poverty would improve health; however, the policy choices discussed in this report were selected for their direct and likely impact on health, rather than for their effectiveness in reducing poverty. Because poor health contributes to poverty, preventing health problems may also help to reduce poverty.

This study recommends many options for improving the health of Kansans. Approaches include new requirements for individuals and institutions, incentives for healthy behavior, and additional state-funded services. Options were selected based on feasibility and likely success. However, they are intended to foster discussion on the prevention of health problems, not to be an exhaustive list of alternatives.

Kansas state government can exercise leadership in preventing certain health problems from occurring and thereby may improve the health of its citizens.

Notes

Introduction

1. Quoted in Kenneth S. Davis, *Kansas* (New York: W.W. Norton, 1976), 170-71.
2. Ibid., 171.
3. Neal R. Peirce and Jerry Hagstrom, *The Book of America* (New York: W.W. Norton, 1983), 585-601.
4. Ibid., 585.
5. U.S. Advisory Commission on Intergovernmental Relations, *Significant Features of Federalism, 1985-86 Edition* (Washington, D.C., February 1986), 19.
6. Ibid.
7. Ibid.

Chapter 1 The Kansas Economy

1. For a more detailed, earlier review of this subject, see Anthony Redwood, Daniel L. Petree, and Gary R. Albrecht, "Long-Term Structural Changes in the Kansas Economy," *Kansas Business Review* 8 (Winter 1984-85):1-9.
2. This section is based on Richard Sexton and John Cita, "The Changing Structure of the Kansas Farm," *Kansas Business Review* 5 (July-August 1982):1-12.
3. This section draws from Richard Sexton and Robert Glass, "Instability in the Kansas Economy," *Kansas Business Review* 6 (March, April-May, June 1983):1-12.
4. Ibid., 1.
5. Shift-share analysis is used to make these estimates of Kansas employment by industry. The methodology for this analysis may be found in Redwood, Petree, and Albrecht.
6. *Impact of Declining Crude Oil Prices on Stripper Oil Wells, Production and Reserves* (Oklahoma City: RAM Group, 1986).
7. David Collins and Colleen Eck, "Economic Aspects of Oil Exploration in Kansas," *Kansas Business Review* 7 (Spring 1984):6.
8. Daniel W. Francke, "Assessing Kansas' Latent Labor Force," *Kansas Business Review* 4 (May 1981):1-6.

194 Kansas Policy Choices

Chapter 2 Economic Prospects for Rural Communities

1. The definition of urban and rural areas used throughout this chapter is as follows: The urban areas in Kansas are the four standard metropolitan statistical areas (SMSAs): Kansas City (Wyandotte, Johnson, Miami, and Leavenworth counties), Wichita (Sedgwick and Butler counties), Topeka (Shawnee County), and Lawrence (Douglas County). Rural areas comprise the balance of the state.

2. Damodar Gujarti, *Government and Business* (New York: McGraw-Hill, 1984), 254.

3. Thomas G. Moore, "Rail and Truck Reform—The Evidence So Far," *Regulation* (November/December 1983):33-41.

4. Unpublished statistics on common carriers maintained by Transportation Division, Kansas Corporation Commission.

5. Data provided by the Transportation Division, Kansas Corporation Commission.

6. Keith Klindworth, Orlo Sorenson, Michael Babcock, and Ming Chow, *Impacts of Rail Deregulation on Marketing of Kansas Wheat* (Washington, D.C.: U.S. Department of Agriculture, Office of Transportation, September 1985).

7. Dodge City, Garden City, Goodland, Great Bend, Hays, Hutchinson, Manhattan, Newton, Pittsburg, Salina, and Wichita.

8. Senator Charles D. Cook, *Business Economic Development and Employment in Rural New York State: An Action Strategy* (Albany: New York State Legislative Commission on Resources, October 10, 1985).

9. One exception is that authority to regulate rails would be turned over to the Departments of Transportation and Justice. See "Washington and the Utilities," *Public Utilities Fortnightly* (March 6, 1986):37.

10. Roger D. Blair, David L. Kaserman, and James T. McClave, "Motor Carrier Deregulation: The Florida Experiment," *Review of Economics and Statistics* 67 (February 1986):159-64.

11. Phillip R. O'Connor, as quoted in *Wall Street Journal,* 26 February 1986.

Chapter 3 State and Local Finance

1. At the federal level, the term "iron triangle" is often used to describe the relationship between an agency, the relevant interest groups, and the appropriations subcommittee handling the agency appropriation.

2. The U.S. Bureau of the Census, Governments Division, collects and publishes government finance data on a uniform basis. General revenue and general expenditure exclude revenues and expenditures of state liquor stores, utilities, and pension funds. Because the Census Bureau aggregates data from many funds of many units of government, it is often difficult to reconcile their data with state and local financial reports. Data are reported on a fiscal-year basis, which differs from unit to unit. The Kansas state government fiscal year begins on July 1, but the fiscal year for local units is the calendar year.

3. The CPI is an index showing the cost of a fixed "market basket" of goods and services that a typical urban family would purchase. The U.S. Department of Commerce computes the price deflator for government purchases—state and local fixed-weight index (hereafter referred to as government purchases deflator) as part of the national income accounts. No price index or deflator perfectly represents all price changes.

4. Direct expenditure is expenditure made directly for programs. Intergovernmental grants are not included as expenditure of the granting government but are included when spent for programs by the grantee government. Kansas has almost completely centralized welfare expenditure, as have two other states. By contrast, highway expenditure is less centralized in Kansas than in any of the comparison states or in the U.S. as a whole.

5. The income elasticity of a tax is a measure of the relationship between changes in personal income and changes in tax collections. Tax yields, even from taxes such as the general sales tax, which is not based directly upon income, usually change in a predictable way as income changes. This relationship commonly is expressed as an index of elasticity, which is computed by dividing the percentage change in the yield of the tax by the percentage change in personal income. The result indicates the percentage change in tax yield that can be expected from a change of 1 percent in personal income. An elasticity of one indicates that a change in state personal income will result in the same percentage change in the yield of the tax, assuming that rates remain unchanged.

The income elasticities of a particular kind of tax vary from time to time and from state to state, because of changes in economic circumstances and differences in the tax laws. As is known, however, income taxes with a graduated rate schedule have elasticities well above one. General sales taxes normally have elasticities somewhat below one. Specific sales taxes imposed on the sale of units of a product, such as packs of cigarettes or gallons of beverage, have elasticities well below one, especially in inflationary periods.

6. There are at least two exceptions to this statement. First, a few levies in Kansas are established by rate in mills. Second, limits imposed on the levies of some funds are also expressed in mills.

7. This reluctance has been powerfully reenforced by the tax lid law of 1970 and by ample evidence that the property tax is unpopular both within the state and nationally.

8. The U.S. Department of Commerce has recently projected that Kansas real economic growth to the year 2000 will average 2.5 percent per year. If we assume an inflation rate of 4 percent, this assumption would be consistent with a current dollar growth of 6.5 percent.

9. "Present level of expenditure" is defined to be present expenditures as a percentage of personal income.

10. Many of the obvious or "easy" sources of current charge income likely have been utilized. Imposing fees and charges for public school education, drastic increase in tuition at the institutions of higher education, or expansion of the use of toll roads could be major sources of revenue, but each would represent a major shift in traditional philosophy and public policy.

11. Average annual percentage changes for revenues and personal income were computed by fitting a log trend line to the data. Daicoff estimates are from unpublished material prepared for the Kansas concensus revenue estimating group.

12. Steven D. Gold, "State Tax Policy: How It Has Changed—Where Is It Headed," preliminary background paper for a Seminar on the Future of State Tax Policy, Seattle, August 4, 1985.

13. This assumption is based on a rate elasticity of one. In other words, the higher sales tax will not decrease sales in the state.

14. The exact date of reappraisal varied from county to county.

15. Personal property as defined for tax purposes in Kansas includes oil and gas operating properties. This property traditionally has been assessed by a for-

mula that uses a "decline curve" to estimate the remaining oil or gas. Just how closely local appraisers have followed the Division of Property Valuation guidelines regarding appraisal of personal property is difficult to know, but a number of instances of taxpayer protest have been triggered by local efforts to do so.

16. The statewide average rate was computed by dividing total tax levies by total assessed values.

17. For a complete description of the bases and the methodology used see U.S. Advisory Commission on Intergovernmental Relations, *1983 Tax Capacity of the Fifty States,* Information Report, M-148 (Washington, D.C., May 1986).

18. For example, the general sales tax base is "retail sales and receipts from selected service industries." Data are obtained from the U.S. Bureau of the Census, *Census of Business* . Sales of food and drugs are omitted because these sales are exempt in many states. Sales of utility services, and the sales of wholesalers and construction contractors, are excluded, although some states tax them. The standardized tax base for the corporate income tax is national corporate net income allocated to the states using a three-factor formula. The federal individual income tax liabilities of residents of the state are used as the individual income tax base.

19. John Shannon is executive director of the U.S. Advisory Commission on Intergovernmental Relations. Robert Kleine was formerly a senior analyst at ACIR.

20. Memorandum to Governor John Carlin and Legislative Budget Committee from Division of the Budget and Kansas Legislative Research Department, 9 November 1985.

22. Advisory Commission on Intergovernmental Relations, *Significant Features of Fiscal Federalism, 1985-86 Edition* (Washington, D.C., February 1986), 160-62.

Chapter 4 Capital Finance and Public Infrastructure

1. Pat Choate and Susan Walter, *America in Ruins: Beyond the Public Works Pork Barrel* (Washington, D.C.: Council of State Planning Agencies, 1981).

2. Ibid., xi-xii.

3. Eugene McQuillin, *The Law of Municipal Corporations,* 3d ed. (Wilmette, Ill.: Callahan, 1985), 358.

4. Second Annual Message, December 6, 1830, in *Messages and Papers of the Presidents,* vol. 3, ed. James D. Richardson (New York, 1897), 509-12.

5. Ibid., 510.

6. The balance of this section on state constitutional history is drawn from B. U. Ratchford, *American State Debts* (Durham: Duke University Press, 1941), 73-134.

7. See A. James Heins, *Constitutional Restrictions Against State Debt* (Madison: University of Wisconsin Press, 1963), 3-12.

8. Rosa M. Perdue, "The Sources of the Constitution of Kansas," in *Kansas Constitutional Convention* (Topeka: Kansas State Printing Plant, 1920), 691-92.

9. *Kansas Constitutional Convention,* 327-28, 332-33.

10. Ibid., 586.

11. This section draws heavily from James Ernest Boyle, *The Financial History of Kansas* (Madison: *Bulletin of the University of Wisconsin,* no. 247, August 1908); and *Summary History of Kansas Finance, 1861-1937,* Publication no. 60 (Topeka: Research Department, Kansas Legislative Council, October 1937).

12. Boyle, 21-23.

13. Ibid., 37-38.

14. *[Kansas] House Journal, 1881,* 56.

15. Note should be made that debt as envisioned by St. John and in the state constitution was debt backed by the taxing power of the state. In the 1800s, the only state tax source was the property tax, and, therefore, any state debt would be guaranteed by the power to tax property. As state government moved away almost entirely from reliance on the property tax as a revenue source, the constitutional concept of state debt became increasingly meaningless. In time, state lawmakers with court sanction would escape constitutional debt limits by inventing new avenues of debt financing—a subject discussed below.

16. Ratchford, 254-57.

17. Boyle, 25.

18. Ibid., 45.

19. Ibid.

20. Ibid.

21. *Compiled Laws of Kansas, 1885,* ch. 52, 509-10.

22. *Leavenworth County* v. *Miller,* 7 Kans. (1871), 479.

23. Boyle, 59-61, 78.

24. *Commercial National Bank of Cleveland* v. *City of Iola,* 9 Kans. (1873), 689.

25. Kenneth E. Beasley, *State Supervision of Municipal Debt in Kansas: A Case Study* (Lawrence: Governmental Research Center, University of Kansas, 1961), 85, 135.

26. This estimate made from data in Boyle, 168, and Beasley, 8.

27. Beasley, 8.

28. *Financing Wastewater Treatment Facilities: A Study of Options for Local Governments in Kansas* (Washington, D.C.: Government Finance Research Center, Municipal Finance Officers Assn., October 1982), III-9.

29. *Session Laws of 1879,* ch. 168, 327-33.

30. *Leavenworth County* v. *Miller,* 7 Kans. (1871), 493.

31. Ratchford, 278.

32. *State* v. *Knapp,* 99 Kans. (1917), 852.

33. See *Summary History of Kansas Finance, passim,* and Mary Rowland, "Kansas and the Highways, 1917-1980," *Kansas History: A Journal of the Central Plains,* 5 (Spring 1982).

34. *Session Laws of 1928, Special Session,* chs. 3, 4.

35. *[Kansas] Senate Journal, 1941,* 57-58.

36. Ibid.

37. Ibid., 311.

38. *[Kansas] House Journal, 1941,* 466.

39. Robert Smith Bader, *The Great Kansas Bond Scandal* (Lawrence: University Press of Kansas, 1982).

40. *[Kansas] House Journal, Special Session of 1933,* 15.

41. *Session Laws of 1933, Special Session,* ch. 98, 123-24.

42. *State, ex rel.,* v. *State Highway Commission,* 138 Kans. (1934), 913.

43. Ibid., 918.

44. *State, ex rel.,* v. *Atherton,* 139 Kans. (1934), 197.

45. *State, ex rel.,* v. *Board of Regents,* 167 Kans. (1949), 590-91.

46. 174 Kans. (1953), 379.

47. Ibid., 380.

48. U.S. Congress, Congressional Budget Office, *The Federal Budget for Public Works Infrastructure* (Washington, D.C.: USGPO, July 1985), *passim* .

49. The construction price index used to adjust capital improvement expenditures into real-dollar values is a composite of two indexes: 1) for the 1972-85
period, the Fixed-Weight Price Index for Government Purchases of structures,
specifically government structures and new construction force-account compensation; and 2) for 1964-72, an index of the value of new construction put in place
for federal, state, and local government. The source for the former is the Bureau
of Economic Analysis, U.S. Department of Commerce; the latter's source is U.S.
Bureau of the Census, *Value of New Construction Put in Place in the United
States* .

50. See, for example, Choate and Walter; Lawrence Litvark and Belden
Daniels, *Innovations in Development Finance* (Washington, D.C.: Council of
State Planning Agencies, 1979); Roger J. Vaughan, *Rebuilding America: Financing Public Works in 1900s* (Washington, D.C.. Council of State Planning Agencies, 1983); and Roger J. Vaughan and Robert Pollard, *Rebuilding America:
Planning and Managing Public Works in the 1980s* (Washington, D.C.: Council
of State Planning Agencies, 1984).

51. This estimate is based on John E. Peterson and Ronald Forbes, *Innovative
Capital Financing* (Chicago: American Planning Association, June 1985),1.

52. See, for example, Choate and Walter; Vaughan; Barbara Dyer and Robert
Pollard, *Investing in Public Works* (Washington, D.C.: Council of State Planning
Agencies, May 1984); and U.S. Congress, House and Senate, Joint Economic
Committee, Subcommittee on Economic Goals and Economic Policy, *Hard
Choices. A Report on the Increasing Gap Between America's Infrastructure Needs
and Our Ability to Pay for Them*, 98th Cong., 2d Sess., 1984.

Chapter 5 Educational Governance and Finance

1. Harold L. Hodgkinson, *All in One System: Demographics of Education—
Kindergarten Through Graduate School* (Washington, D.C.: Institute for Educational Leadership, 1985), 3. The discussion on demographic trends affecting
education draws from Hodgkinson's analysis.

2. Ibid.

3. Ibid.

4. Ibid., 8.

5. Ibid., 10

6. Max Casey, "Occupational Employment Growth Through 1990,"
Monthly Labor Review 104 (August 1981):48.

7. Aims C. McGuinness, "The Search for More Effective Policy Leadership
in Higher Education," *Grapevine* (April 1986):2054-58. The following discussion
draws from McGuinness' analysis.

8. Ibid., 2055.

9. Ibid.

10. Ibid., 2055-56.

11. Hodgkinson, 11.

12. U. S. Department of Education, National Institute of Education, *How
States Compare in Financing Higher Education, 1984-1985: Estimates for Public
Institutions* (Washington, D.C.: Government Printing Office, May 1985), 28.

Chapter 6 Better Health for Kansans

1. Charles Howes, *This Place Called Kansas* (Norman: University of Oklahoma Press, 1952), 125-26.

2. Statewide Health Coordinating Council and Kansas Department of Health and Environment, *The 1984 Plan for the Health of Kansas* (1984), 6.

3. Howard Leichter and Harrell Rodgers, Jr., *American Public Policy in a Comparative Context* (New York: McGraw Hill, 1984), 67.

4. Kansas Action for Children, *Adolescent Pregnancy Childwatch* (Topeka, 1985), 6.

5. American Association of Retired Persons, "A Profile of Older Americans" (Washington, 1985), 1.

6. *The 1984 Plan for the Health of Kansas*, 122.

7. Kansas Department of Health and Environment, *A Healthy Start for Kansas Families* (1984), 1.

8. *Adolescent Pregnancy Childwatch*, 1.

9. *The 1984 Plan for the Health of Kansas*, 241.

10. *A Healthy Start for Kansas Families*, 3.

11. *The 1984 Plan for the Health of Kansas*, 240.

12. "A Need for Care," *Wichita Eagle-Beacon*, 20 October 1985, 1E.

13. Kansas Department of Social and Rehabilitation Services, *A Kansas Agenda for Investing in Women and Children* (1985), 35.

14. Susan Ripley, "Perspectives 20 Years Later: From the Pioneers of the N P Movement," *Nurse Practitioner* 10 (January 1985):78.

15. California State Department of Health, *Child Health and Disability Prevention Referral Study* (1978), 1.

16. Judith Singer, John Butler, Judith Palfrey, "Health Care Access and Use Among Handicapped Students in Five Public School Systems," *Medical Care* 24(January 1986):1.

17. *A Kansas Agenda for Investing in Women and Children*, v.

18. Darrell Lang, *Study of Health Behaviors of Kansas Students* (Emporia, Kans.: Emporia State University [1984]), sects. 3, 7-8.

19. George Christenson et al., "Preface" to "Results of the School Health Education Evaluation" issue, *Journal of School Health* 55 (October 1985):296.

20. Kansas Department of Health and Environment, "School Health Questionnaire 1980-81" (1981), 1.

21. Mary Noak, *State Policy Support for School Health Education: A Review and Analysis* (Denver: Education Commission on the States, 1982), 13.

22. Kristin A. Moore and Richard F. Wertheimer, "Teenage Childbearing and Welfare: Preventive and Ameliorative Strategies," *Family Planning Perspectives* 16 (November/December 1984):285.

23. *Adolescent Pregnancy Childwatch*, 1.

24. Ibid, 5.

25. Elsie Jones et al., "Teenage Pregnancy in Developed Countries: Determinents and Policy Implications," *Family Planning Perspectives* 17 (March/April 1985):61.

26. Ibid, 54.

27. 1985 Wisconsin Act 56.

28. *A Kansas Agenda for Investing in Women and Children*, 37.

29. U.S. Department of Health and Human Services, *Healthy People: The Surgeon General's Report on Health Promotion and Disease Prevention* (1979), 9.

30. Kansas Department of Health and Environment, *Annual Summary of Vital Statistics* (1981), 56.

31. *The 1984 Plan for the Health of Kansas*, 61-62.

32. *American Public Policy in a Comparative Context*, 65-66.

33. Metropolitan Official Health Agencies of the Kansas City Area, *Market Analysis of Kansas City Metropolitan Employers' Health Promotion Needs*, Executive Summary (1983), 3.

34. Health Insurance Association of America, *Survey of Health Promotion Insurance Underwriting Practices*, Research and Statistical Bulletin 1-86 (1986), 1; *USA Today*, "Stay Fit, Pay Less Insurance," (17 January 1985):10.

35. *The 1984 Plan for the Health of Kansans*, 113; Kansas Department on Aging, "The Older Kansan," 1.

36. Barbara Conant, "Home Care Not Widely Recognized, Study Shows," *Current Report of the Kansas Hospital Association* 14 (April 4, 1986): 2.

37. "The Older Kansan," 1.

38. Jo Spangler, St. John's Hospital, in attachment to letter to Lyndon Drew, Kansas Department on Aging, 15 November 1985.

39. Executive Office of Elder Affairs, *The Massachusetts Home Care Program* (1985), 13.

Glossary

ad valorem tax. A tax levied in proportion to the value of property.

Aid to Families with Dependent Children. A federally-assisted, state-administered program that provides cash assistance and counseling to low-income families.

assessed value. Value assigned to property by appraiser or assessor. In Kansas, assessed value is, by law, 30 percent of market value, although in practice, it is often much lower.

assessment/sales ratio. A ratio (percentage) obtained by dividing the assessed value of a property by its sales price.

bond. Evidence of the issuer's obligation to repay a specified principal amount on a certain date (maturity date), together with interest at a stated rate, or according to a formula for determining that rate. Bonds are distinguishable from notes, which usually mature in one year or less.

Bus Regulatory Reform Act of 1982 (PL 97-261). A federal law designed to provide more effective regulation of motor carriers hauling passengers, one of many steps taken by Congress to reduce unnecessary and burdensome government regulation.

capital assets. Assets having significant value and a useful life of several years.

capital budgeting. A plan of proposed capital expenditures and the means of financing them.

capital expenditure. Expenditure for the acquisition of capital assets.

capital finance. The method or methods of financing used by governments to acquire or construct public infrastructure, i.e., capital assets owned by public authorities.

cash basis law. Kansas law requiring that local governments spend or obligate no money before it is actually received by the government.

circuit breaker. Property tax relief to low-income, aged, or disabled taxpayers.

classification. Separation of property into groups to which different levels of assessment apply.

constant dollars. Dollars adjusted in value relative to a certain point in time.

Consumer Price Index (CPI). An index computed by the U.S. Department of Labor showing the cost of purchasing a fixed "market basket" of goods and services such as would be purchased by a typical urban family.

cross-subsidy. Provision of a service or product in one marketplace at a reduced price, while raising prices in other markets. The latter are said to cross-subsidize the former. This situation may occur if the higher-priced market is, effectively, without substantial competition, that is, a protected, regulated market.

current charges. Amounts received for performance of specific services benefiting the person charged and from sales of commodities and services (except by government utilities and liquor stores).

debt. All long-term credit obligations incurred and outstanding in the name of the government or its dependent agencies, whether backed by the government's full faith and credit or nonguaranteed, and all interest-bearing short-term credit obligations including judgments, mortgages, "revenue" and "earnings" bonds, and special-assessment obligations as well as general-obligation bonds, notes, and interest-bearing short-term warrants.

debt limit. The maximum amount of debt that a governmental unit may incur under constitutional, statutory, or charter authorizations. The limitation is usually a percentage of assessed valuation, planned expenditures, or revenues.

debt service. Interest requirements plus the stipulated payment of principal on outstanding debt, usually reported on an annual basis.

depreciation. Expiration of the service life of capital assets attributable to wear and tear, deterioration, inadequacy, or obsolescence. Also, a periodic charge against current income for a portion of the cost of capital assets.

direct expenditure. Payment to final recipients of government payments, in other words, all expenditure other than intergovernmental expenditure.

durable goods. Goods of relatively long usefulness such as appliances and cars.

earmarked. Set aside for special use.

economies of scale. Cost per unit falls as output increases.

equalization aid. Monies received through the state equalization aid formula and distributed to school districts.

equalization formula. A formula established by the Kansas School Equalization Act of 1973 that is used to distribute funds for elementary and secondary education throughout the state; the formula's purpose is to equalize funding among poorer and wealthier school districts.

excise taxes. Taxes levied on sale of specific products or services.

full faith and credit debt. All long-term obligations for which the credit of the government, the power of taxation, is unconditionally pledged.

general revenue. All government revenue except utility revenue, liquor store revenue, and employee-retirement and other insurance trust revenue. The basis for distinction is not the fund or administrative unit receiving particular amounts but, rather, the nature of the revenue sources concerned.

general sales tax. A tax levied on the sales of all final goods and services, often including both consumption and investment goods.

hyperopia. Difficulty in seeing at near-point such as reading a book.

income elasticity. The index of income elasticity shows the relation of changes in the tax yield to changes in personal income and is calculated by dividing the percentage change in the yield of a given tax by the percentage change in personal income.

income taxation. A tax imposed on salaries, wages, fees, profits, rents, and other income.

income tax credits. A provision of the law that allows for reduction in tax liabilities.

income tax deductions. A provision of the law that allows for reduction in taxable income.

infant-mortality rate. The number of infants per 1,000 who die before their first birthday.

industrial recruitment. The process of targeting and recruiting industries to locate in an area.

intergovernmental revenue. Amounts received from other governments as fiscal aid, as reimbursements, or in lieu of taxes.

Interstate Commerce Commission. An agency of the U.S. government for the regulation and supervision of interstate commerce.

Kansas Corporation Commission. An agency of the State of Kansas for the regulation and supervision of certain industries such as electric power, telephone services, and intrastate trucking, among others.

Kansas Department on Aging. An agency of the State of Kansas that administers state aging programs and federal funding under the Older Americans Act.

Kansas Department of Social and Rehabilitation Services. An agency of the State of Kansas that administers programs for the needy, such as medicaid, food stamps, aid to families with dependent children, alcohol and drug abuse, and related programs.

Kansas School Equalization Act of 1973. A state law that provides for the equalization of school funding among school districts.

labor force. People aged sixteen and over who are employed or are actively seeking employment.

levy. To impose or collect by legal authority, often in reference to a tax.

low birth-weight. Below five-and-one-half pounds at birth.

median. The middle value in a distribution, above and below which lie an equal number of values.

medicaid. A federally assisted, state-administered program that provides medical care for low-income persons.

medicare. A federal program that pays for the medical care of persons over age 65 or otherwise eligible.

miscellaneous revenue. Public revenues from interest earnings, property sales, and special assessments.

Motor Carrier Act of 1980 (PL 96-296). A federal law that provides for regulation of motor carriers of property.

natural monopoly. A market in which economies of scale are so persistent that a single firm can serve the market at lower unit cost than two or more firms.

neonatal intensive care. Specialized hospital care designed to treat infants born with life-threatening conditions.

net present value. The dollar value of revenues expected to be received in the future discounted by the time-value of money less the dollar value of expenditures discounted by the time-value of money.

nondurable goods. Goods of relatively short usefulness such as food and clothing.

nontax revenue. Revenue generated by fees, licenses, intergovernmental grants, and sources other than taxation.

nurse practitioner. A registered nurse with advanced education who takes on additional responsibilities such as performing physical examinations and formulating a plan of care for ill persons.

Older Americans Act. A federal law that provides funds for state and local programs serving older persons.

outmigration. Emigration; the departure of persons from their native surroundings

pay as you go. Financing all capital outlays from current revenues rather than by borrowing.

pay as you use. Those who benefit from a public facility pay for its development and operation; the amount paid is related to the level of use.

personal disposable income. Personal income minus taxes.

personal income. Total income, including wages, salaries, investment income, and transfer payments.

physician assistant. A person who has received academic and practical training to provide patient services under the direction and supervision of a licensed physician.

prenatal care. Physician or nurse monitoring of maternal and fetal health and development, education about nutrition and lifestyle, and referral for needed services.

progressive taxes. Tax as a percentage of income increases as income increases.

property tax. Taxation of real estate and tangible and intangible property of residents of a governmental unit, sometimes referred to as ad valorem tax.

public infrastructure. Capital assets which have both substantial value and a useful life of several years and which are integral to the delivery of public services.

public utility commission. A commission with authority appointed to regulate public utilities; in Kansas, this commission is called the Kansas Corporation Commission.

Railroad Revitalization and Regulation Act of 1976 (PL 97-468). A federal law designed to rehabilitate and maintain the physical facilities, improve the operations and structure, restore the financial stability of the railway systems of the U.S., and to foster competition.

rate elasticity. The index of rate elasticity shows the relationship of changes in tax yield to changes in the rate of a tax and is computed by dividing the percentage change in the yield of a given tax by the percentage change in the rate.

real dollars. Dollar adjusted in value relative to a certain point in time.

real property. Land and property permanently affixed to land.

regental institutions. Educational institutions governed by the Kansas Board of Regents.

revenue bond. A bond that is payable from a specific source of anticipated revenue and to which the full faith and credit of an issuer with taxing power is not pledged.

revenue source. Generators of income such as taxes, fees, grants, and other revenues of a governmental unit.

risk capital. Financing used for business ventures.

rural communities in Kansas. All areas of Kansas except the standard metropolitan statistical areas, that is, Kansas City (Wyandotte, Johnson, Miami, and Leavenworth ċounties), Wichita (Sedgwick and Butler counties), Topeka (Shawnee County), and Lawrence (Douglas County)

severance taxes. Taxes applied to minerals taken from the ground, such as oil and gas.

SMSAs. Standard metropolitan statistical areas defined by the U.S. Bureau of the Census; each consists of a single county or a group of contiguous counties.

Staggers Rail Act of 1980 (PL 96-448). A federal law that provides for the restoration, maintenance, and improvement of the physical facilities and financial stability of the rail system of the U.S.

stripper well. An oil well producing small quantities of oil, usually five barrels of oil per day or less.

tangible personal property. Moveable tangible property; for tax purposes in Kansas, oil, gas, and utility property are also classified as personal property.

tax base. The measure to which a tax rate is applied to determine the taxes due, for example, sales, assessed value, or income.

tax capacity. The ability of a governmental unit to raise revenue.

tax effort. Tax collected in relation to tax capacity.

tax structure. The relation of property, income, sales, and other taxes within a given governmental unit.

user fees. Fees charged for the use of a facility.

Index